Sex and the Contract

Nijhoff International Trade Law Series

VOLUME 5

Sex and the Contract

From infamous commerce to the market for sexual goods and services

By

Vincenzo Zeno-Zencovich

MARTINUS NIJHOFF PUBLISHERS

LEIDEN • BOSTON
2011

This book is printed on acid-free paper.

Library of Congress Cataloging-in-Publication Data

Zeno-Zencovich, Vincenzo.
Sex and the contract : from infamous commerce to the market for sexual goods and services / by Vincenzo Zeno-Zencovich.
p. cm. -- (Nijhoff international trade law series, 1877-7392 ; v. 5)
Includes bibliographical references and index.
ISBN 978-90-04-20178-1 (hardback : alk. paper)
1. Sex-oriented businesses--Law and legislation. 2. Prostitution. I. Title.
K5295.Z46 2011
343'.08553067--dc22

2011000997

The author welcomes comments and criticisms at zeno-zencovich@uniroma3.it

ISBN 1877-7392
ISBN 978 90 04 20178 1

PRINTED BY A-D DRUK BV - ZEIST, THE NETHERLANDS

Homo sum: humani nihil a me alienum puto
Publius Terentius Afer, *Heautontimorumenos* I, 1, 25

A young scholar is well aware of the debt of gratitude he owes his mentors, and endeavours to pay back, through his work, the trust that has been bestowed on him. A scholar in his prime discovers that certain debts are never really extinguished. On the contrary they grow with the years and he realizes that he would never have reached his achievements 'but for'. It is however a light and pleasant obligation to acknowledge the enduring tutelage and encouragement of Basil Markesinis and Guido Alpa. I would like to add to them Pietro Rescigno whose works, also on the topic examined in this book, have profoundly influenced my view of legal issues with significant social and ethical implications

CONTENTS

Table of cases ix

Chapter One
An Introduction to Sex Markets 1
a. What are "sex markets"? 2
b. Law and economics in sex markets 10

Chapter Two
Sexual Services 13
a. Prostitution 13
b. Contracts related to prostitution 19
c. Striptease, lap-dancing, peep-shows 23
d. Sex over the phone and the Internet 25

Chapter Three
Sexual Goods 29
a. Pornography 29
b. Sex-enhancing products 33
c. Aphrodisiacs 36

Chapter Four
Sex and Property Rights 39
a. Property of obscene objects 39
b. Copyright 40
c. Trademarks, patents and other forms of protection of intellectual property 44

Chapter Five
Sex Industries 49
a. Producers of pornographic films 50
b. Adult entertainment TV 51
c. "Red light" cinemas, night-clubs, privés, sex shops 53
d. Licensing and zoning 55
e. Sex tourism 59

Chapter Six
The Protection of Sex Consumers 63
a. The parties 63
b. Sale of goods 64

c. Services ... 65
d. Payment ... 66
e. Unfair terms and deceptive practices ... 66
f. The applicable law ... 67

Chapter Seven
Sex as a Profession ... 69
a. Human dignity and the validity of acts of disposal of one's body ... 69
b. The disposability of one's sexual features ... 71
c. The 'commodification debate' ... 74
d. The reality of sex workers ... 76
e. The quest for respectability ... 78

Chapter Eight
Of Sex and of Love ... 83
a. Cohabitation, premarital, marital, and post-marital agreements ... 84
b. Marriage brokerage ... 88
c. On-line dating services ... 94

Chapter Nine
A Comparative View ... 97
a. The *In pari causa turpitudinis* and *Ex turpi causa non oritur actio* rules ... 97
b. The prohibitionist/feminist approach ... 101
c. The market approach ... 107
d. European perspectives: Towards a 'common market'? ... 109
e. International trade issues ... 113
f. Regulation and reform ... 115
g. Social norms ... 117

Concluding Remarks ... 119
a. Interdisciplinarity and plurality of legal approaches ... 119
b. Non-market sex ... 121
c. Sex and sexual ability as a human right ... 124
d. Sexual freedom ... 125
e. Sexual immorality: A notion that has made its time? ... 126

Bibliography ... 127
Index ... 139

TABLE OF CASES

Common Law Jurisdictions

181 South Inc. v. Fischer, 454 *F.3d* 228 (3rd Cir.2006)
American Equitable Assurance Co. v. McWhirter, 133 *So.* 664 (1931) (Miss. S. Ct.)
Andrews v. Parker [1973] Qd. R. 93
Anheuser-Busch Brewing Asso. v. Mason, 46 *N.W.* 558 (1890) (Minn. S. Ct)
Armhouse Lee v. Chappell [CA, 1996]

Bartle v. Nutt, 4 *Pet.* 45 (1830)
Belfast City Council v. Miss Behavin' Limited [HL 2006]
Blackman v. Hustler Magazine, Inc., 620 *F. Supp.* 792 and 1501 (D.D.C. 1985)
Bonenfant v. American Fire Ins. Co. 43 *N.W.* 682 (1889) (Mich. S. Ct.)
Broder v. Zeno Mauvais Music Co., 88 *Fed.* 74 (N.D. Cal. 1898)
Brumley v. Pfizer, Inc., 149 *F. Supp. 2d* 305 (S.D.Tex.,2001)

Calderon v. Buffalo, 397 *N.Y.S.2d* 655 (1977) (N.Y. S. Ct)
Chassman v. People Resources, 573 *N.Y.S.2d* 589 (1991)
Chatham Foot Specialist v. Health Care Service, 837 *N.E.2d* 48 (2005)
Collins v Blantern, 2 *Wils.* 341 [1767]
Coral Leisure Group v. Barnett [1981] I.C.R. 503
Coughler v. Fackler, 510 *SW2d* 16 (1974)(Ky)

Devils Films, Inc. v. Nectar Video, 29 *F. Supp. 2d* 174, 176 (S.D.N.Y. 1998)
Director of Public Prosecutions v. Collins [HL, 2006]
Doctor John's, Inc. v. City of Sioux City, 389 *F. Supp. 2d* 1096 (2005) (N.D. Ia)
Donovan v. Scuderi, 443 *A2d* 121 (1982) (Md)
Dottie's Dress Shop v. Village of Lyons, 313 *Ill. App. 3d* 70 (2000)
Duval v. Wellman, 26 *N.E.* 343 (1891)

Eastern Distributing Corp. v. Lightstone 241 *N.W.* 189 (1932)
Eliza v. Mahood, 26 *La. Ann.* 108 (1874) (La. S. Ct)

Fox v. Encounters International, 318 *F. Supp 2d* 279 (2006)
Fugate v. Greenberg, 189 *N.Y.S.2d* 948 (1959)

Ghaidan v. Godin-Mendoza (HL, 2004)
Glyn v. Weston Feature Film [1916] 1 Ch. 261)
GMC, Inc. v. Chrisofolli, 381 *N.E.2d* 217 (1978) (Oh. C.A.)

Ham v. Wilson, 86 *So*. 298 (1920) (Miss. S. Ct.)
Hermann v. Charlesworth [1905] 1 *KB* 24
Hewitt v. Hewitt, 394 *N.E.2d* 1204 (1979) (Ill. S. Ct.)
Hock v. Hock (1971) 3 *Rep. Fam. L.* 353 (B.C. C.A.)

In re Mavety Media Group, Ltd., 33 *F.3d* 1367 (Fed. Cir. 1994)
In re McGinley, 660 *F.2d* 481, 485 (CCPA 1981)
In re Runsdorf, 171 USPQ 443, 443-44 (TTAB 1971)
In Re The Boulevard Entertainment, 334 *F.3d* 1336 (2003)

Jartech v. Clancy, 666 *F.2d* 403 (1982)
Jespersen v. Harrah's Operating Co., 444 *F.3d* 1104 (9th Cir. 2006)

Lawrence v. Smith, 37 *Eng. Rep*. 928 (1822)
Lewis v. Lewis 44 *N.B. Rep.(2d)* 268 (1983)
Long v. Marino, 441 *S.E.2d* 475 (1994)

Manes Co. v. Glass, 102 A. 964 (1918) (R.I. S. Ct.)
Marvin v. Marvin, 557 *P. 2d* 106 (1976)
Menger v. Thompson, 91 *So*. 40 (1922) (Miss. S. Ct.)
Mitchell Brothers Film Group v. Cinema Adult Theatre, 604 *F.2d* 852 (5th Cir. 1979)
Muflahi v. Musaad, 522 *N.W.2d* 136(1994) (Mich.App.)

Network Communications v. Michigan Bell Tel. Co., 703 *F. Supp*. 1267 (1989) (E.D. Mich.)
New Zealand Post Ltd v Leng. [1999] 3 *NZLR* 219 (HC)
Norfolk 302, LLC v. Vassar, 524 *F.Supp.2d* 728 (E.D.Va.,2007)

Pacific Maxon, Inc. v. Wilson, 619 *P.2d* 816 (1980) (Nev. S. Ct.)
Paris Adult Bookstore II v. City of Dallas, 493 *US* 215 (1990)
Pearce v. Brooks (1866) LR 1 Ex 213
People v. Janini, 89 *Cal. Rptr.2d* 244 (1999) (Cal. C.A.)
Phenix Insurance Co. v. Clay, 28 *S.E.* 853 (1897) (Ga. S. Ct.)
Philip Levy and Others v. Davis, 80 *S.E.* 791 (1914) (Va. S. Ct)
Poplett v. Stockdale, 171 *Eng. Rep*. 1041 (1825)

R. v. Brown (HL 2004)
R. v. Coutts (HL 2006)
R. v. Registrar of Companies, ex p. Att. Gen [QB 1991]
Rainbow Int'l Marriage Serv. v. Ping Cui (2002 Mass. App. Div. 34)
Reed v. Brewer, 37 *S.W.* 418 (1896) (Tx. S. Ct.)
Rehak v. Mathis, 238 *S.E.2d* 81 (1977)
Reliable Consultants Inc. v. Earle, 517 *F.3d* 738, 744 (5th Cir.2008)

Samples v. Monroe 358 *S.E.2d* 273 (1987)
Shook v. Daly, 49 *How. Pr.* 366 (N.Y. Sup. Ct. 1875)
Southey v. Sherwood, 35 *Eng. Rep.* 1006 (1817)
State v. Clark, 638 *P.2d* 890 (1981) (Ida. S. Ct.)
State ex rel. Wayne County Prosecuting Attorney v. Dizzy Duck, 511 *N.W.2d* 907 (1993) (Mich.C.A.)
State v. One 1985 Gray Buick Auto (Ct. Super. Ct. 1993 – on Lexis)
State ex rel. Miller v. Private Dancer, 613 *N.E.2d* 1066 (Oh. C.A.) (1993)
Stephens v. Avery (Ch. 1988)
Stockdale v. Onwhyn 108 *Eng. Rep.* 65 (1826)
Stratton v. Drumm, 445 *F. Supp.* 1305 (1978) (Ct.)

Taylor v. Chester [1869] LR 4 QB 309
The Lady Cox's case, 3 *P. Wms.*339 (1734)
Tol-o-Matic, Inc. v. Proma Produkt-Und Marketing Gesellschaft, 945 *F.2d* 1546 (Fed. Cir. 1991)

Uphill v. Wright, 1 *KB* 506 (1911)

Walker v. Perkins, 97 *Eng. Rep.* 985 (1764)
Wallis v Duke of Portland, 3 *Vesey Junior* 494, 30 *ER* 1123 (1797)
Whistler Corp. v. Autotronics, Inc., 14 *U.S.P.Q.2d* (BNA) 1885 (N.D. Tex. 1988)
Whorton v. Dillingham, 248 *Cal.Rptr.* 405 (1988)
Williams v. Morgan, 478 *F.3d* 1316 (11th Cir. 2007)

European Court of Human Rights

Beck, Copp and Bazeley v. UK (22.10.2002)
Dudgeon v. UK (22.10.1981)
Lustig-Prean and Beckett v. UK (27.9.1999)
Smith and Grady v. UK (27.9.1999)
Tremblay v. France (11.9.2007)
Wackenheim v. France (Petition n. 29961/96 rejected October 16, 1996)

European Court of Justice

Case C-34/79 (14.12.1979) *R. v. Henn and Darby*
Case C-121/85 (decided 11.3.1986) *Conegate v. HM Customs & Excise*
Case C-158/98 (decided 29.6.1999) *Coffeeshop Siberie*
Case C-268/99 (decided 20.11.2001) *Jany v. Netherlands Secretary of Justice*
Case C-168/00 (decided 12.3.2002) (*Leitner v. TUI*)
Case C-117/01 (decided 7.1.2004) *K.B. v. National Health Service*

France

Cour de Cassation

Cass. civ., 1.5.1855, in *DP* 1855, 1, p. 147
Cass. req., 1.4.1895, in *DP* 1895, 1, 263 and in *S.* 1896, 1, 289
Cass. req., 4.5.1903, in *Gaz. Pal.* 1903, 2, p. 394
Cass. req. 17.7.1905, in *DP* 1906, 1, 72
Cass. req., 27.12 1944, in *D.* 1945, p. 121; and in *S.* 1945, 1, p. 32
Cass. crim. 7.6.1945 (in *D.* 1946, jur. p. 149, JCP 1946,II, 2955
Cass. soc., 29.10 1957, in Bull. civ. IV, n° 1027
Cass. soc., 8.1. 1964, in *JCP G* 1964, II, 13546
Cass. 1re civ., 15.2. 1967, in Bull. civ. I, n° 67
Cass. crim. 23.1.1979, in *JCP G* 1979, II, 19143
Cass. 1re civ., 22.7.1987, in *D.* 1988, jurispr. p. 172
Cass. soc. 6.4.1995, *Galdéano v. CRAMIF* (N° 92-22.089)
Cass. soc. 19.12.1996, *URSSAF v. Tremblay* (JurisData : 1996-005145)
Cass. 1re civ., 3.2. 1999, in *JCP G* 1999, I, 143
Cass. 3.4.2003, *Copper communications v. URSSAF* (JurisData : 2003-018666)
Cass. ass. plén., 29.10.2004, no. 519 P, *Galopin v. Floréal*, in *JCP G* 2005, II, 10011
Cass. 1re civ., 4.4. 2006, *Comm. com. électr.* 2006, comm. 88

Other Courts

Conseil d'Etat, 13.12.2006, n. 267782 (*Eroshop v. Ministère de l'Economie*)
Appel Amiens 1.7.1901, in *Gaz. Pal.* 1901, 2, p. 644
Appel Poitiers, 8.2.1922 in *DP* 1922, 2, 33 and in *S.* 1922, 2, p. 116
Appel Montpellier 8.6.1982 in *D.* 1983 Jur. 607
Appel Bordeaux 23.5.1990, *Renard* (JurisData : 1990-042430)
Appel Montpellier 30.4.1992, *Lopez v. Farudjia* (JurisData : 1992-034235)
Appel Orléans 4.6.1998, *Hameon v. Niamke* (JurisData : 1998-045327)
Appel Montpellier 28.9.1999, *Gimenez v. France Telecom* (JurisData : 1999-117622)
Appel Paris 24.1.2000, *Laik* (JurisData: 2000-111383)
Appel Paris 21.11.2001, *Franklin v. Calypso* (JurisData : 2001-159664)
Appel Paris 27.11.2001 *Perez v. Societe Marc Dorel* (JurisData : 2001-163440)
Appel Paris 9.1.2002, *Zilberberg v. Soc. Edimat* (JurisData : 2002-167420)
Appel Paris 16.5.2003, *URSSAF v. Tremblay* (JurisData : 2003-212888)
Appel Paris 23.5.2003, *Vitec v. Cora* (JurisData : 2003-216188)
Appel Paris 18.2.2004, *Chemouny* (JurisData 2004-243542)
Appel Toulouse 12.4.2005, *Societé Suisse Accidents v. Calmels Millet* (JurisData : 2005-270883)
Appel Paris 27.4.2006, *Sylvialize v. Ramarolahy* (in *JurisData* : 2006-299897)

Appel Toulouse 5.9.2006, *Swisslife Assurance de Biens v. Benoit sarl* (JurisData : 2006-323416)
Appel Douai 14.6.2007, *GD Concept v. Camif* (JurisData: 2007-347545)
Appel Rennes 26.6.2007, *Leclerc v. Quilfen* (JurisData : 2007-342165)
Tribunal Comm. Marseille, 7.11.1913 in *Gaz. Pal.* 1914, 1, p. 266
Tribunal civ. Seine, 16.6.1928, in *DP* 1928, 2, p. 187
Tribunal Grande Instance Paris 8.11.1973, in *D. 1974,* somm. p. 30, *Rev. Trim. Dr. Civ.* 1974, p. 806
Tribunal Grande Instance Nanterre, 25.10.1977 (*Hanselmann c. Benazeraf et Sté Production du Chêsne*)
Tribunal Comm. Paris 9.2.1993, *S.té Connection v. France Telecom* (JurisData : 1993-040577)
Tribunal Grande Instance Paris, 25.11.1993, *PIBD* 1994, III, 185, *Etam*

Germany

Bundesverfassungsgericht (Constitutional Court)

BVerfG 9.7.1986, in *NJW*, 1987, p. 3246

Bundesgerichthof (Court of Cassation)

BGH 9.6.1998, in *NJW,* 1998, p.2895
BGH 13.7.2006, in *JZ,* 2007, p. 477
BGH 8. 11. 2007, in *NJW* 2008, 140

Other Courts

BVerwG 15.12.1981, in *NJW,* 1982, p. 664
BVerwG 23.3.2009, in *NVwZ* 2009, 909
BVerwG 30.1.1990, in *JZ*, 1990, p. 382
OLG Schleswig 13.5.2004, in *NJW,* 2005, p. 225
AG Essen, 13.7.1989, in *NJW*, 1989, p. 3162
LG Mannheim, 18.5.1995, in *NJW,* 1995, p. 3398

Italy

Corte di Cassazione (Court of Cassation)

Cass. civ. 13.7.1982, n. 4107
Cass. civ. 1.8.1986, n. 4927
Cass. pen. 30.11.1986, Benedetti, in *Foro it.* 1987, II, 697
Cass. pen. 26.9.1991, Rebuffat

Cass. pen. 10.6.1993, Teso
Cass. pen. 21.1.1994, Cannata (in *Foro it.* 1996, II, 18)
Cass. 24.3.1995, n. 5606, Gasparato (in *Foro it.* 1996, II, 17)
Cass. Sezioni Unite Penali 25.9.1995, n. 3027, Calamai, in *Cass. pen.* 1996, 2968)
Cass. pen. 20.5.1998, n. 7608, in *Riv. pen.* 1998, 876)
Cass. pen. 13.1.1999, n. 2296 (in *Cass. pen.* 2000, 1428)
Cass. pen. 19.5.1999, n. 8600, in *Cass. pen.* 2001, 640
Cass. pen. 26.11.1999, n. 285
Cass. pen. 11.2.2000, n. 7734
Cass. pen. 14.2.2001, n. 16536 (in *Riv. pen.* 2001, 633)
Cass. pen. 12.2.2003, n. 13039
Cass. pen. 11.3.2003, n. 19644
Cass. pen. 16.4.2004, n. 23657
Cass. pen. 22.4.2004, n. 25464 (in *Cass. pen.* 2004, 3577)
Cass. pen. 14.5.2004, n. 30582, in *Riv. pen.* 2005, 160
Cass. pen. 3.6.2004, n. 36157 (in *Foro it.* 2006, 32)
Cass. pen. 8.6.2004, n. 35776
Cass. pen. 9.11.2004, in *Cass. pen.* 2005, 1892
Cass. civ. 23.3.2005, n. 6276
Cass. civ. 10.5.2005, n. 9801 (in *Giust. civ.* 2006, 93)
Cass.civ. 20.1.2006, n. 1202 (in *Foro it.* 2006, 1406)
Cass. civ. 7.3.2006, n. 4876
Cass. pen. 21.3.2006, n. 15158

Other Courts

Appello Roma 29.11.1993 (in *Diritto informazione e informatica* 1994, 299)
Tribunale Piacenza 31.7.1950 (in *Foro it.* 1951, I, 987)
Tribunale Firenze 6.11.1985 (in *Foro it.* 1988, II, 400)
Tribunale Milano 1.7.1993 (in *Gius* 1994, 5, 103)
Tribunale Bergamo 7.5.2003, (in *Foro it.* 2003, II, 642)
Pretura Catania 10.4.1992 (in *Giur. merito* 1993, 1051)
Pretura Modica 22.12.1994, (in *Riv. pen.* 1995, 376)
Commissione Tributaria Milano 22.12.2005, n. 272 (in *Giur. merito* 2006, 1795)

CHAPTER ONE

AN INTRODUCTION TO SEX MARKETS

We live in a society in which we are assailed from all sides by invitations to sexual stimulation, whether explicitly or more indirectly. On sidewalks at night, at newsstands, on web pages, on TV programmes, on advertising hoardings, leaflets and stickers sexual services and sexual goods are offered to us. One only has to pay and one receives – more or less – what has been asked for.

At the same time we are encouraged to improve our sexual appearance through perfumes and beauty creams, beauticians and cosmetic surgeons, intimate lingerie and gymnasiums, and exhibit it into practice in bars, discotheques, holiday resorts and the like.[1] More often than not advertising, even if it is not selling sex, has a sexual innuendo.[2]

Although difficult to define, there are sex markets and sex industries, which over the last two decades have been attracting increasing attention from economists and sociologists.

Lawyers, on the whole, and especially in Europe, have been much less interested in the topic of sex markets[3] and have mostly concentrated their analysis on specific aspects, generally of criminal law, such as human trafficking and child pornography.

The purpose of this book is to try to offer a comprehensive view of the legal aspects of the sex industry, considered outside of the shadow of criminal activities. And this, historically, is the field of contract law.

This is not at all an easy task not only because of the necessarily variable (in time and in space) enforcement of penal laws by the authorities to whom this task is entrusted, and their interpretation by the courts. The answer to what is legal in the sex market – and therefore can be the object of a contractual

[1] See Sanders, *Paying for Pleasure. Men who Buy Sex*, Willan Pub., Cullompton, 2008: "The sex industry is bound to interrelated systems of other institutions, specifically the interplay between the labour market and the leisure economy" (at p. 191). See also the prologue "The Sexual Landscape of the New Millennium", in Hawkes, *Sex & Pleasure in Western Culture*, Polity, Cambridge 2004, p. 5 ff.

[2] The phenomenon has increased through the years: compare Courtney, Whipple, *Sex Stereotyping in Advertising*, Lexington Books, Lexington, Mass. 1983, with Reichert, Lambiase (eds.), *Sex in Advertising: Perspectives on the Erotic Appeal*, Lawrence Erlbaum Ass., Mahwah, N.J., 2002, and Reichert, *The Erotic History of Advertising*, Prometheus, Amherst, N.Y., 2003.

[3] I have anticipated a few of the topics examined in this book in the article "*Sex and the contract*": *dal mercimonio al mercato*, in *Riv. trim. dir. proc. civ.* 2007, 1191. In a feminist but not prohibitionist perspective see Marella, *Bocca di Rosa, Roxanne e le altre: considerazioni in tema di sesso, mercato e autonomia privata*, in 2 *Polemos*, issue 2/2008, p. 35.

relationship – depends on a vast amount of specific elements which have to be taken into account and on the deliberate penumbra in which these activities are left. The less spoken, the better, it would seem, and silence comes not only from academic scholars but also from legislators and governmental authorities – at a national or a local level – who prefer not to tackle, unless under strong public pressure and in a restrictive direction, the thorny question.

The lack of a systematic non-penal approach is even more noticeable in European civil law jurisdictions where private lawyers appear to be comfortably resting on century-old Latin maxims (whose present day actual effectiveness will be discussed further on). If one looks at traditional handbooks or treatises, when confronted with dealings that are "contrary to morality", mainstream writings cling, as if to a lifeline, to the notion that such dealings do not exclusively comprise those offensive to "sexual morality" and confine their attention to those that are not. Scholars thus avoid having to write about sex in case they would sully their pens with a disreputable topic.[4] And yet, wherever the subject is discrimination between male and female employees, workplace harassment, breach of the duty of conjugal fidelity, impairment of the ability to enjoy married life, what is being discussed, directly or indirectly, if not questions of sex? Common modesty should not be allowed to inhibit debate, and in any case, *honni soit qui mal y pense*.

a. *What are "sex markets"?*

Criticism of the current state of legal debate is, however, sterile if one does not try to offer a different starting point. Rather than embarking on the slippery task of establishing that today's moral standards are different from those of the past and therefore require different rules, the attempt that will be made in this work is to offer some extra-legal elements drawn from other social studies – mainly economics and sociology – and to show how the reality of sex markets is perceived by other scholars. This obviously does not automatically mean that things *are* how they are described, but at any rate presents a different perspective which should be taken into account.

---

[4] If the phenomenon is, as we shall see, so widespread, it is fairly unlikely that lawyers as a social category (particularly the males among them) have been excluded from it and that none of them has ever – to take just a few of the most trivial examples - bought a pornographic magazine, visited an erotic chat-room or used a sex aid. It would seem that hypocrisy even more than morality is the reason that the topic remains hidden from their view. On the double (sexual) life of a great jurist such as Oliver Wendell Holmes, see Markesinis, *The Duality of Genius*, Jan Sramek Verlag, Vienna, 2008, at p. 269 ("Holmes the public man was not the same as Holmes the private one". Incidentally Holmes, in *The Path of the Law* (reprinted in *The Collected Works of Justice Holmes*, U. Chicago Press, 1994 vol. 3, at p. 391) expressed the view that "it would be a gain if every word of moral significance could be banished from the law altogether".

If we are to apply the criteria commonly used by the abundant literature of economic theory and wish to treat the 'sex market' as a market like any other,[5] we are interested in knowing the figures on businesses, workers, clients, and turnover; types of goods and services on offer; collateral activities, whether upstream or downstream, the number of economic operations; and the mean *per capita* spend.

At the same time one should identify the relevant markets; see to what extent the "sex market" can be subdivided into component markets; to what extent goods and services are substitutable; what (if any) the barriers to entry are; the price dynamics; and the (certainly not negligible) influence of regulation.[6]

This approach, it should be noted, is only gradual (as it is also among scholars of social sciences) and is still far from reaching consolidated and widely accepted results. One can group three lines of research.

i. The first line of research, chronologically is statistical research into sexual behaviour and deviation, prompted mainly by the flourishing criminological studies which had already started towards the end of the 19th century.[7] Clearly those researches were interested mostly in aspects related to prostitution and were aimed – following the intellectual fashion of the time – at outlining the character of the "delinquent woman" *par excellence*, the prostitute. However, looked at over a century's distance, we have an impressive amount of data and of methodological indications, which were meant to be used, or at least should have been used, in regulating the market (in those many jurisdictions where brothels were legal and public authorities controlled the health of prostitutes), or in curbing it, promoting policies of social "redemption" of both *filles de joie* and their clients. This wealth in statistical and social data was lost when – principally after World War II – brothels were closed and prostitution became or an individual "business" or, later on, one of the main activities of powerful and difficult to eradicate criminal organizations specialized in the trafficking of women to be used as a low cost labour force in the prostitution market.

---

5 According to Posner, *Sex and Reason*, Harvard U.P., Cambridge, Ma., 1992, p. 335 "If the Constitution itself distinguished between sexual markets and other markets, this would be answer enough to a proposal to equate the two types of market. But it does not – or rather it gives *more* protection to property than to liberty" [italics in original]. It is however not altogether clear why matters which concern the sale and purchase of sexual services and goods should be more a question of "liberty" rather than a question of "property".

6 Anticipating current trends see already Reynolds *The Economics of Prostitution*, C.C.Thomas, Springfield, Ill., 1986: "Someone contemplating the business of prostitution would likely form some concept of the legal environment in different locations in evaluating money-making possibilities" (at p. 51)

7 For a good example see Kneeland, *Commercialized Prostitution in New York City*, Grant Richards, London, 1913 which contains a vast amount of empirical data.

More or less at the same time as the prostitution market enters a grey zone, which is difficult to control and quite impossible to monitor through the classical economic indicators which have been listed above, other sexual industries come to the forefront.[8] The most important of these is pornography, mostly thanks to the widespread use at low cost, of coloured print and the production of electronic apparatuses, which can be bought at consumer prices and boost the market for porn videos. This market will grow at an impressive rate when digital techniques are introduced and telecommunication networks open what is commonly called the Internet age. From an economic point of view this is not only a different product/service, but also one that requires a more skilled labour force, including technical staff to direct, film and produce the videos. Technical equipment is required and marketing policies and distribution channels must be put into action. One can easily detect all the typical elements of a firm. Although even here data are difficult to collect,[9] it is very clear that one is faced with a different market and that the prostitution model is no longer the most important and cannot any longer be used as the yardstick for sexual enterprises.

Alongside pornography, other sex industries started to develop thanks to increased mobility and more relaxed mores, mostly related to the entertainment industry. Here again we have different features, different forms of organization, and a different mix of the various factors of production.

One of the main difficulties researchers of statistical data encounter is that although most of these activities are legal – in the sense that there is no prohibition, criminal or administrative, on their undertaking – those who run them prefer on the whole to remain in the penumbra.[10] What would be typical in other new and growing sectors – *i.e.* an association grouping the different businesses and promoting their interests towards decision-makers and their image towards the public – is completely absent. From an economic research point of view this means that all the data that generally industry and trade associations collect from their members and disseminate through the public are lacking.[11]

---

[8] But they are not always detected: see *e.g.* Poulin, *La mondialisation des industries du sexe. Prostitution, pornographie, traite des femmes et des enfants*, Interligne, Ottawa 2004 who gives (at p. 48) an extremely vague definition of sex industries.

[9] For an attempt see Ropelato, *Pornography statistics 2007*, available at: www.internet-filter-review.toptenreviews.com with tables annexed that refer not only to the USA but to other countries as well. The data are copious and interesting. However, the author takes care to warn that "Statistics are compiled from the credible sources mentioned. In reality, statistics are hard to ascertain". For further economic data see Halavais (ed.), *Cyberporn and Society*, Kendall/Hunt, Dubuque, 2006.

[10] "Statistical evidence on the influence of various factors on the demand for prostitution services is rare due to the lack of fully tolerant legality and the presence of stigma" (Cameron, *The Economics of Sin. Rational Choice or No Choice At All?*, Edward Elgar, Cheltenham 2002, at p. 191).

[11] Posner, *Sex and Reason*, Harvard U.P., Cambridge, Ma., 1992, at p. 438 notes the "relative paucity of *reliable* data on sex" [italics in original].

One therefore has to use rough estimates that do not allow one to compare and rank sex markets with others that are somehow related (the entertainment sector, the publishing sector, *et caetera*). Although this information may not be essential in order to establish the applicable (private) law, it is extremely relevant in a regulatory perspective, for which dimensions, social impact, forecasts are the points of departure and of guidance.

The scarcity of general and uniform statistical data has one very important consequence on the construction of a legal framework within which sexual transactions can fit: the arguments used – in favour of one solution rather than its opposite – can easily ignore the facts, or be founded upon some scarce and non-significant facts. Passion and ideology – whether in favour of prohibitionist, feminist or *laissez-faire* theories – prevail over reasonable law-making, which is a long way from perfection but surely better than deciding through prejudice.

ii. The second line of research is the very wide-ranging sociological investigation on the different aspects that surround sex life, including what is not considered "regular" sex (*i.e.* between spouses). There is here an apparent paradox: the information on sexual habits was much richer as regards what happened outside the married couple's bedroom and was mostly retrieved by interviewing prostitutes. Only later when the ground-breaking researches by Kinsey and by Masters and Johnson were published, was the gap filled. What is important to note here is that, quite properly from a sociological point of view, sex is sex,[12] and the fact that it is satisfied outside a "market" or thanks to "market procedures" is only an aspect of a biological and physiological need.[13]

Sociological research therefore has had an extremely important role in keeping together "market" and "non-market" sex, which previously were kept far apart and unrelated.[14] The latter fell under the shroud of the sanctity of marriage which could not be investigated without infringing the deepest secrets of a family. The former, instead, was the land of lewdness, debauchery and crime inhabited by pimps, prostitutes and men with no moral values.

---

[12] Sanders, *Paying for Pleasure. Men who Buy Sex*, Willan Pub., Cullompton, 2008: "The pull factors of the sex industry obviously revolve around the constructions of female sexuality that permeate everyday life" (at p. 196).

[13] For a recent survey containing a great deal of data on the sexual behaviour of Italians see Vaccaro, *I comportanenti sessuali degli italiani. Falsi miti e nuove normalità*, Franco Angeli, Milan, 2003.

[14] This contiguity may have its drawbacks: The "conceptual ambiguity over what actually constitutes a *sex market* or a *marriage market* currently hinders the study of the formation, organization and dissolution of partnerships" [italics in original] (Laumann, Ellinson, Mahay, Paik, Youm, *The Sexual Organization of the City*, U. Chicago Press, Chicago, 2004, at p. 10f.).

We now know that clients of a sex market are ordinary people – both male and female – who conduct normal lives and who for various reasons – the most important and common being pleasure – buy sexual goods and services.[15] Their going to the market does not in any way imply that they do not have a stable sexual relationship and, apart from issues relating to conjugal fidelity, that they are "perverted".[16]

This research offer us a precious insight into the demand-side of the market, enabling us to understand what people expect from sexual experience,[17] how they satisfy their needs,[18] and to what extent the market supplements "ordinary", non-market sex life.[19]

Moreover, the supply-side is also investigated: starting with the reasons that bring a person to prostitute his or her body,[20] the motivation that keeps them in the "trade"; apprenticeship and careers in the "porn-star" system; to what brings a dancer or a ballerina to cross the line and enter into the nude entertainment business.

Although this research is typically sociological, and therefore follows the extremeley diversified methodologies of this kind of study, it offers precious elements for what today is one of the leading theories in economics, so-called behavioural economics. It is quite understandable that applying a classic

---

[15] For the most important and recent research on the point see Sanders, *Paying for Pleasure. Men who Buy Sex*, Willan Pub., Cullompton, 2008: "Men who buy sex are ordinary citizens who are upstanding members of the community in terms of employment, obeying the law and fulfilling family obligations. Yet it is this 'type' of man that is clearly in the firing line for their corrupt sexual habits and 'using' women" (at p. 143) And at p. 34ff. see the rich sociological data on sex buyers. See also, for an Australian survey, Pitts, Smith, Grierson, O'Brien, Misson, *Who Pays for Sex and Why? An Analysis of Social and Motivational Factors Associated with Male Clients of Sex Workers*, 33 *Archives of Sexual Behavior* 353 (2004) (In a setting where commercial sex is legally available from brothels, it would appear that clients are unremarkable in their social characteristics and are motivated mainly by the ease of the commercial sex encounter, the absence of engagement with another, and because they feel in need of sexual relief).

[16] Sanders, *Paying for Pleasure. Men who Buy Sex*, Willan Pub., Cullompton, 2008: "Where all men who buy sex are considered dangerous and all sex workers as dishevelled victims or rational, calculating criminals, a discourse is produced (some would call this propaganda) that is barely short of man-hating" (at p. 10.)

[17] Monto, *Why Men Seek out Prostitutes*, in Weitzer (ed.) *Sex for Sale: Prostitution,Pornography, and the Sex Industry*, Routledge,New York, 2000, p. 67ff.

[18] Lever, Dolnick, *Clients and Call Girls: Seeking Sex and Intimacy*, in Weitzer (ed.) *Sex for Sale: Prostitution, Pornography, and the Sex Industry*, Routledge, New York, 2000, p. 85ff.

[19] See e.g. Laumann, Ellinson, Mahay, Paik, Youm, *The Sexual Organization of the City*, U. Chicago Press, Chicago, 2004 (at p. 18) who distinguish "*Direct sexual marketplaces*: bars and dance clubs, bathhouses, personal ads, and such informal settings as private parties and public parks" from "*mediated sexual marketplaces* (blind dates, singles nights)" [italics in original]. And Sanders, *Paying for Pleasure. Men who Buy Sex*, Willan Pub. Pub., Cullompton, 2008: "Men, particularly heterosexual men, are often not explored as subjects in their own right, as sexual beings with legitimate desires, attractions and pleasures" (at p. 11).

[20] See Lemoncheck, *Loose Women, Lecherous Men*, Oxford U.P., New York 1997 (in particular Ch. 4, at p. 110ff, entitled "I Only Do It for the Money"). Can one prostitute one's voice? See Rich, Guidroz, *Smart Girls Who Like Sex: Telephone Sex Workers*, in Weitzer (ed.) *Sex for Sale: Prostitution, Pornography, and the Sex Industry*, Routledge, New York, 2000, p. 35ff.

economic model (as if the rationale for choosing a box of detergent and a porn video were the same) leaves us unsatisfied and that the outcome is bound to be strained.

All the results that we are provided with have (or should have) a direct influence on some of the most discussed legal issues. While nearly everybody agrees that the notion of what is immoral varies with time and place, and we all recall the witty dictum of the Australian judge on the mystery of how bikinis stay in place,[21] it is extremely difficult to provide solid evidence of the changes in mores and to establish, in advance (and not with hindsight,) what can be the object of a legal contractual relation.

iii. The third line of research is the latest that has been developed, rather gradually, over the last quarter of a century[22] with a surge in the last decade.[23] Full fledged economists have put their intellectual instruments and their econometric models[24] into action and have tried to understand what sex markets are, how they work and how the various factors combine.[25] The first market to be investigated has been that of prostitution,[26] quite clearly defined and on which

---

[21] "Surely, what is immoral must be judged by the current standards of morality of the community. What was apparently regarded with pious horror when the cases were decided would, I observe, today hardly draw a raised eyebrow or a gentle 'tut-tut'. George Bernard Shaw's Eliza Doolittle (circa 1912) thought the suggestion that she have a bath in private with her clothes off was indecent, so she hung a towel over the bathroom mirror. One wonders what she would have thought and said to the suggestion that she wear in public one of today's minuscule and socially accepted bikinis, held miraculously in place apparently with the aid of providence, and, possibly, glue" (*Andrews v. Parker* [1973] Qd. R. 93, per Stable J.).

[22] See the wide-range research by Reynolds *The Economics of Prostitution*, C.C.Thomas, Springfield, Ill., 1986.

[23] There are still several aspects that appear insufficiently examined such as the public finance profile. Arguing from the fact that little interest is paid to the amount of tax revenue from the control of prostitution, the conclusion of Cameron, *The Economics of Sin. Rational Choice or No Choice At All?*, Edward Elgar, Cheltenham 2002 (at p. 199) is that "The main policy issues that emanate from this market are then not financial ones, rather those of health, particularly contagious diseases, and the exploitation and abuse of vulnerable entrants".

[24] For some examples see Cameron, *The Economics of Sin. Rational Choice or No Choice At All?*, Edward Elgar, Cheltenham 2002, at p. 189; Edlund, Korn, *A Theory of Prostitution*, 110 *J. Pol. Econ.* 181 (2002) (at p. 192ff); Collins, Judge, *Client Participation and the Regulatory Environment*, in Munro, Della Giusta (eds.), *Demanding Sex: Critical Reflections on the Regulation of Prostitution*, Ashgate, Burlington, Vt, 2008 (at p. 144) [the book must be mentioned also for the vast bibliography at pp. 211–229]; Della Giusta, Di Tommaso, Strøm, *Sex Markets. A Denied Industry*, Routledge, Abingdon 2008 (at pp. 19ff. and 41 ff); Albert, Gomez, Gutierrez Franco, *Regulating Prostitution: A Comparative Law and Economics Approach* [2007], published online at http://www.fedea.es/pub/Papers/2007/dt2007-30.pdf (at p. 25f).

[25] This is clearly stated by Reynolds *The Economics of Prostitution*, C.C.Thomas, Springfield, Ill., 1986 in the introduction to her work: "Economic concepts should apply to individuals' reactions to incentives and disincentives, whether they are engaging in legal or illegal enterprises. Supply and demand, opportunity costs, and profit maximization can all be used to think about prostitution, just as any other economic sphere" (at p. *vii*).

[26] See the opening definition in Edlund, Korn, *A Theory of Prostitution*, 110 *J. Pol. Econ.* 181 (2002): "Prostitution is low-skill, labor intensive, female, and well paid".

the data, both statistical and social, was available.[27] Obviously this requires that one abandons, at least at the beginning, moral prejudices and tries to understand the functioning of the market.

What was roughly labelled "infamous commerce" had therefore to be destructured in its various elements, moments, components, interactions.[28] Examining prostitution or pornography means focusing on much more than the simple act through which the service or the goods are bought, and it requires extending the inquiry to the different aspects that surround it.[29]

At the same time economists, much better than lawyers, have been able to understand to what extent sex markets are regulated markets, mostly by the external – and very misty – boundaries of criminal law, but also by the uncertainty of private and administrative law. What appears indifferent to the law under the *In pari causa turpitudinis* rule, is correctly perceived as an element that shapes the market and drives it in certain directions.

Moreover economic research, investigating on the motivation behind the individual consumption of sexual goods and services, is able to explain the reasons for its globalization, which is related to the simple reason of the profit one can make by moving one's body from where its value is practically nil to where the price paid is ten times more, whatever the levy that must be given to some organization or person offering entry into the market and "protection".[30] This same research points at sex tourism as an effect of the different purchasing power between developed and non-developed countries.[31]

[27] Understandably research begins with micro-economic models: see *e.g. The Theory of Sex Markets* in Laumann, Ellinson, Mahay, Paik, Youm, *The Sexual Organization of the City*, U. Chicago Press, Chicago, 2004 (based on a study of Chicago). Or Dickson, *Sex in the city: mapping commercial sex across London*, The Poppy Project, London 2004; Mullings, *Globalization, Tourism and the International Sex Trade*, in Kempadoo (ed.) *Sun, Sex, and Gold. Tourism and Sex Work in the Caribbean*, Rowman & Littlefield, Lanham Md, 1999 (at p. 55ff analysis of the market in Jamaica). For a first example of demand/supply approach see Flexner, *Prostitution in Europe*, Grant Richards, London, 1914 (at p. 39ff).

[28] See for prostitution market segmentation, Reynolds *The Economics of Prostitution*, C.C.Thomas, Springfield, Ill., 1986, at p. 14ff. And for diversification of male prostitution markets Cameron, Collins, Thew, *Prostitution services: an exploratory empirical analysis*, 31 *Applied Economics* 1523 (1999). Albert, Gomez, Gutierrez Franco, *Regulating Prostitution: A Comparative Law and Economics Approach* [2007], published online at http://www.fedea.es/pub/Papers/2007/dt2007-30.pdf (at p. 28f) distinguish between escort and call girls, brothels, house prostitution, street prostitution.

[29] *E.g.* Cameron, *The Economics of Sin. Rational Choice or No Choice At All?*, Edward Elgar, Cheltenham 2002: "In terms of welfare economics we are dealing with its [*viz.* prostitution] role as an externality abatement technology" (at p. 185).

[30] For the "economics of pimps" see Reynolds *The Economics of Prostitution*, C.C.Thomas, Springfield, Ill., 1986, (at p. 24ff). Their importance in defining key factors of the market (such as prices) is underlined by Albert, Gomez, Gutierrez Franco, *Regulating Prostitution: A Comparative Law and Economics Approach*, [2007] published online at http://www.fedea.es/pub/Papers/2007/dt2007-30.pdf (p. 13f).

[31] See Manderson, Jolly (eds.), *Sites of Desire, Economies of Pleasure. Sexualities in Asia and the Pacific*, U. Chicago Press, Chicago, 1997; Altman, *Global Sex*, U. Chicago Press, Chicago, 2001.

A further element, which at the same time encourages and is the object of economic research is the fact that nowadays sex markets are mass markets.[32] The general increase in spending power; the wider availability of services and goods; the diversification of products as to quality, price and consumer satisfaction, together with sheer demographic growth involve a much larger number of people on the demand side, and therefore also on the supply side. This means not only that sex markets are no longer a niche, but also that they share the characteristics of other mass markets, becoming an ordinary commodity rather than a rare and marginal element in individual spending.

Although it may appear that the economic analysis of sex markets is scarcely interested in moral values,[33] one can easily see how these are an important factor to be considered in an objective way. Sex markets are – in most cases – reputation markets, where not only is the reputation of providers at stake but also of clients.[34] Being a prostitute, a porn actor/actress or a nude entertainer implies difficult choices that, once taken, are not easy to change and revert.[35] And at the same time – quite differently from other markets – the decision to satisfy one's needs through services or goods on the sex market may have, if made public, a shaming effect.[36] This factor has significant economic side-effects, such as sex tourism, which is chosen not only because of lower cost of services, but also because of the reduced risk of stigmatization.

A further typical aspect of economic research is that of pricing policies.[37] They quite clearly differ according to whether we are considering bodily

---

[32] Bernstein, *The Meaning of the Purchase. Desire, Demand and the Commerce of Sex*, 2 *Ethnography* 389 (2001) at p. 411 describes the "shift from a relational to a recreational model of sexual intimacy, by the symbiotic relationship between the information economy and commercial sexual consumption, by the ways tourism and business travel facilitate the insertion of men into the commercial sexual marketplace".

[33] *Rectius* "should not include moral considerations": Albert, Gomez, Gutierrez Franco, *Regulating Prostitution: A Comparative Law and Economics Approach*, [2007] published online at http://www.fedea.es/pub/Papers/2007/dt2007-30.pdf (at p. 15). The authors however indicate the moral implications in the evaluation of negative externalities.

[34] The perspective is amply presented in Della Giusta, Di Tommaso, Strøm, *Sex Markets. A Denied Industry*, Routledge, Abingdon 2008, at p. 17ff.

[35] "The moral decision to engage in prostitution is a sunk cost to the prostitute once he or she has begun" (Reynolds *The Economics of Prostitution*, C.C.Thomas, Springfield, Ill., 1986, at p. 188)

[36] For an analysis of naming-shaming policies in UK see Sanders, *Paying for Pleasure. Men who Buy Sex*, Willan Pub., Cullompton, 2008, at p. 149ff; in the US Teichman, *Sex, Shame, and the Law: An Economic Perspective on Megan's Laws*, 42 *Harv. J. on. Legis.* 355 (2005).

[37] Again see Reynolds *The Economics of Prostitution*, C.C.Thomas, Springfield, Ill., 1986, on costs, profit maximization, and career changes (at p. 16ff). However after fifteen years of research on the topic Cameron, *The Economics of Sin. Rational Choice or No Choice At All?*, Edward Elgar, Cheltenham 2002, at p. 197–199 lists twelve possible reasons for high prices in the prostitution market and concludes: "Some of the above factors are intimately linked to the degree of legality and tolerance of the market. It is not possible to predict a priori whether greater legal accommodation would push up the pay as it would seem likely to expand both the supply and the demand. Unfortunately we have no real idea of the relevant supply or demand elasticities, although probably the major factor which might decrease supply would be an improvement in women's labour market opportunities elsewhere".

services which require the presence in the same place of supplier and of client; consumer goods, such as those ordinarily found in a sex shop; or on-line services. Except for the latter – which suffer the same near-to-free pressure of most digital services, whatever their content – it is quite clear that the "forbidden" nature of what is bought justifies the acceptance by the client of a higher – compared to equivalent products or services – price.[38] From a legal point of view, analyzing price trends in the sex markets[39] helps understand how and what can effectively be regulated through intervention on price sensitive factors.[40] At the same time, from a strictly contractual point of view, the price paid by the consumer is relevant in order to understand if ordinary enforcement and redress measures are of any significance and to help us compare sex consumers with any other consumer.

b. *Law and economics in sex markets*

It should by now be clear why a general knowledge of the relevant sociological and economic literature on sex markets is essential for examining, on new basis, the relationship between contract theory and the provision of sexual goods and services.

Even if one is not an *aficionado* of the Law & Economics school of thought,[41] the relationship between the two aspects could not be more clear and sheds

---

[38] According to Edlund, Korn, *A Theory of Prostitution*, 110 *J. Pol. Econ.* 181 (2002) the reason for high prices is that "prostitution must pay better than other jobs to compensate for the opportunity cost of forgone marriage markets earnings" (at p. 182). However if one looks at the European street prostitution markets where prices are fixed and invariable within the local market, the impression is that the prices are established by the organizations behind the sex workers (mostly Eastern European or African), and are not left to the sophisticated calculations that the two authors suggest. The theory is labelled as "somewhat curious" by Collins, Judge, *Client Participation and the Regulatory Environment*, in Munro, Della Giusta (eds.), *Demanding Sex: Critical Reflections on the Regulation of Prostitution*, Ashgate, Burlington, Vt, 2008 (at p. 138).

[39] Cameron, *Space, risk and opportunity: the evolution of paid sex markets*, in 41 *Urban Studies* 1643 (2004).

[40] Do red light districts encourage competition between businesses and therefore level prices towards the bottom? If one considers the amount of information consumers receive, it would appear that the answer is affirmative. For an analogous situation see Reynolds *The Economics of Prostitution*, C.C.Thomas, Springfield, Ill., 1986: "The consequence of [a business] going underground is that a prospective customer will have a more difficult time finding out where a prostitution market is located, what services are offered, and what the prices are. Information becomes difficult to obtain and competition is much less active, since a primary way to compete involves overtly telling prospective clients about markets" (at p. 41). See also Albert, Gomez, Gutierrez Franco, *Regulating Prostitution: A Comparative Law and Economics Approach*, [2007] published online at http://www.fedea.es/pub/Papers/2007/dt2007-30.pdf (at p. 7).

[41] It is curious to note that the extremely long and wide-spanning book by Posner, *Sex and Reason*, Harvard U.P., Cambridge, Ma., 1992 is *not* a L&E inquiry into the legal aspects of sex, although one does find some references in this line (at p. 115ff). The reason may be that the distinguished author's view is that "sex markets" are governed by the principle of liberty, rather than by that of property (at p. 335). The grounds of this statement are not altogether clear and appear to be disproved by all the literature and empirical research which is cited in this work.

a very crude, but less rhetorical, light on the scene. Setting aside or objectivizing moral considerations allows us to understand what we are really talking about, instead of embarking on philosophical discussions of high-flying principles.

At the same time, however, one should be reminded that, in general law, is explicitly permeated with moral values, and contract law is no different. *Bona fides*, reasonableness, implied duties and obligations, cooperation, mitigation of damages *et caetera* (the list is as long as the table of contents of any handbook on contract, whether from a civil law or a common law jurisdiction) are expressions of a world of principled businessmen, who certainly are trying to maximize their respective profits but, at the same time, know that the law and the courts are policing their activities and will more often than not give a hand to the party that they feel has been oppressed.

Even if one holds a sceptical view on "immoral contracts" as a useful category, one should not forget that law is intrinsically moral and therefore it is impossible to set aside entirely values and principles.

This is the main reason why lawyers, although needing to know economic, statistical and social facts and figures, when it comes to setting a rule that which looks to the future, and therefore must guide human conduct, roads must part and decisions be taken.

It is therefore rather *naïf* to expect that the legal regulation of sex markets follows mechanically the results of social studies.[42] And while it is quite pointless for a social scientist to like or dislike what he or she is examining and it carries the risk of biased opinion, a lawyer, of necessity, must take sides, favour certain interests, restrict others.

Therefore when one passes from a descriptive role – typical of sociologists and economists – to a prescriptive role – typical of lawyers – the vast amount of information that has been gathered on sex markets needs to be used in function of the goals pursued. A certain number of highly value-ridden decisions are generally taken through penal legislation. The fight against human trafficking for sexual services implies a very strong moral stance which puts at its centre the protection of human beings. And the same may be said with regards to child pornography and the decision to prosecute not only those who produce, distribute and sell the videos, but also those who hold a physical or digital copy.

Explicitly, instead, for a L&E approach, see Albert, Gomez, Gutierrez Franco, *Regulating Prostitution: A Comparative Law and Economics Approach*, [2007] published online at http://www.fedea.es/pub/Papers/2007/dt2007-30.pdf. The balanced conclusion (at p. 42) is that "there is no single best Law and Economics response for the problems posed by prostitution".

[42] Brooks-Gordon, *The Price of Sex: Prostitution, Policy and Society*, Willan Pub., Cullompton, 2006.

Using social and economic data as a starting point does not, therefore, imply that one necessarily adheres to a *laissez-faire* approach. As a matter of fact – as will be analyzed more in detail in the following pages – it is, rather, the traditional category of immoral contracts that expresses a very simplified and unregulated market-driven approach.[43]

Therefore, while lawyers are freer to use deontic tools, they must also carefully consider the consequences of suggested rules and their coherence with their theoretical premises.

Quite clearly this study is – and wishes to be – experimental and therefore open-ended. Preferences are expressed but with the understanding that opposing ones can equally be well argued and founded. Tolerance in the field of studies concerning sex and the law, is much more than an intellectual posture and should be a methodological choice.[44]

[43] However quite appropriately Albert, Gomez, Gutierrez Franco, *Regulating Prostitution: A Comparative Law and Economics Approach*, [2007] published online at http://www.fedea.es/pub/Papers/2007/dt2007-30.pdf (at p. 10) underline that a contractual approach to prostitution implies that prostitutes enjoy contractual rights.

[44] "Academic disagreement does *not* imply lack of respect and admiration" (italics in original): Markesinis, Fedtke, *Engaging with Foreign Law*, Hart, Oxford 2009, p. vii (the quote is referred to René David's work, but can and should be extended to all academic debates).

CHAPTER TWO

SEXUAL SERVICES

a. *Prostitution*

Prostitution has always (being the 'oldest profession'[1]) served as the example of a contract "contrary to morality", and is typically associated with keeping a disorderly house. Before examining the contract more closely, it is appropriate here to mention how the perception of prostitution as archetypal has influenced all sex contracts and dragged them along with it into the domain of illegality. A careful process of distinguishing is, however, necessary in order to avoid generalized conclusions.

The other element to be considered – as has often proved the case with private law – is the strong tendency for private law rules to be modified in the wake of penal law.[2]

To the extent that it is suppression by penal statutes – and its associated case law – that lays down the determining elements of a given instance, private law

[1] Historical studies on prostitution are numerous. For some typical 19th - early 20th century encyclopaedic approaches see Dufour *Histoire de la prostitution chez tous les peuples du monde depuis l'antiquité la plus éculée jusqu'a nos jours*, (3 volumes), Paris, Seré Editeur,1851–1852. The introduction is explicit: "Ce trafic sensuel, que la morale reprouve, a existé dans tous les siècles et chez tous les peuples; mais il a revêtu les formes les plus variées et les plus étranges, il s'est modifié selon les moeurs et les idées; il a obtenu ordinairement la protection du législateur; il est entré dans les codes politiques et même parfois dans les cérémonies religieuses; il a presque toujours et presque partout conquis son droit de cité" (p. 6f); or Acton, *Prostitution considered in its moral, social, and sanitary aspects in London and other Large Cities and Garrison Towns with proposal for the control and prevention of its attendant evils*, Churchill, London (Ist ed. 1857, 2nd 1870); Sanger, *The History of Prostitution: Its Extent, Causes and Effects Throughout the World*, The Medical Pub., New York 1910; Flexner *Prostitution in Europe*, Grant Richards, London 1914.

For later comprehensive works see Scott, *A History of Prostitution*, Torchstream Books, London, 1954 (the author notes, over half a century ago, that "there are, too, many establishments which although they are virtually brothels existing solely for the purpose of prostitution, manage to avoid the law by various expedients. There are 'employment agencies', 'service flats', 'dancing academies', 'massage parlours', 'manicure and lady-barbering establishments', turkish baths', 'language-schools', 'teashops'" (at p. 12); Henriques, *Prostitution and Society. A Survey*, MacGibbon & Kee London 1963; Davis (ed.) *Prostitution. An International Handbook on Trends, Problems and Policies*, Greenwood Press, Westport, Ct, 1993; Gangoli –Westmarland, *International Approaches to Prostitution. Law and Policy in Europe and Asia*, Policy Press, Bristol 2006. For an updated survey of French criminal law on prostitution see Py, *Prostitution, Proxénétisme, Racolage*, in *Rep. Pen. Dalloz*, Paris, 2006.

[2] For a comparative analysis of criminal laws concerning prostitution see Decker, *Prostitution: Regulation and Control*, Littleton, Co., Rothman, 1979

aspects will inevitably be influenced, all the more so in cases where, as here, the central question is the legality or otherwise of the activity itself and hence of the contract.

We must therefore attempt to establish the relevant connections, but also the appropriate distinctions, between offences, torts wrongs, and business dealings. Not a simple undertaking, given that it is based essentially on debatable or at least flexible theoretical premises.

Let us start from the historically consolidated notion of prostitution, which was considered as the dealings for money that a woman undertakes with her own body. The inadequacy and general nature of the formula is immediately apparent, beginning with the arbitrary assumption that the activity is carried out only by women when since antiquity there have been male prostitutes as well, albeit in smaller numbers.[3]

But the most perplexing part is the reference to "her own body".[4] Does this require that in providing the service within the definition there be contact of *corpore corpori* (body with body), or does it include situations where there is no actual contact, *e.g.* looking but no touching? The distinction is not merely academic, because criminal statutes and case law might or might not qualify as acts of prostitution the carrying out of sexual acts upon oneself without any physical contact taking place between the parties[5] and sexual acts at a distance calculated to satisfy, directly and immediately, the libido of the person who has ordered the service.[6]

As can be seen, there is a graduated progression from actual intercourse to the satisfaction of a sexual urge without physical contact.[7] But there is another systematic obstacle: if it is true that the private law description of prostitution is strongly influenced by criminal law,[8] it is also true that many statutory laws

---

[3] see Aggleton, *Men who sell sex*, UCL Press, London, 1998; Doais, *Travailleurs du sexe*, VLB, Montreal, 2003. Can one discriminate against male (homosexual) clients? See Comment, *The Hunkiest Little Whorehouse in Town is Looking for a Few Good Men, but Only to Work: The Constitutional Implications of Heidi Fleiss's Female Brothel*, 14 *Vill. Sports & Ent. L.J.* 77 (2007)

[4] See Honoré, *Sex Law in England*, Hamden, Ct., Archon Books 1978, p.111: "A prostitute is sometimes said to sell herself or her body, but this is inaccurate. She makes with her client a contract for services, like that between a dentist, repairer or cinema owner and their customers". Calabresi, *An Introduction to Legal Thought: Four Approaches to Law and to the Allocation of Body Parts,* in 55 *Stanford L. Rev.* 2113 (2003) at p. 2147 points out the tendency to consider surrogacy contracts as a form of prostitution.

[5] See for an Italian case Cass. pen. 21.3.2006, no. 15158 (holding that sexual services carried out in video-conference via chat websites are equal to prostitution).

[6] For some examples see the Italian cases Cass. pen. 3.6.2004, no. 36157 (in *Foro it.* 2006, 32); Cass. pen. 22.4.2004, no. 25464 (in *Cass. pen.* 2004, 3577) (another case involving web chat).

[7] For an extremely detailed sociological description of the interpretation, execution, enforcement and discharge of a sexual contract between a prostitute and her client see O'Connell Davidson, *Prostitution, Power and Freedom*, Polity, Cambridge, 1998, pp. 88 ff.

[8] For this approach in a typical civil law system see Comporti, *Negozio giuridico immorale e irripetibilità della prestazione "ob turpem causam" ex art. 2035 c.c.*, in *Giur. compl. cass. civ.* 1955, VI, 148, at p. 153 according to whom the offences against public morals set out in the penal code involve "absolute immorality".

repressive of prostitution state that the act of prostitution is not in itself an offence.[9] It should be pointed out that this solution has generally been justified from a social point of view, in consideration of the derelict position of most prostitutes and to avoid them being the main – and most obvious – targets of police and legal suppression.[10] The wrongdoing targeted by prostitution laws is therefore the exploitation of prostitutes, what we might call the entrepreneurial aspect of the phenomenon.

It is clear that legality under criminal law does not necessarily imply the same under private law[11] (on the contrary, one is normally dealing with situations that are completely distinct from one another[12]). Therefore the fact that a certain juridical act is not qualified as a crime does not mean that it is a valid transaction or does not entail any responsibility. But the query immediately arises as to whether civil law should, in order to properly construe these types of contract, embrace the criminal interpretations that have arisen out of different situations. In other words, given that an individual prostitute plying his/her trade is not committing an offence, does that necessarily entail that the civil analysis of such activity should coincide with the criminal account? Or is it possible to have distinct civil and criminal concepts of prostitution? The consequences of the reply to this question are clear when we recall that criminal case law has extended the concept of prostitution to activity in which no physical contact takes place between the parties. In concrete terms, from the point of view of the validity of the contract, is the conclusion to be drawn the same whether the relationship is the 'common' one between prostitute and client or an individual offer of a sexual service at a distance (*e.g.* a peep-show, or online via a webcam)?

---

[9] The ECJ in the *Jany* decision (analyzed in detail in Chapter 9, para. d) has noted that in the majority of member states prostitution is not illegal *per se*. In Great Britain "It is not a criminal offence to engage in prostitution" Rook – Ward, *Rook & Ward on Sexual Offences. Law and Practice*, London, Sweet & Maxwell, 2004,[3] p. 353. In Irish law "Prostitution in itself is not illegal: a person may lawfully perform a sexual act with another in return for payment provided the act is not otherwise illegal": O'Malley, *Sexual Offences. Law, Policy and Punishment*, Dublin, Sweet & Maxwell, 1996, p. 182. For Italian case law, see Cass. pen. 8.6.2004, no. 35776 (legality of performing sexual acts, "even if done with a view to monetary gain").

[10] One should note that in France and in Italy the bills in favour of the closing of brothels were presented and strongly campaigned for by "feminist" MPs of their time, whose names are still associated with the law: in France Law 13.4.1946 n° 46-685 (loi Marthe Richard); in Italy Law 20.2.1958 n. 75 (legge Merlin) (For the latter see Bellassai, *La legge del desiderio. Il progetto Merlin e l'Italia degli anni Cinquanta*, Carocci, Rome 2006)

[11] See the case decided in Germany by the OLG Schleswig 13.5.2004, in *NJW*, 2005, p. 225

[12] Comporti, *Negozio giuridico immorale e irripetibilità della prestazione "ob turpem causam" ex art. 2035 c.c.*, in *Giur. compl. cass. civ.* 1955, VI, 148, notes at p. 152, that "even dealings of which the subject matter is an offence contrary to public morals may not in itself be contrary to morality, when the activity itself, despite being subject to penal sanctions, is not intrinsically and objectively contrary to the moral principles of a given society, in the sense that it is not offensive to the commonly held sense of decency."

The answer might indeed be affirmative. It does not however seem appropriate to arrive at it via the irrefutability of criminal statute or case law without considering the different perspectives presented by the concerns and methods of the private law system.

The core of the problem is the inter-relation between the various branches of the law. When we think of a modern criminal offence we have in mind, generally, a clearly defined set of cases – defined by statute law in their essential elements, and expressed in clear, and not broad, language – which must be verified, in accordance with very strict procedural rules – especially on evidence and fairness – by a court, with or without the assistance of a jury. From a logical and systematic point of view there is a crime only when the criminal trial is held and ends with a decision on the guiltiness of the accused. But can a civil court, which is examining the matter from a completely different point of view (generally on the basis of a claim of restitution, performance or damages) and which uses quite different standards of evidence, decide that the facts which are at the basis of the claim are to be considered a crime and therefore illegal according to private law?

If, therefore, from a general point of view and returning to the topic of this paragraph, the violation of the law on prostitution can be declared only by a criminal court, it would appear more coherent if civil courts fashioned their own notions of illegality and immorality, without becoming the self-proclaimed enforcers of statutes that are not addressed to them.

However the law in action is much more complex and less orderly. It is quite common – not only in this field – that the courts find their grounds for voiding or not enforcing an agreement on a supposed violation of criminal statute law following the maxim *ubi maior minor cessat* (or its French version: *le penal tient sur le civil*).

One can therefore easily understand that when criminal case law extends the scope of prostitution laws to facts which originally were not contemplated (male or transgender prostitution, no physical contact between parties, no money paid but only services rendered in consideration[13]), civil courts will hastily use these holdings to declare the immorality of the agreement or of the act. Judicial decision-making – from a legal-realist perspective – has a great deal to do with rhetorical argumentation and criminal law weighs heavily as an authority and it is rather difficult – for the sustainability of a decision in front of both of higher courts and public opinion – to hold that what *in abstracto* could/would be considered an offence by a criminal court is, instead, a regularly enforceable agreement.

---

[13] See however *State v. Clark*, 638 *P2d* 890 (1981) (Ida. S. Ct.) (services rendered to a prostitute while receiving her earnings cannot serve as consideration because of their immoral purpose)

This way of reasoning should, however, have an obvious side-effect: when the law de-criminalizes a behaviour that formerly was the object of criminal pursuit, one could argue that the related transactions should now be considered valid.

This approach can be applied to the various situations that arise from the scope of prostitution laws.[14]

One can, with rough approximation, outline four different regimes:[15]

i. Jurisdictions where prostitution – intended as the provision of sexual services in exchange for money or other utility – is *ipso facto* considered a criminal offence for both parties or for one of them.
ii. Jurisdictions where prostitution is not a crime, but gives rise to an unenforceable agreement.
iii. Jurisdictions where the contract for sexual services between a prostitute and his/her client is a valid and enforceable contract.[16]
iv. Jurisdictions where prostitution is legally organised by business entities.[17]

While in cases *iii.* and *iv.* few doubts should remain as to the validity of the various agreements that surround prostitution,[18] in the cases that fall under *i.* pragmatic – rather than systematic – reasons lead to the opposite conclusion (*i.e.* the contract will be held illegal and void).

---

[14] The literature on the subject is vast: inter alia see Decker, *Prostitution: Regulation and Control*, Littleton, Co., Rothman, 1979; Bindel, Kelly, *A Critical Examination of Responses to Prostitution in Four Countries: Victoria, Australia, Ireland, the Netherlands, and Sweden*, London Metropolitan University 2003 (available at www.endviolenceagainstwomen.org.uk); Danna (ed.), *Prostitution and Public Life in Four European Capitals*, Carocci, Rome 2007 (and available on-line at http://www.danieladanna.it/).

Although largely sociological, one of the most interesting studies on the subject is certainly "*Paying the Price: A Consultation Paper on Prostitution*", issued in June 2004 by the UK Home Office, which includes a substantial raft of legal statistics, a thorough summary of British legislation concerning prostitution and a summary of the law in 18 other European and non-European countries. See also the report by the Scottish administration, *Being Outside – Constructing a Response to Street Prostitution* (December 2004), especially chapter 11 which compares the various legislative solutions.

[15] For a similar subdivision see Reynolds *The Economics of Prostitution*, C.C.Thomas, Springfield, Ill., 1986, at p. 25ff. (Four models: laissez faire model, control model where police enforce prostitution laws, zoning model, regulation model); and Matthews, *Prostitution, politics and policy*, Routledge, London 2008 where four policies concerning prostitution are listed and analyzed: regulation, decriminalisation, legalisation, prohibition (p. 95ff.)

[16] This is the present German solution, discussed further on at Ch. 9, para d).

[17] This is the case of the state of Nevada in the US: Bingham, *Nevada Sex Trade: A Gamble for the Workers*, 10 *Yale J.L. & Feminism* 69, at 93f (1998); Note, *The Best Little Whorehouse Is Not in Texas: How Nevada's Prostitution Laws Serve Public Policy, and How Those Laws May Be Improved*, 6 *Nev. L.J.* 217 (2005). And in the state of Victoria in Australia: See Murray, *Labour Regulation in the Legal Sex Industry in Victoria*, 16 *Austr. J. Labour L.* 321 (2003)

[18] However, it has been held in European jurisdictions where brothels, mostly before World War II, were legal and subject to police authorisation that the agreements that were reached within were immoral: see Rescigno, "*In pari causa turpitudinis*", in *Riv. dir. civ.* 1966, 1, at p. 52. For some French decisions in this sense see Cass. 1re civ, 15.2.1967, in *JCP G* 1967, IV, 46; Appeals Paris, 22.3.1923, in *D.* 1923, 2, 118.

The most complex situation is that under *ii.* because the relation between private law and criminal law is – as we have seen – unsettled. And as these jurisdictions are the majority it is extremely important to understand if and when (and why) we are confronted with an immoral contract.

This discussion is particularly relevant considering that prostitution, traditionally, is the model of immoral contracts. If one were to conclude that the provision of sexual services which fall under the notion of prostitution is (no longer?) immoral, there would be significant consequences for the other contracts for sexual services and goods.

Pursuing the private law analysis further, if we were to assume that prostitution is not a crime but is an unenforceable agreement, one could ask whether this unenforceability is on both sides. According to the well known and century-old maxim, applied in all Western jurisdictions, *In pari causa turpitudinis melior* (or *potior*) *est condicio possidentis* (or *defendentis*). Therefore none of the parties can claim for the breach or the enforcement of the contract. But if one looks at parliamentary intention in enacting laws that de-criminalise prostitution, given that they were meant to protect the (weak) prostitute against the (powerful) pimp and client,[19] one could argue that we are faced with what is nowadays called a "*nullité de protection*", *i.e.* the possibility only for one party (the weak one) to claim that the contract is void, and not for the other.

This principle – which is widely applied in consumer law (only the consumer can ask for the contract to be voided) – if applied to prostitution contracts would mean the prostitute, who is not considered '*in pari causa*', might ask for payment of sums or services due, but the pimp (or, less likely, the client) may not claim breach, damages and/or restitution.[20]

There is a further way to get around the *In pari causa turpitudinis* rule in relations between the prostitute and his/her procurer. If the purpose of most criminal statutes which make exploitation of prostitution a crime, is that of protecting public morality but also the prostitute, the latter might bring – in those jurisdictions which allow the *partie civile* in a criminal trial – a claim for damages arising from the violation of the law.[21] The claim, therefore, would not be grounded in contract, but in tort. One could argue that, in the latter field, the ancillary principle of *Ex turpi causa non oritur actio* should apply.[22]

---

[19] For a summary of the arguments in favour of the abolition of legalized bordellos in Italy (enacted by Parliament in 1958) see Bellassai, *La legge del desiderio. Il progetto Merlin e l'Italia degli anni Cinquanta*, Carocci, Rome 2006

[20] This leads in some cases to the agreement being voidable (*i.e.* only the party which has suffered can act) rather than void: Bellizzi, *Contratto illecito, reato e irripetibilità ob turpem causam*, Giappichelli, Turin, 1999, pp. 6ff.

[21] For an Italian case (where, as in France, the victim may claim damages in the criminal trial) see Cass. pen. 26.11.1999, no. 285 (the prostitute is "prospective injured party and victim").

[22] See Enonchong, *Illegal Transactions*, LLP, London, 1998, p. 93ff

Therefore the immorality of the relation between prostitute and pimp would be a defence for the latter. But at the same time the counter-argument could be that the two parties are not *In pari delicto* and therefore, at least, the prostitute should be able to claim restitution of the sums confiscated as proceeds of the crime.[23]

These and many more hypothetical questions could be put relating to the private law consequences of prostitution agreements.[24] The aim of this paragraph, however, was not to embark on a would-be treatise on prostitution contracts, but to outline the many issues that a private law approach raises and that require a reply consistent with the general principles of the law applicable to contracts and other obligations.

b. *Contracts related to prostitution*

For a long time, prostitution has been the most important and most widespread immoral contract. Pornography, on-line sex and live sexual entertainment had a marginal role or were non-existent.

Focusing attention on prostitution has therefore brought to question the validity and enforceability of other contracts which were considered ancillary to prostitution.

The list is infinite: the lease of the premises where the prostitute holds his or her business;[25] the rental of a carriage to receive clients "on the road";[26]

---

[23] Honoré, *Sex Law in England*, Hamden, Ct., Archon Books 1978, p.131: "It is more doubtful whether the prostitute, if she has handed over the money [to the pimp], may claim it back in this case. The law in this case is arguably intended not merely to penalise the pimp but to protect her, and she is claiming not the reward of prostitution but the return of money paid without good cause". It would appear that this is the French position: see Cass. Crim. 7.6.1945 (in *D.* 1946, jur. p. 149, with comment by the great French lawyer René Savatier; and in *JCP* 1946,II, 2955, with comment by Hemard). More recently Appeals Bordeaux (criminal division) 23.5.1990, Renard (JurisData: 1990-042430) in which the act of the pimp extorting by violence money from the prostitute enables the latter to bring an action in tort. The *in pari delicto* rule cannot be used as a defence in order to avoid payment of non pecuniary damages.

[24] *e.g.* what are the effects of working as a prostitute on the property regime within marriage? See the Italian cases – described as 'aiding and abetting' – decided in Cass. pen. 11.3.2003, no. 19644 and Cass. pen. 11.2.2000, no. 7734

[25] Honoré, *Sex Law in England*, Hamden, Ct., Archon Books 1978, p. 125. The French position is equally clear: "La location d'un immeuble pour servir de maison de prostitution est nulle, comme contraire aux bonnes mœurs" (see *ex multis* Cass. soc., 29.10 1957, in *Bull. civ.* IV, n° 1027; or Cass. 1re civ., 15.2. 1967, in *Bull. civ.* I, n° 67). But where a building is leased knowingly for the purposes of prostitution by a lone person there is no offence (according to Italian law) because "the existence of a form of organisation, however rudimentary" is required (Cass. pen. 16.4.2004, no. 23657; and Cass. pen. 19.5.1999, no. 8600,in *Cass. pen.* 2001, 640).

[26] *Pearce v. Brooks* (1866) LR 1 Ex 213 (The Court thought the evidence given on the fact that the carriage had been used as part of the prostitute's display to attract men supported the verdict and, applying the *Nemo auditur* rule declined to intefere).

the provision of food and beverages;[27] the transport to and from the place where the streetwalker waits for her clients;[28] supplying condoms;[29] selling furniture;[30] insurance contract on a disorderly house;[31] employment as porter for a prostitute;[32] *et caetera.*

---

[27] *Anheuser-Busch Brewing Asso. v. Mason*, 46 *N.W.* 558 (1890) (Minn. S. Ct) (When a vendor sold beer to a vendee with knowledge that the beer would be used in the vendee's brothel, the vendor was not barred from recovering the price of the beer because the vendor had not actively aided the vendee in her unlawful activity). The French position appears to be unfirm: see T. com. Marseille, 7 nov. 1913 in *Gaz. Pal.* 1914, 1, p. 266; but *contra*, T. civ. Seine, 16.6.1928, in *DP* 1928, 2, p. 187, with comment by Minvielle; and Appeals Poitiers, 8.2. 1922 in *S.* 1922, 2, p. 116).

[28] According to the criminal division of the Italian Court of Cassation the client who "after having sexual relations with the prostitute, accompanies her back to the place where she carries out her trade" is not guilty of aiding and abetting (Cass. pen. 9.11.2004, in *Cass. pen.* 2005, 1892), Cass. 14.2.2001, n. 16536 (in *Riv. pen.* 2001, 633). The problem has also arisen in the USA: see the Comment, *Sex on the Internet: A Legal Click or an Illicit Click*, 38 *Cal. W.L.Rev.* 527 (2002). And for the use of a third party's car see *State v. One 1985 Gray Buick Auto.* (Ct. Super. Ct. 1993 – on Lexis 3502) (The State failed to prove that the automobile was used as a means of committing the crime of solicitation of prostitution; the use of the automobile was not instrumental to the solicitation of an undercover police officer).

[29] For a – frustrated – Italian attempt to extend the offence of aiding and abetting to persons who "being in possession of a regular business licence, supply packets of condoms at current market prices to persons engaging in prostitution, even if the transaction occurs at the same place as the prostitution activity" (Cass. pen. 14.5.2004, n. 30582, in *Riv. pen.* 2005, 160).

[30] See *Ham v. Wilson*, 86 So. 298 (1920) (Miss. S. Ct.) (Sellers who sold furniture on an account to buyer who was a prostitute could not recover the furniture in a replevin action when prostitute was unable to pay balance due after one seller, the mayor of town, ordered all prostitutes out of town, because sellers knew intended use of furniture and the contract was for an immoral purpose and was void). And for the same Court *Menger v. Thompson*, 91 So. 40 (1922) (A furniture merchant could not collect from an owner of a house of prostitution in his action for recovery of furniture sold to the owner and for the balance of the purchase price because the owner was engaged in an illegal business, and the merchant knew of it. He could not enforce a contract based on illegal proceeds). See also *Reed v. Brewer*, 37 *S.W.* 418 (1896) (Tex. S. Ct.) (Note endorsee was not entitled to recover amounts due under notes, given for the use of furniture, where the endorsee was charged with notice that the notes were to be repaid with proceeds from prostitution and were, thus, illegal contracts); and *Philip Levy and Others v. Davis*, 80 S.E. 791 (1914) (Va. S. Ct) (The seller sought to recover the possession of certain furniture and other household goods sold and delivered to the buyer. The seller alleged that payment had not been made by the buyer. The evidence showed that the furniture would be used in the buyer's house of prostitution, and the seller was aware that the buyer's only means of payment would be income from that illegal business. The trial court entered a judgment for the buyer. On appeal the court held that, as a general rule of law, a court could not aid a party to enforce an illegal contract. As such, the seller could not recover damages for the breach of the contract at issue because it was unenforceable on public policy grounds). But the opposite view was taken in *Eliza v. Mahood*, 26 *La. Ann.* 108 (1874) (La. S. Ct) (A furniture seller was awarded judgment against her buyer for the amount due even though both kept public houses of prostitution, and the seller knew that the furniture would be used for an immoral purpose, which use did not vitiate the contract).

[31] See *Bonenfant v. American Fire Ins. Co* 43 *N.W.* 682 (1889) (Mich. S. Ct.) (A fire insurer was entitled to new trial because the court erred in not submitting to the jury the question of whether a purchaser of a house from the insured kept it as a house of prostitution and lewdness, rendering the fire risk more hazardous). More than a century later the same argument echoes in a French decision: Appeals Toulouse 12.4.2005, *Societé Suisse Accidents v. Calmels Millet* (JurisData: 2005-270883), in which it was held that the insurer should have been informed of the particular use of the building because it implied an extension of the risk. Not having done

Some of these cases fall – or might fall – under penal law statutes incriminating those aiding, abetting or pandering. But other cases are not considered by prosecutors.

From an objective point of view the argument that has been used for holding these contracts immoral is that they are instrumental to prostitution and therefore are legally contaminated by the immorality of the latter.[33]

With the exception of the lease of a house used as a brothel,[34] the argument does not overcome an attentive private law examination.

The general principle of validity of contracts is more than an abstract rule. It is a value on which modern society rests. Voidness and voidability are exceptions and are restrictively interpreted. Unenforceability, especially if one party has already suffered a detriment, is an unwelcome decision because it undermines stability of business agreements and the millenary rule that *pacta sunt servanda*. Extending invalidity (or unenforceability) to other contracts – which theoretically could be without limits – is much more laden with policy concerns than the question of immorality itself.[35]

---

so, the contract was declared void. But in *Phenix Insurance Co. v. Clay*, 28 *S.E.* 853 (1897) the Georgia Supreme Court took a different view. The insurance company issued to the insured a policy of insurance on a house that the insured rented out. The insurance company argued that the fact that the house was rented to a woman with the knowledge of the insured that the property was to be used for prostitution defeated the insured's action on the policy. The court noted that neither party to the policy benefited by the illegal use of the insured property. The contract of insurance did not grow out of and was not connected with the illegal use of the house. The purpose and object of the contract of insurance was not in contravention of the public interest, and the contract was not against public policy as tending to promote an illegal and immoral business. For a similar, French, decision see Appeals Amiens, 1.7. 1901, in *Gaz. Pal.* 1901, 2, p. 644; and in further instance Cass. req., 4.5.1903, in *Gaz. Pal.* 1903, 2, p. 394. But more recently see Appeals Toulouse 5.9.2006, *Swisslife Assurance de Biens v. Benoit sarl* (JurisData: 2006-323416) in which the contract was held void and unenforceable by third parties damaged when the building caught fire.

[32] For an Italian case see Cass. pen. 13.1.1999, n. 2296 (in *Cass. pen.* 2000, 1428) (holding the contract valid). For the opposite French view see Cass. soc. 8.1. 1964, in *JCP G* 1964, II, 13546

[33] See *Coughler v. Fackler* 510 *SW2d* 16 (1974)(Ky) (no recovery of monies if agreement was founded upon prostitution); and *Donovan v. Scuderi*,443 *A2d* 121 (1982) (Md) and all the cases cited by Williston, *A Treatise on the Law of Contracts* (4th edition by Lord), Lawyers Coop., Rochester, N.Y., 1997, at pp. 514ff..

[34] For some cases see: in France Cass. 1re civ., 3.12.1963, in *Bull. civ.* 1963, I, n° 531 (lease is void if the building is used for an illegal or immoral purpose such as a gaming house or a brothel); or Cass. civ. 15.11.1938, in *Gaz. Pal.* 1939, 1, 194; Cass. civ. 27.12.1945, in *Gaz. Pal.* 1946, 1, 88; Cass. soc., 29.10.1957, in *Bull. civ.* IV, n° 1027 (purchase of a house with the purpose of using it as a brothel); Cass. req., 1.4.1895, in *DP* 1895, 1, 263 and in *S.* 1896, 1, 289; Cass. req. 17.7.1905, in *DP* 1906, 1, 72; Appeals Poitiers, 8.2.1922, in *DP* 1922, 2, 33 and in *S.* 1922, 2, p. 116 (loan to buy a building to be used as brothel). One should however consider that the application of nullity to the lease implies not only non-refundability of rent paid, but also (in most European jurisdictions) non-applicability of fixed terms imposed by various rent acts, no possibility of pre-emption rights, *et caetera*.

[35] On the tendency, already evident several decades ago, to exclude connected contracts from the scope of immoral contracts, see Rescigno, "*In pari causa turpitudinis*", in *Riv. dir. civ.* 1966, 1, at p. 51.

However, not only invalidity should – and actually is – used sparingly, but it is also extremely difficult to explain why contracts collateral to prostitution should be considered immoral.[36] The transaction in itself has nothing obscene or lewd in it. Millions of similar ones are made every day without anyone questioning their validity. How should one detect those which are immoral? One does not need to delve the vast literature on the subject to reach the conclusion that few areas of contract law are more shrouded in the mist of uncertainty than the intent of the parties.

Moreover, if one applies general – albeit complicated – rules of causation it is extremely difficult to establish a link between the collateral contract and that of prostitution. Can one reasonably assert that the act of prostitution is a significant consequence of the contract which is considered ancillary to it?[37] Would one usually apply the same criteria in an ordinary tort case?

The reason for the development of the tendency to declare unenforceable contracts somehow related to prostitution is, to look at things realistically, the quality of the parties, or rather, of one of them, the prostitute.[38]

Once the Court is aware of his or her profession the social stigma is transformed into legal rule. The judge avenges public morality by punishing not so much the prostitute – who is irredeemable – but those who take significant legal commitments with him or her.

From a systematic point of view this position – however well argued in public policy – is hardly tenable because it implies that, contrary to the principle of equality in front of the law, a certain class of persons (prostitutes) has a limited contractual capacity which affects all those who are aware of such a condition.[39]

---

[36] Honoré, *Sex Law in England*, Hamden, Ct., Archon Books 1978, p. 131 (on contracts which supply prostitutes with the necessities of life); for the American view see Corbin, *Corbin on Contracts. Illegal Bargains*, LexisNexis, Newark, NJ, 2002, vol 15, at p. 548f.: "any bargain to render service. To lend money, or to supply goods or buildings for the purpose of aiding to maintain such a business" is to be considered unlawful. However "It is not unlawful to sell goods to one who conducts the immoral business, even though the seller knows the buyer will use the goods in the business, if the goods sold are such as have lawful uses and the seller does not participate in the immoral purpose"

[37] On this line see *American Equitable Assurance Co. v. McWhirter*, 133 *So.* 664 (1931) (Miss. S. Ct.) (Insured's use of her insurance contract to obtain credit to purchase household goods that she then allegedly used in her house of prostitution did not render the insurance contract void as against public policy, her use of the contract in this manner was too remote to have rendered the contract void as against public policy).

[38] Buckley, *Illegality and Public Policy*, Sweet & Maxwell, London, 2002, at p. 92: "It must be very doubtful, however, whether other contracts related to her activities would nowadays be regarded as 'contrary to public policy'" (…) "The better view is therefore that, on grounds of pragmatism as well as principle, the category of contracts contrary to public policy on grounds of 'immorality' should be kept within a narrow compass: with *Pearce v. Brooks* being regarded as a doubtful authority"

[39] And not only in contracts: see the Italian case decided by Cass. 13.7.1982, n. 4107 on entrusting the care of minors to a mother who is a prostitute

Again the remarks that have been made do not tend to set out the rules that govern – or should govern – contracts.

c. *Striptease, lap-dancing, peep-shows*

The extent to which the criminal law framework can be onerous is shown whenever we turn from what is traditionally regarded as prostitution (offering one's own body upon payment for the satisfaction of another's sexual requirements) and examine different ways in which a body and sexual requirements play a part, but where the latter are satisfied without bodily contact.[40]

The difference is not, however, confined to this physical particularity.

We are generally dealing here with activities that are not performed for individual consumption but are part of a complex, and hence entrepreneurial, trade.

It is clear that the widening scope of criminal law enforcement has had significant consequences for civil interpretations of the relations involved. But, here again, distinctions should be made. Indeed, certain services have, since some time ago, become permitted by the criminal law in the form of shows and theatrical acts. There would be no point in discussing the legality of contracts between *Crazy Horse* and *Les Folies Bergères* in Paris and their respective '*artistes*' on the one hand and their numerous loyal customers on the other. It will be said that this is due to the importance of the artistic context – the music, dance routines and scenery – in which use is made of the body. But in response to this it is clear that what attracts such a large audience to these places, instead of the *Opéra* and *Chaillot*, is certainly the sexual urge excited, and perhaps satisfied, by the displays of nudity.[41] And note that in the majority of cases one is a long way from the refinement of the famous venues mentioned above, and outside effects are usually confined to a light show – trained on the artistes in a darkened hall - with mood music and a series of more or less stereotyped movements. It suffices that the show does not cross the imperceptible threshold of obscenity for it to be considered legal in every respect.[42]

---

[40] Where does the border stand? For a sociological perspective see Bullough - McAnulty, *The Sex Trade: Exotic Dancing and Prostitution*, in McAnulty - Burnette (eds.), *Sex and Sexuality*, vol. I, Praeger, Westport, Ct., 2006, vol. I, at p. 299

[41] See Posner, *Sex and Reason*, cited above at fn11, p. 364.

[42] For a possible example of striptease being illegal under article 528 of the Italian penal code (obscene performance) because it is "accompanied by poses and attitudes provocatively and continuously invoking sexual relations" see Trib. Roma 5.5.1986 (in *Foro it.* 1986, II, 672). With similar arguments see *State ex rel. Miller v. Private Dancer* (613 *N.E.2d* 1066) (Oh. C.A.) (1993) (A nuisance existed at a nightclub because lap dancing was lewd and tended to incite sensual desire or imagination. "Lewdness" was not void for vagueness because it put a person of ordinary intelligence on notice of what actions were prohibited). But *contra* see *State ex rel. Wayne County Prosecuting Attorney v. Dizzy Duck*, 511 *N.W.2d* 907 (1993) (Mich.C.A.) (Nude dancing and lap dancing that did not involve employees masturbating patrons, were not within the

And here we need to establish a criterion whereby the concept of obscenity, important in criminal law, can be related to the civil concept of "contrariety to morality".[43] The question is a simple one: is everything that is obscene also contrary to morality, while anything that is not obscene is also not contrary to morality? And this question transforms itself into the equally simple judicial dilemma: is the accompanying contract valid or not? An example: if the dancers are ill but the musicians, singers and other entertainers are all available, can the customer claim compensation for non-performance of the contract on the grounds that the presence of the dancers was of the essence? What if the strip artiste is replaced by a male colleague? What if the show is tedious and does not satisfy the client's sexual demands?

The uncertainty as to limits clearly affects the case of 'lap-dancing' in which the performance lays yet more stress on the sexual aspect and the artiste allows herself to be touched fleetingly or does so herself, the public showing their appreciation usually by tucking banknotes into her diminutive G-string.[44] In some jurisdictions criminal case law has held that such conduct comes under the same heading as prostitution and organising it is thus illegal.[45] This however is not always the case. While it seems easy to conclude that money conferred by the clients to the artiste is thus in the nature of a gift (similar to the ubiquitous practice of 'tipping') and so cannot be claimed back under any circumstances, different considerations apply to the service in itself. The contract

---

statutory definition of lewdness and were not abatable nuisances). In a not-so-recent decision which reflects pre-sexual revolution mores, a French court has held that a contract between the owner of a night-club and a strip-tease artist was void and therefore the former could not claim damages for an unjustified repudiation by the latter (Trib. Gr. Instance Paris 8.11.1973, in *D. 1974*, somm. p. 30 and 1975, p. 40, with comment by Puech; and in *Rev. Trim. Dr. Civ.* 1974, p. 806,with comment by Loussouarn)

[43] Another way to avoid the issue is considering nude dancing within the very wide spectrum of freedom of expression: see the US Supreme Court case concerning nude dancing *Barnes v. Glen Theatre* 501 US 560 (1991) (nude dancing is a form of expressive activity; however an Indiana public indecency statute was justified despite the incidental limitations on such expressive activity because it was unrelated to the "erotic message" the dancers seeked to convey). From this, exclusively American, point of view, see Sklar, *Nude Dancing*, 5 *Geo. J. Gender & L.* 95 (2004); Case, *Lewd and Immoral: Nude Dancing, Sexual Expression, and the First Amendment*, 81 *Chi.-Kent L. Rev.* 1185 (2006). The rule is set forth in *People v. Janini*, 89 Cal. Rptr.2d 244 (1999) (Cal. C.A.) (Convictions of defendant lap dancers and defendant theater managers for ordinance violations and prostitution reversed; ordinance violations were pre-empted by state law, and performances enjoyed free speech protection).

For an Australian perspective on tabletop dancing and lap dancing see Murray, *Labour Regulation in the Legal Sex Industry in Victoria*, 16 *Austr. J. Labour L.* 321 (2003).

[44] For another Italian case, which confirms the variety of opinions, "Fleetingly touching the dancers on the arms, legs, buttocks, hips and breast" does not constitute "a sexual service" (Trib. Bergamo 7.5.2003, in *Foro it.* 2003, II, 642).

[45] Bullough, *The Sex Trade: Exotic dancing and prostitution*, (ch. 12 in McAnulty, Burnette (eds.), *Sex and sexuality*, Greenwood Press, Westport, Ct. 2006). Roach, *Stripping, Sex, and Popular Culture*, Berg, Oxford, 2007. According to the criminal division of the Italian Court of Cassation (Cass. pen. 12.2.2003, n. 13039) the "conduct [is] intended to promote and profit from services that are objectively calculated to stimulate the sexual instinct".

is made between the management of the venue and the client, and the entry fee gives the client the right to attend the spectacle and, sometimes, also the right to a drink. In criminal terms the contract is an element of the *actus reus* (the continuing and organised aspect of it) but it is reasonable to ask if such contracts might nevertheless produce effects (for example where a ticket is paid for but the customer is not able to enter the hall).

With the peep-show, we move onto another level: the client pays to be present, alone or with others, at a person's sexual acts, unable to touch the participants, but usually able to indulge in auto-erotic practices. Although the contact of body upon body is not involved, there is no doubt that one party is providing a representation of a sexual act with the main purpose of satisfying the urges of the other contracting party. Apart from the similarities with prostitution, there are clear elements of obscenity/contrariety to public morals and satisfaction of sexual needs. The conclusion thus seems obvious.[46] And yet if the means of availing oneself of the 'show' are changed only to the extent of watching it on recorded media instead of being present in person the whole legal aspect changes: one is permitted to ask why the mere fact of being present in person makes the legal relationship void?

An integrated consideration of transactions "for sexual purposes" thus leads us to question the reasons for the differences, their rationale, and whether there are any criteria for making the distinctions.

d. *Sex over the phone and the Internet*

With the development of communications networks, sexual services – along with almost all other kinds – are now obtainable through this medium.[47] These are characterised by the distance between the supplier and the user, neutralised for sound and vision by the technology. In the first, still widely used, version, the client looking for auto-erotic release telephones a number and speaks to an operator. The service consists of an exclusively sexual conversation. More recently, images have been added to the voice, so the service now generally consists of the representation of a naked body and of a sexual act.[48]

---

[46] But confirming that in these matters the Latin maxim *quot capita tot sententiae* is still valid see the French decision Appeals Paris (crim. division) 18.2.2004, Chemouny (JurisData: 2004-243542) holding that there was no criminal offence of deceit towards a mentally disturbed person of age who had paid over 15,000 FF (€ 2300,00) to have access to ten peep-shows. The decision indirectly holds that the contracts were valid.

[47] For some data on the phone sex industry see Flowers, *The Fantasy Factory. An Insider's View of the Phone Sex Industry*, U. Penn. Press, Philadelphia 1998 p. 3ff

[48] For a history of phone sex see ch. 5 in Lane, *Obscene Profits. The Entrepreneurs of Pornography in the Cyber Age*, New York, Routledge, 2000, p. 149. But from a sociological point of view one question could be: is cybersex sex ? For a perplexed answer see Waskul –Douglass –Edgley, *Outercourse: Body and Self in Text Cybersex*, in Waskul (ed.), *Net.sexxx.*

We have seen how criminal case law tends to regard such activity as equivalent to prostitution and so treats the organising enterprise as exploitation. Yet if the defining element of prostitution is the "use of one's own body" without any bodily contact necessarily occurring, a problem immediately arises when the service consists entirely of a conversation, in which what counts is the content and tone of voice. The two techniques – telephone and computer – even though the latter is a development of the former, would be subject to distinct legal regimes.[49] Moreover, assuming for the moment that both are contrary to morality, there is a far from negligible technical consideration which impinges on the validity of the obligations undertaken and on their effectiveness.[50] Usually, indeed, the payment for such services is made through a scheme of delegated payment in the form of an addition to the user's telephone bill. Once the contract between supplier and user has been completed, usually by the means of automatic devices, the service is rendered and payment will be made by the client when it is requested by the telecommunications company and thence transferred to the due recipient. In the first place, one could question the validity of such delegated dealings, given that the telecoms operator agent cannot hide behind an alleged blissful ignorance of the content of the 'value added' services he has facilitated.[51] Their voidness would obviously drastically

Readings on Sex, Pornography and the Internet, Peter Lang, New York, 2004, at p.13; and Waskul, *The Naked Self: Body and Self in Televideo Cybersex*, *ibidem*, at p.35.

[49] Consider Lord Brown's *dictum* in *Director of Public Prosecutions v. Collins* [HL, 2006] at para. 27: "I confess that it did not at once strike me that such a telephone conversation would involve both participants in committing a criminal offence. I am finally persuaded, however, that section 127(1)(a) is indeed intended to protect the integrity of the public communication system: as Lord Bingham puts it at paragraph 7 of his speech, "to prohibit the use of a service provided and funded by the public for the benefit of the public for the transmission of communications which contravene the basic standards of our society". (Quite where that leaves telephone chat-lines, the very essence of which might be thought to involve the sending of indecent or obscene messages such as are also proscribed by section 127(1)(a) was not explored before your Lordships and can be left for another day.)"

[50] For the French debate on the point see Raymond, *Messageries roses et droit des contrats*, in *Contrats, conc. consom.* 1994, chron. 4

[51] This argument is discussed in the English case examined in *Armhouse Lee v. Chappell* [CA, 1996] according to which (Lord Brown J.) the contract between the client and the advertised telephone sex line might not be enforceable; but the contract between telephone sex line and a third party for advertising services is. For a US decision incidentally examining a similar situation see *Network Communications v. Michigan Bell Tel. Co.* 703 *F. Supp.* 1267 (1989) (E.D. Mich.) (holding that the telephone company's termination of a billing and collection agreement for allegedly sexually-explicit and/or obscene recorded telephone messages was not a state action). French case law is much more to the point: see Appeals Montpellier 28.9.1999, *Gimenez v. France Telecom* (JurisData: 1999-117622): one cannot invoke the fact that the main use of the telephone line has been to access on-line porn services. The telecoms operator is not obliged to control the use of the line for good morals and no evidence has been provided that the reason for which service has been subscribed to is to access pornographic sites. The contract is therefore valid and the bills have to be paid. However, *les bonnes moeurs* can be invoked from the other party to the contract: see T. Comm. Paris 9.2.1993, *S.té Connection v. France Telecom* (JurisData: 1993-040577), which held valid the repudiation of the contract by France Telecom on the grounds that its network was being used for a homosexual porn site. It would however

alter the type of service that is offered under a pre-payment formula (the client buys an amount of credit, which is progressively used up as he avails himself of one erotic service after another) or is paid for by credit card whose details have been supplied.

The second consideration is that the case of erotic services via telephone and computer is unique among dealings for sexual purposes with the final user, since the payment is made after, rather than before the service is performed. Thus in theory the client, having received the service, could invoke the immorality of the contract and require the telecoms operator not to pay the provider for the erotic service.[52] If this does not in practice happen, one may conclude it is because the client has no wish to advertise his 'consumer choices'.

The services in question exhibit a further peculiarity, which is typical in the world of telecommunications, and that is that the party with whom the contract is made is seldom situated in the country where the client resides. From here the communication is re-directed to the client's country where generally the person offering the service resides, especially if the use of the native language is an essential feature of the service (one can well imagine that an 'erotic line' phone call conducted in some strange and foreign language would hardly satisfy the dialler's requirements). The remote sourcing does not seem to pose questions of private international law, because various factors, not least consumer law, lead us to consider the client's law applicable and any input from foreign law and jurisdiction of no consequence, if only for lack of the necessary formal requirements.

More to the point, one must acknowledge the national legal system's limited reach – not to mention the frailty of attempts at self-regulation – in this zone known as cyberspace, where even if laws are shown to apply any chance of enforcing them is slight.

---

appear that porn hot-lines are legal as they are subject to specific (albeit higher) taxation: Article 235 of the CGI (Code Général des Impôts) states that "1. Il est institué une taxe sur les personnes qui fournissent au public par l'intermédiaire du réseau téléphonique des services d'informations ou des services interactifs à caractère pornographique qui font l'objet d'une publicité sous quelque forme que ce soit. - 2. Cette taxe est égale à 50 % des sommes perçues en rémunération des services qu'elles mettent à la disposition du public".

[52] In Germany, after the enactment of the Prostitutionsgesetz of 2002 (see further Ch. 9, para. d) the BGH (decision of 8. 11. 2007, in *NJW* 2008, 140) has stated that after the reform the contracts concerning porn chat-lines cannot be any longer considered void because they are contrary to *bonos mores* according § 138 BGB. This article must be interpreted in accordance with fundamental rights and the social context. The legislative change is a clear indication on how social standards have changed. Therefore a contract for a service named 'Erotik Line' is valid and the creditor has action for payment of the sums due (€ 15,165). For a critical comment of the decision see Majer, *Sittenwidrigkeit und das Prostitutionsgesetz bei Vermarktung und Vermittlung*, in *NJW* 2008, 1926.

CHAPTER THREE

SEXUAL GOODS

In the sex market there is a vast number and variety of services, but also a significant range of products that are designed directly and unmistakeably to stimulate and satisfy sexual activity. The issues raised by this are obviously different: sale of goods rather than services issues, guarantee for defects rather than non-performance, and a different criminal law frame of reference.

a. *Pornography*

Discussions about pornography generally – and especially in the United States – are centred on the conflict that repressive legislation raises with freedom of expression issues. In this conflict in balance there is, on the one side, the protection of morals, and on the other the freedom to express and disseminate ideas.

From one viewpoint, that which places all the different forms of expression at the same level, the answer would clearly be in favour of freedom of expression. Showing representations of copulation between humans as distinct from that of animals; describing it in scientific as distinct from literary terms or recording it live are all equivalent activities and thus to be equally protected. Moving along this line, the boundaries of licit pornographic expression are incrementally enlarged and regulation appears inadmissibly discriminatory in respect of other forms of expression.[1] The feminist reaction is the criminalization of pornography as the depiction of an act of violence against women.[2]

This dominant opinion is not however followed in this paragraph. If one adopts a more realistic point of view, according to which all expressive content is not in fact entitled to the same treatment[3], it becomes possible to point out

---

[1] For a social history of pornography in the last five decades in the US see Streitmatter. *Sex Sells! : The Media's Journey from Repression to Obsession*, Westview Press, Boulder, Co,2004

[2] But one should remember that pornography is not only for men, but also for women: see Shamoon, *Office Sluts and Rebel Flowers: The Pleasure of Japanese Pornographic Comics for Women*; and Butler, *What Do You Call a Lesbian with Long Fingers? The Development of Lesbian and Dyke Pornography*, in Williams (ed.), *Porn Studies*, Duke U.P., Durham, 2004, pp. 77 and 167. And involves not only women as models but also men in homosexual pornography: Stychin, *Law's Desire. Sexuality and the Limits of Justice*, Routledge, London, 1995, p. 55 (chapter 3 devoted to "*The Porn Wars. Feminism and the Regulation of Gay Male Pornography*"); Thomas, *Gay Male Video Pornography: Past, Present, and Future*, in Weitzer (ed.) *Sex for Sale: Prostitution, Pornography, and the Sex Industry*, Routledge, New York, 2000, p.49.

[3] I have tried to set out these views in a more comprehensive way in *Freedom of Expression. A Critical and Comparative Analysis*, London, Routledge-Cavendish, 2008 (in particular in chapter 7)

the meagre expressive content of pornographic representation which is essentially about consumer products designed to satisfy not intellectual but primarily physical needs. Interventions limited to the conditions of circulation (the whether, when and how) are moreover justified in the same way as with any other product to which warnings as to use apply. This is certainly a grey area in which artistic expression and the pornographic can become mixed, but this is a physiological point and is not of sufficient weight to dictate the rules.

Pornography is therefore considered here as a product,[4] not as the expression of a fundamental human right.[5] One will assume that – subject to the proportionality test – limitations to its dissemination are legitimate.[6] What we are interested in is how such limitations affect the contracts through which such products circulate among the general public.

As with prostitution, the first point one should examine is the impact of criminal law on pornographic production.[7] In most Western jurisdictions it would appear that there is indeed a large body of law on obscene publications, plays or videos, according to which the trade in products with pornographic content is illegal *per se*.[8] The consequences for the sale contract should thus be

---

[4] For a history of the pornographic industry see Lane, *Obscene Profits. The Entrepreneurs of Pornography in the Cyber Age*, Routledge, New York, 2000; Brown, *Commercial Sex: Pornography* (ch. 11 in McAnulty, Burnette (eds.), *Sex and Sexuality*, Greenwood Press, Westport, Ct. 2006).

[5] See *Belfast City Council v. Miss Behavin' Limited* (HL 2007): "If article 10 and article 1 of Protocol 1 [of the ECHR] are engaged at all, they operate at a very low level. The right to vend pornography is not the most important right of free expression in a democratic society and the licensing system does not prohibit anyone from exercising it" (*per* Lord Hoffmann).

[6] One of the main arguments by feminist writers in favour of laws restricting pornography is based on its "effects", insisting on the fact that it can cause violence (see Mason-Grant, *Pornography Embodied. From Speech to Sexual Practice*, Rowman & Littlefield, Lanham, Md., 2004, at p.62). This approach appears to miss the central point: pornography is meant to induce directly sexual excitement and satisfaction; it can therefore be considered a product, not much different from a snack or a cold drink. Hence its regulation. At any rate the argument is challenged: see *Does Pornography Cause Violence? The Search for Evidence*, in Church Gibson – Gibson (eds.), *Dirty Looks. Women, Pornography, Power*, British Film Institute, London, 1993, p. 5 ("It is time for feminists, and their supporters, who want to act against men's greater use of violence and sexual coercion, and their continuing social dominance, to abandon the search for some spurious causal link with 'pornography' – however we define it", at p. 18)

[7] The tendency – by scholars (especially feminist) - to consider pornographic films as a form of prostitution is widespread: see Garb, *Sex for Money is Sex for Money: The Illegality of Pornographic Film as Prostitution*, 13 *Law & Ineq*. 281 (1994)

[8] For the US see Williston, *A Treatise on the Law of Contracts* (4th edition by Lord), Lawyers Coop., Rochester, N.Y., 1997: "The sale or bargain to sell anything in itself immoral or obscene, or an agreement to manufacture or publish anything of the kind, is invalid" (vol. 7, § 16.23, p. 530). For an old English case see *Poplett v. Stockdale*, 171 *Eng. Rep*. 1041 (1825) ("I must now take notice of the character of this book. It professes to be the history of a common prostitute, and to detail her real or pretended amours. I have no hesitation in saying, that no person who has contributed his assistance to the publication of such a work can recover in a Court of Justice any compensation for labour so bestowed. The person, who lends himself to the violation of the public morals and laws of the country, shall not have the assistance of those laws to carry into execution such a purpose. It would be strange, if a man could be fined and imprisoned for doing that, for which he could maintain an action at law. Every one who gives his aid to such a work,

nullity and the application of the principle *In pari causa turpitudinis*: no protection for the purchaser if the item is damaged or unusable, or the contents are entirely different from what was requested, or the contents are identical to another item marketed under a different name.

There are however a few points that need to be clarified: the first is the scope of the penal statute. Does it contemplate the production of obscene publications and videos? Or does it punish their exposure to the public? Or their trade? These are extremely important features because they may exclude from the scope of criminal law the transfer of pornographic materials from one person to another outside a commercial relation.

The second point is the effect that the findings of a penal judgment may have in a private-law controversy. If a crime has been found, the solution is the nullity of the contract.[9] But let us assume that the court has found that the material is obscene but not the other requirements for applying the provision (*e.g.* the publication was not shown to the public[10]): should it be considered obscene, and therefore illegal, by a civil court? If a product is pornographic, the many ways through which it may be disseminated (*e.g.* whether it is sold where it will be seen by all comers or in a place where only adults will be exposed to it) appear irrelevant from a private law perspective. The intrinsic contrariety to morality of the product drags the associated contract towards invalidity, whatever the surrounding circumstances may be.

The main problem that a legal-realist approach has to face is the fact that notwithstanding the enormous amount of legislation purporting to repress pornography,[11] obscene publications and video are sold in their millions each day in the Western world, at newsstands, in bookstores, in video-rental outlets,

---

though as a servant, is responsible for the mischief of it. No man can doubt the double object of this work, the corruption of youth, in the first place, by the exhibition of licentious scenes; and the extortion of money from exalted individuals, by holding over them the fear of having themselves described as persons of immoral habits. I have no power here to punish these parties, but I will not consent, that the plaintiff shall have the assistance of this Court, to obtain remuneration for labour directed to such scandalous purposes", *per* Best CJ). For some among many cases decided by Italian criminal law courts in the sense see Cass. pen. 21.1.1994, Cannata (in *Foro it.* 1996, II, 18); Cass. pen. 10.6.1993, Teso; Cass. pen. 26.9.1991, Rebuffat; Pret. Modica 22.12.1994, (in *Riv. pen.* 1995, 376) (despatch of catalogues of products that were "obscene and for intimate use"); Pret. Catania 10.4.1992 (in *Giur. merito* 1993, 1051).

[9] For a US example see *Fugate v. Greenberg*, 189 *N.Y.S.2d* 948 (1959) (Defendant publisher could not offset plaintiff author's breach of contract claims, as indemnification agreement did not insure against defendant's intentional act of distributing obscene books, to which it had pled guilty).

[10] See the Italian case decided by the joint criminal divisions of the Court of Cassation 24.3.1995, n. 5606, Gasparato (in *Foro it.* 1996, II, 17)(no crime of "trade in obscene items, where this is carried out in a sufficiently discrete and cautious manner")

[11] And where pornography is not an offence there are numerous proposals to introduce new criminal offences. See *e.g.* the Report of the [New Zealand] Ministerial Committee of Inquiry into Pornography, 1989, at p. 138, proposing imprisonment and severe monetary penalties for running a business in "prohibited materials" and for advertising them.

on-line. It is difficult to argue that we are not faced with real pornography (it is sufficient to browse the covers and the titles). And it is quite unsatisfactory to hold that these millions of transactions are valid only if spontaneously performed, but cannot ever be enforced by the courts. Or at least the argument could only be accepted if one decides that – as a matter of policy – they should exist outside or at the margins of the legal world.

One solution – albeit rather artificial – could be that of separating the material object involved in the trade – an obscene film, say – from the principle of contrariety to morality. The latter would not necessarily be the consequence of the former but would require an extra element (*e.g.* a lewd motive on both sides of the contract), which would have to be proven and which is not necessarily entailed in an over-the-counter sale.

Although one is quite accustomed – especially in the continental European legal doctrine – to such intellectual acrobatics, which are often excogitated by the courts in order to avoid otherwise unwelcome solutions, it is quite clear that they are quite inadequate in the face of the size of the phenomenon.

In some cases the legislature intervenes, exempting from criminal sanctions intermediaries such as newsagents[12]; or exempting Internet providers from a duty to control over what is being transmitted on their networks or sites.[13] It is however clear that excluding criminal sanctions or liability in tort does not, in itself, mean that a contract is valid.

One should also consider that the commerce of pornographic material does not seem to attract the same generalised opprobrium that greets the frequenter of prostitutes.[14] Is it possible to maintain that the social conscience validates these contracts and requires for them, as for any other contract, the protection of the law?[15] The answers may differ, but they are clearly more difficult in jurisdictions – such as civil law ones – where the civil code includes a specific provision on the unenforceability of immoral contracts. One is well accustomed to the fact that in these countries also it is up to the courts to specify the content of the rule and to adapt it to the changing mores.[16] However it is difficult to ask

---

[12] See *e.g.* the Italian law 17.7.1975, n.355 which provides that newsstands are not liable for the sale of pornographic publications provided the public cannot immediately see the obscene parts and they are not sold to minors under 16.

[13] See article 15 of Directive 00/31 on e-commerce ("Member States shall not impose a general obligation on providers, when providing the services covered by Articles 12, 13 and 14, to monitor the information which they transmit or store, nor a general obligation actively to seek facts or circumstances indicating illegal activity").

[14] See Williams (ed.), *Porn Studies*, Duke U. Press, Durham 2004 ("Facile fantasy about the root evil of pornography, one that can only persist in ignorance of the genre's history and its close analysis", at p.12).

[15] However the social investigation and related data are debatable: see Soble, *Pornography and the Social Sciences*, in Soble – Power (eds.), *The Philosophy of Sex. Contemporary Readings*, V ed.,Rowman & Littlefield, Lanham, Md. 2008, at p. 433

[16] For a way out found by a US judge see *Eastern Distributing Corp. v. Lightstone* (241 N.W. 189) (1932) (A seller is entitled to compensation from a distributor for legitimate magazines sold under the terms of a written contract because the contract was divisible, and the delivery of obscene material did not render the entire contract void).

a judge to decide *contra legem* and to take upon himself the burden that should rest on Parliament's shoulders.

Ultimately, one is left with an unpleasant dilemma: either pornography does not really exist; or the whole legal system – including criminal law, administrative law, private and procedural law – is quite unable to enforce rules which appear to be rooted in deeply felt moral principles.

b. *Sex-enhancing products*

All over the Western world there are commercial outlets (so-called sex-shops or porno-shops) which sell a variety of products related to sexual activity: items of clothing, models of sex organs, equipment used in various extreme practices (typically, sado-masochism), stimulation enhancers and the like. The legality of sale contracts for such goods should be based on the principle of sexual freedom, if and when it is ingrained in our legal order.[17]

Understandably the issue is not so easily disposed of, as it requires clarification of various points.

i. In the majority of European legal systems there is no ban either on homosexuality or on allegedly 'unnatural' sexual practices. This point is made by way of contrast with the legislative position in other undoubtedly free countries – free also in this arena – such as the United States.[18]

ii. The first fundamental premise for the legitimate exercise of sexual freedom is having attained majority. Sexual activity between minors raises delicate questions of parental responsibility, while between adults and minors it raises the question of criminal acts.

iii. The second fundamental premise is founded on consent, without which the spectre of sexual violence is present. Yet even in the case of consenting adults it is reasonable to ask how far this extends: as far as permitting actual bodily harm, as can occur with sado-masochistic or other extreme sexual practices[19]?

---

[17] See Honoré, *Sex Law in England*, Hamden, Ct., Archon Books 1978, p. 172f

[18] See the survey edited by Posner, Silbaugh, *A Guide to America's Sex Laws*, U. Chicago Press, 1996.

[19] Compare the tragic cases of erotic bondage games resulting in the death of one of the partners decided by the House of Lords in *R. v. Coutts* (2006) and by the Trib. Firenze 6.11.1985 (in *Foro it.* 1988, II, 400). The problems arising from such practices are analysed by Koppelman, *Eros, Civilization, and Harry Clor*, 31 *N.Y.U. Rev. L. & Soc. Change* 855 at 860ff (2007) and by Pa, *Beyond the Pleasure Principle, The Criminalization of Consensual Sadomasochistic Sex*, 11 *Tex J. Women & L.* 51 (2001). However not so long ago as 1994 the House of Lords in *R. v. Brown* held that these acts were punishable as crimes, and that consent was no justification: "In my opinion sado-masochism is not only concerned with sex. Sado-masochism is also

iv. The third premise is that sexual freedom is to be exercised so as not to outrage decency, typically by avoiding performing acts in public or in places open to the public.

If then these products are incidental to the legitimate exercise of a fundamental freedom and have always, as the literary and graphic tradition in the field tells us, been used together with inoffensive objects (*e.g.* bottles and other

---

concerned with violence. The evidence discloses that the practices of the appellants were unpredictably dangerous and degrading to body and mind and were developed with increasing barbarity and taught to persons whose consents were dubious or worthless" (*per* Lord Templeman). "I have no doubt that it would not be in the public interest that deliberate infliction of actual bodily harm during the course of homosexual sado-masochistic activities should be held to be lawful" (*per* Lord Jauncey). "Sado-masochistic homosexual activity cannot be regarded as conducive to the enhancement or enjoyment of family life or conducive to the welfare of society. A relaxation of the prohibitions in sections 20 and 47 can only encourage the practice of homosexual sado-masochism, with the physical cruelty that it must involve (which can scarcely be regarded as a 'manly diversion'), by withdrawing the legal penalty and giving the activity a judicial imprimatur. As well as all this, one cannot overlook the physical danger to those who may indulge in sado-masochism. In this connection, and also generally, it is idle for the appellants to claim that they are educated exponents of 'civilised cruelty.'" A proposed *general* exemption is to be tested by considering the likely *general* effect. This must include the probability that some sado-masochistic activity, under the powerful influence of the sexual instinct, will get out of hand and result in serious physical damage to the participants and that some activity will involve a danger of infection such as these particular exponents do not contemplate for themselves. (…) There is no legal right to cause actual bodily harm in the course of sado-masochistic activity" (*per* Lord Lowry). One can wonder if Lord Mustill's dissent would today be considered in a more favourable light: "What I do say is that these are questions of private morality; that the standards by which they fall to be judged are not those of the criminal law; and that if these standards are to be upheld the individual must enforce them upon himself according to his own moral standards, or have them enforced against him by moral pressures exerted by whatever religious or other community to whose ethical ideals he responds. The point from which I invite your Lordships to depart is simply this, that the state should interfere with the rights of an individual to live his or her life as he or she may choose no more than is necessary to ensure a proper balance between the special interests of the individual and the general interests of the individuals who together comprise the populace at large. Thus, whilst acknowledging that very many people, if asked whether the appellants' conduct was wrong, would reply "Yes, repulsively wrong," I would at the same time assert that this does not in itself mean that the prosecution of the appellants under sections 20 and 47 of the Offences against the Person Act 1861 is well founded.(…) if it were to be held that as a matter of law all infliction of bodily harm above the level of common assault is incapable of being legitimated by consent, except in special circumstances, then we would have to consider whether the public interest required the recognition of private sexual activities as being in a specially exempt category". And similarly Lord Slynn's dissent: "as the law stands, adults can consent to acts done in private which do not result in serious bodily harm, so that such acts do not constitute criminal assaults for the purposes of the Act of 1861. My conclusion is not based on the alternative argument that for the criminal law to encompass consensual acts done in private would in itself be an unlawful invasion of privacy. If these acts between consenting adults in private did constitute criminal offences under the Act of 1861, there would clearly be an invasion of privacy. Whether that invasion would be justified and in particular whether it would be within the derogations permitted by article 8(2) of the European Convention on Human Rights, it is not necessary, on the conclusion to which I have come, to decide". It is a pity that the case is not discussed in the very complex approach to the problem in *Consent to Sexual Relations* by Wertheimer (Cambridge, Cambridge U.P. 2003). It is commented upon in Archard, *Sexual Consent*, Westview Press, Boulder, Co. 1998 (at p.110 ff.)

household objects; fruit and vegetable) in sexual activity, then no legal obstacles should be raised to their being validly sold.

These premises are, however, far from granted and there are many jurisdictions (typically Southern US states[20]) in which the sale – if not also the simple possession – of these objects is a criminal offence.[21]

Let us then assume that the law does not criminalise, directly or indirectly,[22] this activity. Does that mean that the contracts through which these objects are distributed and sold are valid? If, then, we subscribe to the interpretation which holds that defining them as sales of obscene objects entails the nullity of contracts for contrariety to morality, the consequences on legal relations in sale of goods would be significant. Indeed the purchaser would be deprived of any of the guarantees normally afforded by contracts of this kind. In practical terms no action would lie in respect of malfunctioning goods, no right to repair or replacement, no compensation for damage caused to property (typically by fires caused by a defective product), and no right of return for goods bought via 'distance marketing'.[23]

---

[20] See below Chapter 5, para. b)

[21] And the related contracts are void: see, in a case which makes one smile thinking of the ingenuity of businessmen, *Manes Co. v. Glass*, 102 *A*. 964 (1918) (R.I. S. Ct.): the honourable justices describe very cautiously the objects: " 'The Manes Company' was engaged in the business of making and selling "toy novelties" and that from time to time he disposed of certain of his products to the defendant, the purchase price of which amounted to the sum of $ 151.61. These novelties were variously designated as 'Bear Charms' or 'Movie Bears', 'Bull Charms' or 'Movie Bulls', 'Modern Dances', and the 'Naked Truth'. Samples of these devices were introduced in evidence and form a part of the record now before us. They are capable of being operated and thus producing effects which would not be apparent so long as they remained in a state of repose. That they are designed and intended to be operated and that such operation would be within the comprehension of children is obvious from a mere casual inspection of the articles. We do not feel warranted in particularly describing the effects which may be produced by the manipulation of these so-called 'novelties'. To do so would only serve to extend the knowledge of and give permanency to obscene and indecent devices." The action by the producer for payment of the price of the "novelties" was dismissed: "Samples of the articles introduced in evidence at the trial bear unmistakable proof of their obscene and indecent character which fully justified the court in its refusal to submit that question to the consideration of the jury. We do not need to cite authorities to the effect that a contract based upon a violation of the statute referred to [*viz*. General Laws of Rhode Island, Chapter 347, Section 13, which make it unlawful for any person to sell anything that may be obscene, indecent or manifestly tends to the corruption of the morals of youth] cannot be enforced in a court of law". Nearly a century later sex toys are still the object of judicial debate: see *Williams v. Morgan*, 478 *F.3d* 1316 (11th Cir. 2007) (Alabama statute e that prohibits the commercial distribution of sex toys upheld). For a Comment, *Substantive Due Process: Sex Toys after* Lawrence, 60 *Fla. L. Rev*. 507 (2008).

[22] See the Italian case decided by the Corte di Cassazione (Cass. SS.UU. pen. 25.9.1995, n. 3027, Calamai, in *Cass. pen*. 1996, 2968) in which the general penal code provision against obscenity was invoked against a phallic sculpture ("There is no violation of article 528 of the penal code where objects of a phallic form displayed and offered for sale are of an evidently ironic or jocose nature such that they cannot be considered obscene")

[23] See further Chapter 6 devoted to the protection of "sex consumers". The problem also exists in other legal systems: see. Biesanz, *Dildos, Artificial Vaginas, and Phtalates: How Toxic Sex Toys Illustrate a Broader Problem for Consumer Protection*, 25 *Law & Ineq*. 203 (2007).

One might reply "*dura lex sed lex*", but the outcome is not at all desirable in terms of legal policy since, in practice, it is tantamount to conferring a privileged and, one may assume, unintended legal privileged position on the producers of "obscene objects", whose circulation, instead, one wishes to limit. To draw a perhaps simplistic law and economics rule, there would be an incentive for producers to announce the "obscene" nature of their products so as to benefit from this regime and/or to ignore duties of the proper functioning of the product.

To avoid such a conclusion, one might take the radical course of excluding the consideration of such objects as "obscene" (though with a few of these, particularly models of sex organs, this would be very difficult) or else offer a better conceptualisation of a contract contrary to morality. Following this line of thought one might, therefore, posit that it is not the physical goods in themselves – *ex hypothesi* "obscene" – that determine contrariety to morality, since the legal regime is indifferent to the purchase of one item rather than another, provided that it circulates in the market legitimately. In other words, if the manufacture and trade of certain items is not prohibited then the various contracts whereby these change hands at different levels of the distribution chain cannot be void.

Questions of invalidity or illegality may arise when a specific and mandatory rule is breached.[24] Where such rules are generic they are not sufficient to render a deal void. The contract would therefore be void if an interest held to be fundamental or inalienable was harmed, such as the dignity of the person, typically, in the case of prostitution. Where "obscene" objects are concerned, private use by consenting adults without any economic purpose in mind would have no effect on the validity and hence legality of the contract by which they were acquired. A "sexual purpose" is not, therefore, necessarily an illicit one.

c. *Aphrodisiacs*

Aphrodisiacs have been used in all cultures at all times, but in recent years the issue of products with (real or alleged) aphrodisiac properties has assumed a prominent social and economic profile. Viagra, the "blue pill", has won a fame that far surpasses that of more established brands.[25] Almost as soon as it appeared, similar products were manufactured (*e.g.* Cialis) and not a day

---

[24] However one should note that the theory of illegal contracts, at least in English law, is fraught with contradictions, owing to its piecemeal development, as pointed out by Buckley, *Illegality in Contract and Conceptual Reasoning*, 12 *Anglo-Am. L. Rev.* 280 (1983) (but the same could be said for most other jurisdictions).

[25] For a "social history" of the product see Loe, *The Rise of Viagra. How the Little Blue Pill Changed Sex in America*, NYU Press, New York, 2004

passes without offers of the original or its imitators arriving online into one's e-mail account[26] These products work (or are intended to) by increasing male sexual potency and staying power.[27]

Given that impotence in its various degrees of severity is a curable medical condition, it is clear that in the normal course of events any medication should be prescribed by and taken under the control of a doctor.[28] No commercial questions of any kind should arise in these circumstances other than the collateral one of whether the drug should be available through the national health service.[29]

The problem occurs when this vast range of types of product, advertised openly as aphrodisiacs, is offered (and bought) outside a medical relationship, regardless of their immense variety ranging from household names like Viagra and Cialis to other product marketed using techniques that recall a quack doctor and his promises of miraculous properties.

Selling of this kind, where medicines available only on prescription are involved, might be considered illegal because they are contrary to the principle of public order.

Indeed, the doctor's prescription has a function in reporting the patient's medical condition and so his or her right to receive the appropriate treatment. Where this is missing, an essential and legitimising element of the transaction is missing also. Thus we could be confronted by a case of invalidity for violation of a mandatory rule.

Can we, however, conclude that such contracts are more generally contrary to morality?

It might be said that this kind of product, when not bought as part of a doctor-patient relationship, serves only to stir an individual into an enhanced state of sexual performance. It is immaterial whether this is brought about through images, physical objects or sex-enhancing products.

To this one can reply that since sexual freedom is one of the most intimate spheres of individual liberty the state has no right to interfere in the ways in

---

[26] See Note, *Patent Law for New Medical Uses of Known Compounds and Pfizer's Viagra Patent*, in 46 *IDEA* 283 (2006).

[27] See the Comment, *Life, Liberty, and the Pursuit of Viagra? Demand for "Lifestyle" Drugs Raises Legal and Public Policy Issues*, in 28 *Capital U.L. Rev.* 837 (2000).

[28] See McLaren, *Impotency: A Cultural History*, Chicago, Chicago U.P. 2007 (in particular chapter 10 devoted to the drugs for the cure of impotence)

[29] This subject has been most intensely debated in the USA: see Haff, *Health Care Coverage: Contraception and Viagra*, 7 *Georgetown J. Gender & L.* 1185 (2006); Chavkin, *Medicaid and Viagra: Restoring Potency to an Old Program*, in 11 *Health Matrix* 189 (2001); Kaminski, *Must Employers Pay for Viagra? An "Americans with Disabilities Act" Analysis Post-Bragdon and Sutton*, in 4 *DePaul J. Health Care L.* 73 (2000); Comment, *Prescription for Fairness: Health Insurance Reimbursement for Viagra and Contraceptives*, 35 *Tulsa L.J.* 399 (2000); Comment, *Mandated Medicaid Coverage of Viagra: Raising the Issues of Questionable Priorities, the Need for a Definition of Medical Necessity, and the Politics of Poverty*, in 44 *Loy. L. Rev.* 611 (1998).

which consenting adults exercise it. There is no place for 'public morals' in the bedroom, as these only apply in public and outside contexts. Whether sexual stimulation is reinforced through physical exercises, consumption of certain foods (such as oysters) or of alcohol, or of other legal substances are matters of no concern to the law.

The case of aphrodisiacs is helpful to point out how in the sex market entirely legal contracts do exist alongside others which, for a variety of reasons, are considered illegal or unenforceable. And at the same time it must be borne in mind that the widespread use of such products results indirectly in a larger market of potential consumers of sexual services, including those who, for reasons of age or dysfunction, can only enter it with difficulty.[30]

[30] See. DeLamater, Still *Sexual Desire in Later Life*, in Stombler, Baunach, Burgess, Donnelly, Simonds (eds.), *Sex Matters. The Sexuality and Society Reader*, II ed., Pearson, Boston, 2007, at p. 375; Gott, *Sexuality, Sexual Health and Ageing*, Maidenhead, Open University Press, 2005; Kirkman, *Ageing and Sexuality. The Final Frontier for Positive Ageing?*, in Hawkes, Scott (eds.), *Perspectives in Human Sexuality*, OUP, Oxford, 2005, p.104 (Viagra "also means that sexual performance remains an issue for men into their old age. This not only has consequences for older men but also for the women partners of these men, who may have looked forward to a time when the 'coital imperative' was no longer as imperative, and that sexuality might involve more options than simply penetrative sex", at p.113); Note, *A New Sexual Revolution?: Viagra as Pandora's Box for the Elderly*, 7 *Elder L.J.* 409 (1999). In *Brumley v. Pfizer, Inc.* 149 *F.Supp.2d* 305 (S.D.Tex., 2001) one of the (rejected) claims was that the drug would cause the patient to engage in sexual activities at an increased energy level with potential risks for his health.

CHAPTER FOUR

SEX AND PROPERTY RIGHTS

The analysis of the validity of contracts concerning the transfer of goods of a sexual nature brings us to a question that can be considered paramount, that is, the ownership of such entities and the possibility to assert property rights over them.

a. *Property of obscene objects*

It would appear reasonable to assume that if one can legitimately own "sexual goods" one can legitimately transfer them.[1] We shall set aside the issue of property rights of one's own sexual features, which will be discussed further on in Chapter 7.

Apparently with regard to material objects there seems to be a distinction between individual ownership of them, and the possibility to trade them. Whilst for the former there are no bans, nor any case law stating that these objects cannot be owned, for the latter, administrative regulations prevail establishing when, where and how such a trade may be run.

The validity of the contract between two individuals depends instead on the interpretation one gives to the general ban on immoral contracts which has been discussed in Chapter 3.

We are therefore in front of rather peculiar property rights: one can own and use an object and be protected in one's right by the ordinary remedies of the law (restitution or damages), but one may not, altogether or under severe limitations, transfer that object by contract. The conclusion however is not surprising.

There are many other objects – *e.g.* works of art, buildings, environmentally protected land – that may be owned but not transferred unless there is compliance with strict regulations. The justifications which are given are all posited in public policy and are meant to protect the general interest.

In the case of property over sexual goods, the ban on transfer – because the contract is immoral – is justified on the basis of public morality. Applying the

[1] Albeit with some legal subterfuge ("ironic or jocose nature" of objects of phallic form): see the Italian case (Cass. SS.UU. pen. 25.9.1995, n. 3027, Calamai, in *Cass. pen.* 1996, 2968). Compare however Williston's view: "The sale or bargain to sell anything in itself immoral or obscene, or an agreement to manufacture or publish anything of the kind, is invalid" [Williston, *A Treatise on the Law of Contracts* (4th edition by. Lord), Lawyers Coop., Rochester, N.Y., 1997, volume 7, § 16.23, p. 530].

principle of proportionality it is, however, difficult to understand how the prohibition of transfer from one individual to another on a non-professional basis could promote the values underlying the public morality principle.

This is a further reason for reconsidering the foundation and the scope of the immorality rule applied to contracts.

The issue gets more complicated when one is confronted with property rights over non-material entities.

b. *Copyright*

Can one assert copyright over an obscene work of art? In this regard, the first question which arises is if the author can claim rights over the result of his intellectual effort and can invoke the full protection of the law. Copyright laws do not contain express provisions banning from their scope works that are deemed immoral.[2] Therefore, whether it be Gustave Courbet's *L'origine du monde* (which finally has found its place in the Quay d'Orsay museum)[3] or a lewd hardcore film, the creation of the work entitles the author to the protection of the law.

Following this line, limitations to the right to reproduce, represent and disseminate the work come after the work has been created and are justified by reasons of public policy, mostly laws against obscenity.[4]

Similarly, a parallel isssue is with works where the content is considered illegal for its subversive or criminal expression (a pamphlet advocating the extermination of a race, a handbook on how to organize a terrorist attack *et caetera*).

It is a crime to disseminate such works, but copyright is not questioned. And one can find an analogy with the rights over Adolf Hitler's writings, which were not declared as non-existing, but were confiscated by the Allies and transferred to the Land of Bavaria, which now holds them.

There is, however, a different approach which has found the approval of the courts. There can be no right over obscene works, and therefore the author cannot invoke the protection of the law.[5]

---

[2] See, for the US, *Jartech v. Clancy*, 666 *F.2d* 403 (1982) ("There is nothing in the Copyright Act to suggest that the courts are to pass upon the truth or falsity, the soundness or unsoundness, of the views embodied in a copyrighted work. The gravity and immensity of the problems, theological, philosophical, economic and scientific that would confront a court if this view were adopted are staggering to contemplate. It is surely not a task lightly to be assumed, and we decline the invitation to assume it.")

[3] For the adventurous history of this scandalous painting, created in 1866, see Savatier, *L'Origine du monde. Histoire d'un tableau de Gustave Courbet*, Bartillat, Paris 2006.

[4] On the use of postal laws to prevent dissemination of obscene materials see Forkosh, *Obscenity, Copyright, and the Arts*, 10 *New Eng. L. Rev*. 11 (1974).

[5] There is a long list of English cases dating back to the beginning of the 19th Century, and stretching well into the 20th: In *Southey v. Sherwood*, 35 *Eng. Rep*. 1006 (1817) (a case of an

This line of thought, therefore, does not distinguish between infringement of copyright and breach of contract. In the latter case, the denial of enforcement or of damages might be justified by the general refusal of immoral contracts. But in the former case what is denied is the existence of a property (copy)right.

The obvious consequences are that anyone can appropriate himself of the work of another, reproduce it in whole or in part without paying any monies, change, modify or adapt it at his pleasure.

The self-proclaimed author would not even have the possibility to claim an indirect protection (typically, passing off) as generally happens with works that do not fall under the notion of works of art, such as games or puzzles.

Although this line of thought[6] does not appear to be attractive, it does have – apart from the approval of some courts – some elements in its favour.

---

apparently libellous poem) Lord Chancellor Eldon's opinion was that "If this publication is an innocent one, I apprehend that I am authorised, by decided cases, to say that, whether the author did or did not intend to make a profit by its publication, he has a right to an Injunction to prevent any other person from publishing it. If, on the other hand, this is not an innocent publication, in such a sense as that an action would not lie in case of its having been published by the author and subsequently pirated, I apprehend that this Court will not grant an Injunction". In *Lawrence v. Smith* 37 *Eng. Rep.* 928 (1822) the defendant had published without the consent of the author a book entitled *Lectures on Physiology, Zoology and the Natural History of Man.* Always according to the Lord Chancellor Eldon "Looking at the general tenour of the work, and at many particular parts of it, recollecting that the immortality of the soul is one of the doctrines of the Scriptures, considering that the law does not give protection to those who contradict the Scriptures, and entertaining a doubt, I think a rational doubt, whether this book does not violate that law, I cannot continue the injunction". In *Stockdale v. Onwhyn* 108 *Eng. Rep.* 65 (1826): "The work professed to be the history of the amours of a courtesan, that it contained in some parts matter highly indecent, and in other matter of a slanderous nature upon persons named in the work. (…) I am certain no lawyer can say that the sale of each copy of this work is not an offence against the law. How then can we hold that by the first publication of such a work, a right of action can be given against any person who afterwards publishes it?" (*per* Abbott CJ).

For some US cases see *Shook v. Daly*, 49 *How. Pr.* 366 (N.Y. Sup. Ct. 1875); *Broder v. Zeno Mauvais Music Co.*, 88 *Fed.* 74 (N.D. Cal. 1898). For other cases see Rogers, *Copyright and Morals*, 18 *Mich. L. Rev.* 390 (1920); and the Note, *Immorality, Obscenity and the Law of Copyright*, 6 *S.D. L. Rev.* 109 (1961). This line of thinking is still alive: see *Devils Films, Inc. v. Nectar Video*, 29 *F. Supp. 2d* 174, 176 (S.D.N.Y. 1998) ("It strains credulity that Congress intended to extend the protection of the copyright law to contraband [hard core pornographic films].")

[6] The question is open to debate: see Phillips, *Copyright in Obscene Works: Some British and American Problems*, 6 *Anglo-Am. L. Rev.* 138 (1977) quoting Halsbury ("It is not clear whether there is no copyright in such works, or whether copyright exists, but will not be afforded protection by the courts (Vol. IX (Copyright), Hailsham ed., 1973, p. 531, para. 833, n.l.)"); and Skone James ("in order to establish such a claim the author must, in the first place, show a right to sell; and this he cannot possibly do, he himself not being able to acquire a property therein (Copinger and Skone James on Copyright, Eleventh ed., 1971, para. 224)", it is "more accurate to say that the ground for refusal by the courts to intervene is that it is against public policy to protect rights of publication and sale of works, where publication and sale would be against the public interest".) These positions appear to be confirmed in more recent legal literature: see Halsbury's *Laws of England*, 4th edition, Butterworths, London, 2006, vol. 9(2), para 64 and fn5.

In the first place one should mention works of which the creation is itself a crime, such as child pornography. Whatever the artistic merits of the author – one can think of photographer David Hamilton – the depiction of children in such a way that satisfies base and paedophile instincts is deemed a crime, and therefore inevitably follows the rules concerning the objects of the crime, i.e. confiscation and destruction. Just as a criminal chemist cannot invoke any property right over his home-made heroin, in a similar way the author of a paedo-pornographic work cannot assert ownership over it.

The second reason is one of policy. If one has to contrast obscenity and immorality, which try to seep into society under the wide cloak of copyright it is preferable to deny the protection of the law from the outset.

It is much more coherent to dissuade pornographers at the beginning of their economic endeavour, rather than accord them, initially, a right which in practice is, and should be, denied. Behind this approach there are however some quite obvious flaws.

If the policy is that of banning obscene works it is up to Parliament to set the rules (criminal, administrative, procedural) and have them applied.

One might doubt that judicial wisdom is able to grasp the whole complexity of the issue. And at any rate the courts would only have a piece-meal approach. At best they would act only when some private controversy about the existence or non-existence of enforceable rights arises.[7] The rule would therefore be very similar to that which exists for prostitution services and copyright would be denied only if and when some party should ask for the court's assistance.

It has also been suggested that the lack of copyright protection would have a multiplying, rather than curbing effect on the dissemination of the works one aims at prohibiting.[8]

There is a further, more general, objection to denying copyright protection to works that are considered immoral. It is an agreed principle that the

---

[7] This is the reasoning of the US 9th Circuit in *Jartech v. Clancy*, 666 F.2d 403 (1982), according to which "Pragmatism further compels a rejection of an obscenity defense. Under the dictates of *Miller v. California*, obscenity is a community standard which may vary to the extent that controls thereof may be dropped by a state altogether. Acceptance of an obscenity defense would fragment copyright enforcement, protecting registered materials in a certain community, while, in effect, authorizing pirating in another locale" (case citations omitted). And what happens if someone removes sex-scenes from films? See Note, *E-Rated Industry: Fair Use of Sheep or Infringing Goat?*, 6 *Vand. J. Ent. L. & Prac.* 291 (2003).

[8] See the Comment, *Constitutional Protection of Obscene Material Against Censorship as Correlated with Copyright Protection of Obscene Material Against Infringement*, 31 *S. Cal. L. Rev.* 301 (1957) ("It is here that the censorship laws against obscene literature must come into play to prevent the increased circulation of such a work. If, however, such censorship laws do not have a co-equal standard of obscenity in common with the copyright limitation, it is manifest that the denial of relief to the author in such a case does not in anyway benefit the public by keeping from them the things which the court thinks they should not have, but has exactly the opposite effect: it multiplies the copies and increases the circulation of something that the court thinks immoral" (at p. 309).

standards through which a court or any other public body establishes the "immorality" or "obscenity" of a work are those of the community which the court or the public body represent. If one considers that copyright is now extended to 70 years after the death of the author, one can easily figure out that protection is denied on the basis of standards that may well be more than a century old.[9]

And it is sufficient to re-examine in the light of present day standards the cases in which a work of art has been qualified as obscene to acknowledge that the result would be different now.[10]

If therefore one accepts the view that copyright can also be granted to grossly obscene works,[11] the consequences for contract law are quite obvious.

---

[9] The argument is amply developed in the US landmark case *Mitchell Brothers Film Group v. Cinema Adult Theatre* [604 *F.2d* 852 (5th Cir. 1979)]: "Denying copyright protection to works adjudged obscene by the standards of one era would frequently result in lack of copyright protection (and thus lack of financial incentive to create) for works that later generations might consider to be non only non-obscene but even of great literary merit") (Godbold J.).

[10] It is sufficient to read the emphasis with which Younger J. argues in *Glyn v. Weston Feature Film* [1916] 1 Ch. 261 (a case of plagiarism from novel to the screen), and smile, thinking of the bygone days: "The episode described in the plaintiff's novel, and which she alleges has been pirated by the defendants, is in my opinion grossly immoral in its essence, in its treatment, and in its tendency. Stripped of its trappings, which are mere accident, it is nothing more nor less than a sensual adulterous intrigue. And it is not as if the plaintiff in her treatment of it were content to excuse or palliate the conduct described. She is not even satisfied with justifying that conduct. She has stooped to glorify the liaison in its inception, its progress, and its results; and she has not hesitated to garnish it with meretricious incident at every turn.

Now it is clear law that copyright cannot exist in a work of a tendency so grossly immoral as this, a work which, apart from its other objectionable features, advocates free love and justifies adultery where the marriage tie has become merely irksome. It may well be that the Court in this matter is now less strict than it was in the days of Lord Eldon, but the present is not a case in which in the public interest it ought, as it seems to me, to be at all anxious to relax its principles. We are constantly hearing of the injurious influence exercised upon the adventurous spirit of our youth by the penny dreadful which presents the burglar in the guise of a hero and so excites the imagination of the juvenile reader that, adopting in the spirit of true adventure the life of his idol, he presently finds himself in the dock branded by an unfeeling world as a common thief. So is a glittering record of adulterous sensuality masquerading as superior virtue, as it does in this book, calculated, with consequences as inevitable as they are sure to be disastrous, to mislead into the belief that she may without danger choose the easy life of sin many a poor romantic girl striving amidst manifold hardships and discouragements to keep her honour untarnished.

It is enough for me to say that to a book of such a cruelly destructive tendency no protection will be extended by a Court of Equity. It rests with others to determine whether such a work ought not to be altogether suppressed". The dictum appears to be widely overruled in *Stephens v. Avery* (Ch. 1988) in which the plaintiff applied for injunctive relief in order to enjoin publication of confidential information on a lesbian relationship. The defendants' defence that conduct was immoral and scandalous and therefore the *Nemo auditur* rule should apply was rejected. According to Browne-Wilkinson VC "there was at the present time no generally held view that homosexual acts between consenting adults were grossly immoral and, in the absence of an act that was in breach of a generally accepted moral code, it was not for the court to determine whether equitable relief should be excluded on the ground of immorality".

[11] This appears to be the attitude of the French courts: see Tribunal Grand Instance Nanterre, 25.10.1977 (*Hanselmann c. Benazeraf et Sté Production du Chêsne* (*droit moral* recognized to interpreters of pornographic film): "Attendu qu'aux termes de la jurisprudence sus relatée, le droit moral reconnu à l'acteur sur son interprétation permet à celui-ci de s'opposer

Limitations to the rights of the author or the copyright holder must be expressly indicated by legislation and, as with any exceptional rule, must be interpreted *stricto sensu*. There is therefore a general presumption of legality of the contracts concerning the exploitation of the work and the circulation of its copies. And at the same time protection is given against infringement.[12] The fact that some forms of dissemination may be forbidden for public policy reasons (typically broadcasting on free-to-air TV) does not validate violation by third parties.

This approach is particularly important if applied to on-line sale of pornographic videos. If these are not protected any business might legitimately get hold of its competitor's library and start offering it, at a lower price, on the Internet. The end result would be that they would be practically free. This might be a policy goal inasmuch as one wishes to destroy the value of the porn industry, but it should be clearly stated.

And there is a further effect on the contracts of those working in the creation of such works (typically porn actors and actresses) which will be examined in Chapter 7.

c. *Trademarks, patents and other forms of protection of intellectual property*

Problems similar to those we have encountered in copyright arise in the case of trademarks. As we know trademarks can be registered but also can be *de facto*. In the first case there might be a preliminary scrutiny on whether it may have an obscene meaning.

This happens quite often – and involuntarily – when an innocent name has a completely opposite meaning in a foreign language.

But one can imagine that – especially in the field of sex goods – the business may choose to operate under an explicit (and obscene) trademark.

In this case – and contrary to copyright laws – legislative intent is made explicit. Section 2(a) of the US Lanham Act provides that no trademark may be refused registration unless it "consists of or comprises immoral, deceptive, or scandalous matter".[13] Section 3(3) (a) of the British Trademark Act states

à la fois à une exploitation non autorisée de son interprétation et à une défiguration de cette interprétation, ce, sur la base des articles 1382 et 1142 du Code civil.

Attendu que dans le film 'Anthologie des scènes interdites, érotiques ou pornographiques' qui constitue une œuvre seconde dans laquelle B. a inclus des extraits du film 'Frustration', celui-ci a, par application des principes plus haut exposés, commis une faute en ne sollicitant pas de l'interprète son autorisation, d'autant plus nécessaire qu'il faisait ainsi de la prestation de l'artiste, une exploitation distincte de celle du film 'Frustration', et de surcroît non rétribuée".

[12] See *Blackman v. Hustler Magazine, Inc.*, 620 *F. Supp*. 792 (on quantum of damages) and 1501 (on merits) (D.D.C. 1985) in which a photographer was awarded $ 431,000 for multiple publication of nude photos by porn magazine without the consent of the author.

[13] The provision raises severe criticism. Generally the American way around the clear legislative wording is by invoking First Amendment rights. See Gibbons, *Semiotics of the Scandalous*

that a trademark shall not be registered if it is "contrary to public policy or to accepted principles of morality". Article 3 of the French trademark law (Loi no 91–7 du n. 1.1991 relative au marques) states, at letter b), that "Ne peut être adopté comme marque ou élément de marque un signe (…) contraire à l'ordre public ou aux bonnes mœurs".

Similar provisions exist in most national legislation pursuant to the provision of Article 6 *quinquies*, letter B) of the Amended Paris Convention on Intellectual Property of 1883 according to which:

> Trademarks covered by this Article may be neither denied registration nor invalidated except in the following cases:
> …
> …
> (iii) when they are contrary to morality or public order.

The same phrasing is found in Article 3 para. 1 lett. f) of the EC Trademark Directive 89/104 of 21.12.1988 which has substantially unified trademark law throughout the European Union.

The consequences are quite obvious. If one cannot be granted a trademark on obscene or immoral terms or signs, no property right can be asserted on such terms or signs. They cannot be transferred or licensed. They are not part of the business assets. There is no infringement.

---

and the Immoral and the Disparaging: Section 2(a) Trademark Law after Lawrence v. Texas, 9 *Marq. Intell. Prop. L. Rev.* 187 (2005) (and a vast number of cases decided by the courts and the trademark commission); Note, *Self-Disparaging Trademarks and Social Change: Factoring the Reappropriation of Slurs into Section 2(a) of the Lanham Act*, 106 *Colum. L. Rev.* 388 (2006); Note, *Trademark Law and Free Speech: Protection for Scandalous and Disparaging Marks*, 42 *Harv. C.R.-C.L. L. Rev.* 451 (2007). Davis, *Registration of Scandalous, Immoral, and Disparaging Matter under Section 2(a) of the Lanham Act: Can One Man's Vulgarity Be Another's Registered Trademark?*, 54 *Ohio St. L.J.* 331 (1993). It is doubted that the provision is stringently applied: see Baird, *Moral Intervention in the Trademark Arena: Banning the Registration of Scandalous and Immoral Trademarks*, 83 *Trademark Rep.* 661, at 728 (1993) ("no reported decision has refused registration of any mark relying solely on the basis of the immorality rubric"). There appears, however, to be a considerable string of case-law opposing this view, and rejecting First Amendment defences: see *e.g. In Re The Boulevard Entertainment* (334 *F.3d* 1336 (2003)) where the various precedents are cited: "To justify refusing to register a trademark under the first clause of section 1052(a), the PTO must show that the mark consists of or comprises "immoral, deceptive, or scandalous matter." *In re Mavety Media Group, Ltd.*, 33 *F.3d* 1367, 1371 (Fed. Cir. 1994). A showing that a mark is vulgar is sufficient to establish that it "consists of or comprises immoral … or scandalous matter" within the meaning of section 1052(a). See *id.* at 1373–74 (analyzing a mark in terms of "vulgarity"); *In re McGinley*, 660 F.2d 481, 485 (CCPA 1981) (quoting with approval *In re Runsdorf*, 171 USPQ 443, 443–44 (TTAB 1971), which refused registration of a mark on grounds of vulgarity). In meeting its burden, the PTO must consider the mark in the context of the marketplace as applied to the goods described in the application for registration. *McGinley*, 660 *F.2d* at 485. In addition, whether the mark consists of or comprises scandalous matter must be determined from the standpoint of a substantial composite of the general public (although not necessarily a majority), and in the context of contemporary attitudes, *id.*, keeping in mind changes in social mores and sensitivities, *Mavety*, 33 F.3d at 1371"

One might also suppose that the undertaking using such words or signs could not claim protection through the rules of unfair competition, because that would circumvent the scope of the law, which is expressly aimed at denying that protection.[14]

As to patents, the UK 1977 Patents Act, at Section 1 (1) states that:

> (3) A patent shall not be granted for an invention the commercial exploitation of which would be contrary to public policy or morality.
> (4) For the purposes of subsection (3) above exploitation shall not be regarded as contrary to public policy or morality only because it is prohibited by any law in force in the United Kingdom or any part of it.

Article L611–17 of the French Code de la propriété intellectuelle states that:

> Ne sont pas brevetables les inventions dont l'exploitation commerciale serait contraire à la dignité de la personne humaine, à l'ordre public ou aux bonnes mœurs, cette contrariété ne pouvant résulter du seul fait que cette exploitation est interdite par une disposition législative ou réglementaire.

At an international level Article 27, para. 2 of the TRIPS Agreement mirrors the cited provisions in national law stating that:

> Members may exclude from patentability inventions, the prevention within their territory of the commercial exploitation of which is necessary to protect *ordre public* or morality, including to protect human, animal or plant life or health or to avoid serious prejudice to the environment, provided that such exclusion is not made merely because the exploitation is prohibited by their law.

Although these provisions have been introduced much later than trademark laws provisions and there is scarce evidence of their practical application,[15] one can easily note, especially from the French text, that the notion of "morality" is given a very wide meaning here and ends up by embracing the many, and difficult, bioethical issues. One can imagine however cases concerning sex-enhancing products; or sex-related drugs for which a request for patent could be refused.

But rather than embark on far-fetched examples (reality is always more creative than imagination), the express prohibition of protection for immoral

[14] And the opposite rule applies in the case in which a porn websites appropriates itself of a trademark used for the sale of completely different items: see the French cases *Vitec v. Cora* (Appeals Paris 23.5.2003) (JurisData: 2003–216188); *Regine* (Appeals Paris 9.1.2002, *Zilberberg v. Soc. Edimat)* (JurisData: 2002–167420); and *Etam* (Tribunal Grande Instance Paris, 25.11.1993, *PIBD* 1994, III, 185). For a similar New Zealand case see *New Zealand Post Ltd v Leng.* [1999] 3 *NZLR* 219 (HC). And passing off of a well known film series by a producer of porn films ("Angelique", Cass. 1re civ., 4.4. 2006, *Comm. com. électr.* 2006, comm. 88, with comment by Caron).

[15] Compare the US cases *Whistler Corp. v. Autotronics, Inc.*, 14 *U.S.P.Q.2d* (BNA) 1885 (N.D. Tex. 1988); and *Tol-o-Matic, Inc. v. Proma Produkt-Und Marketing Gesellschaft*, 945 *F.2d* 1546 (Fed. Cir. 1991).

trademarks and inventions suggests a useful comparison with copyright based on the evaluation of the impact of legislation and on a law and economics approach.

In the former case, where property rights are *de jure* or, at least, *de facto* granted to obscene works of art, the market seems to greatly profit from the protection of the law. Admittedly, there has always been – since antiquity, as Greek vases demonstrate – a great request for erotic visual arts, and their success, presumably, is scarcely related to allocation rules. One can also add that copyright is a costless protection, if compared with the registration procedures required for patents and trademarks.

There is probably a disincentive to apply for IP protection when one does not know in advance whether the request will be accepted or refused and might result in a lower growth rate, especially in the field of patentable inventions, with a very low level of innovation, widespread imitation of goods and practically no brand value.[16]

Obviously these remarks are not meant to suggest that human ingenuity could and should devote itself to the field of sex-related inventions,[17] but simply to show what the effects of different forms of regulation can be.

Returning to a contract perspective the current state of the law may help explain why in the sector of sexual goods we have mostly the sale of unprotected objects, without any sort of restrictions on their use. Passing off is a common feature of the trade, and investment made by one producer is profited from all the others.

This could justify – from the point of view of cost structure – higher prices than those one would expect for that kind of product.

Conclusively, property rights over both tangibles and intangibles are not immune from aversion towards sex. This is not surprising as one could expect that concern over the morality of juridical acts is addressed to all the various aspects, and not only towards contracts. This is especially true when – as in the case of patents and trademarks – there are "gatekeeper" procedures upon which entitlement depends.

---

[16] See Bolen, *When Scandal Becomes Vogue: The Registerability of Sexual References in Trademark and Protection of Trademarks from Tarnishment in Sexual Context*, 39 *IDEA* 435 (1999). But see also the case decided by the House of Lords *Belfast City Council v. Miss Behavin' Limited* [2007] ("This case must take the prize for the most entertaining name of any that have come before us in recent years" (per Baroness Hale).

[17] Anecdotic but instructive of market trends Levins, *American Sex Machines. The Hidden Story of Sex at the US Patent Office*, Cincinnati, Adams Media 1996.

CHAPTER FIVE

SEX INDUSTRIES

By concentrating on prostitution and criminal elements associated with it, it is easy to forget that in the 'sex market' – and this could hardly be otherwise – there are enterprises where the activities are completely legal although many people may find them improper and the companies themselves prefer to retain a low profile.

The concept of 'sex industries'[1] obviously implies the existence of capital (both financial and human), structures, equipment and organisation dedicated to offering services and/or to production or exchange of goods.

And if we accept the legal-realistic viewpoint which sees an enterprise as a "nexus of contracts" we cannot then avoid the question of the legitimacy of these contracts or whether the charge of contrariety to morality levelled at dealings with the end customer does not as a result overwhelm the entire complex on which these depend and undermine the legitimacy of the enterprise as a whole.[2]

The issues to be raised here, starting from examination of the contracts, thus address whether and how these enterprises can and ought to operate. Obviously anyone who starts out with the view that the 'sexual' goods and services on offer are immoral will find it difficult to accept[3] that it is possible in

---

[1] Spector (ed.), *Prostitution and Pornography. A Philosophical Debate about the Sex Industry*, Stanford U. P., Stanford, 2006.

[2] On illegal partnerships and companies in English law see Enonchong, *Illegal Transactions*, London, LLP, 1998, p. 56ff. See *R. v. Registrar of Companies, ex p. Att. Gen*, [QB 1991] in BCLC 476 in which the company was struck off the Register:"It is well settled that a contract which is made upon a sexually immoral consideration or for a sexually immoral purpose is against public policy and is illegal and unenforceable. The fact that it does not involve or may not involve the commission of a criminal offence in no way prevents the contract being illegal, being against public policy and therefore being unenforceable. Here, as the documents clearly indicate, the association is for the purpose of carrying on a trade [prostitution] which involves illegal contracts because the purpose is sexually immoral and as such against public policy" (*per* Ackner L.J.).

[3] And this is the approach adopted by the European Parliament in its draft report "on the consequences of the sex industry in the European Union" dated 9.1.2004 (2003/2107(INI)). The first recital yields the following definition: "*the sex industry can be defined as an undertaking which legally or illegally puts in the market sexual services and/or products and exploits the human body, mainly of women and children, for profit-making*", and included in its explanatory statement is this list: "*This exploitation includes organised prostitution – for example escort services, call girls, operation of brothels, street prostitution, internet prostitution, massage parlours, strip clubs, telephone sex, marriage bureaus, sex tourism, pornography, and sex fairs.*" Hence the request for a campaign focused on "*combating the degrading act of the buying and using of female bodies by men*". The point which seems to escape the report's authors is how to reconcile this

this sector to speak of efficiency and competitivity, ideal company size, return on capital and even of social responsibility.

But from the legal point of view – and from that of business law in particular – once the activity in question has been recognised as legal there is no reason to ignore this fact when it comes to applying the same principles that are relevant in any other sector about which people have moral qualms about, such as the armaments or chemicals industries, or businesses that tend to have an unappealing image, such as funeral services or abortion clinics.

a. *Producers of pornographic films*[4]

In the preceding pages the legality of audiovisual pornographic products has been discussed. It has been argued that trading in these is legal, in some jurisdictions, provided it is done in ways that do not offend public decency.[5] The issue that now arises is whether all of the activity involved in pornographic film production is legal: actors and technicians need to be engaged; the set to be rented; and all the editing and post-production completed in readiness for distribution. We shall assume that the product is pornographic and that the 'harder' it is, the more satisfied the customer will be.

The plot that the actors play out before the camera and the spotlights is highly simplified, but such as it is it is undeniably obscene, consisting of sexual acts of all kinds. Can the economic project involving various persons, all linked by a raft of contracts, be considered legal in private law terms?[6] The concept of 'public morals' and its sanitising function is sorely tested since all the participants in the different deals well know the nature of the product and how its purpose is fulfilled.

If the enterprise is organised in the form of a company, then its corporate object will be a continuous output of such productions and will be described as 'video production' qualified with the adjective 'pornographic'. Any queries on the parts of a jurist could perhaps be met by the factual observation that awareness of the uncertainty as to legality leads to production taking place overseas and only distribution of the finished item being carried out in

approach with the fact that many of these enterprises – as they are forced to admit – operate "*legally*".

[4] For a history of the pornographic industry see Lane, *Obscene Profits. The Entrepreneurs of Pornography in the Cyber Age*, New York, Routledge, 2000.

[5] Obviously this conclusion cannot be reached by those who consider pornographic films as a form of prostitution: see Garb, *Sex for Money is Sex for Money: The Illegality of Pornographic Film as Prostitution*, 13 *Law & Ineq*. 281 (1994).

[6] The temptation to resolve the problem by introducing new criminal offences is strong around the world. See *e.g.* Report of the [New Zealand] Ministerial Committee of Inquiry into Pornography, Auckland, 1989, p. 138 [imprisonment and severe monetary penalties for running a business in "prohibited materials" and for advertising them].

countries with a repressive legislation of pornography. But this is hardly a satisfactory reply as it evades the problem by intellectual sleight of hand.

The solution seems to require us to grasp the matter by either one horn or the other horn. Either we recognise (and it is hard not to) that such films are intentionally obscene, vulgar and scurrilous and the actors are 'selling their bodies', not in some theatrical fiction, but in a real sense abhorrent to human dignity. If so, there are inescapable consequences for the company, the legal relations created and its profits (for how could a shareholder aware of the situation legitimately ask for part of them?). Or else it is the concept of contrariety to morality, as well as its effects that is to be amended without diminishing its range but restricting its use to where it is appropriate to direct it.

A normative response to these questions is often found in taxation law, which often considers the pornographic nature of the film produced to deny special tax rebates or benefits. Therefore pornographic films are subject to ordinary taxes on company income. The consequence is quite coherent: as the state does not (and cannot from an ethical point of view) tax criminal and other illicit activities, the production of obscene videos may well be considered disreputable but not against the law.[7]

b. *Adult entertainment TV*

The natural outlet for porn films and one of the most profitable forms of their exploitation is on adult entertainment television. In this case the business behind the provision of pornographic video services is much more complex

[7] The argument is quite frequent in European and French law: see *e.g.* the European Convention on Cinematographic Co-Production (Strasbourg 2.10.1992) according to which (article 5, para. 3) "Projects of a blatantly pornographic nature or those that advocate violence or openly offend human dignity cannot be accorded co-production status" [which opens the possibility of obtaining special funding]. And article 91 of the Loi n. 2007-1824 of 25.12.2007 according to which "N'ouvrent pas droit au bénéfice du crédit d'impôt les jeux vidéo comportant des séquences à caractère pornographique ou de très grande violence, susceptibles de nuire gravement à l'épanouissement physique, mental ou moral des utilisateurs." The special and derogatory taxation of pornographic activities has been held not discriminatory or contrary to the ECHR: see Conseil d'Etat, 13.12.2006, n. 267782 (Eroshop v. Ministere de l'Economie) ("Les dispositions précitées n'étaient pas non plus contraires aux articles 10 et 14 de la convention européenne de sauvegarde des droits de l'homme et des libertés fondamentales qui, respectivement, garantissent la liberté d'expression et interdisent les discriminations dans l'exercice des droits fondamentaux, dans la mesure où l'application du taux majoré de taxe sur la valeur ajoutée prévue par ces dispositions ne pouvait être regardée comme apportant à la liberté d'expression une restriction disproportionnée au but qu'elles poursuivaient, alors même que les activités ainsi taxées étaient, en outre, soumises à une réglementation restrictive dans l'intérêt de la protection de la jeunesse"). Or Cass. crim. 23.1.1979, in *JCP G* 1979, II, 19143 (If a tax law imposes a special tax on the products of a certain activity, the latter cannot be considered illegal and fall under the sanction of criminal law against obscene films).

than on the Internet.[8] Generally there is a wide catalogue of selected long-running films which are made available through a satellite or a cable provider. Sometimes there is direct access to the porn channel; but often this is hosted by a general content provider who produces his own programmes and hosts others. In these cases there is a general agreement between the parties, which may also include the collection of the price paid by the clients; and a contract with the viewer, usually on a pay-per-view basis but occasionally through subscription.

What should be noted is that in this way pornographic services are included in a 'respectable' environment in which the company which runs the cable or satellite television must ensure towards their customers certain standards of quality, respect of contractual agreements and, especially, compliance with the relevant legal provisions.

From this last point of view one should mention that in the European Union these services are regulated, albeit indirectly, by the 2007/65 Directive, which at Article 3h provides that on-demand audiovisual services which "might seriously impair the physical, mental or moral development of minors" may only be made available to the public "in such a way that ensures that minors will not normally hear or see such on-demand audiovisual media services". This provision, as all EU norms, must be read in the light of the preambles of the Directive. In this case para. 45 clearly states that "Measures taken to protect the physical, mental and moral development of minors and human dignity should be carefully balanced with the fundamental right to freedom of expression as laid down in the Charter on Fundamental Rights of the European Union. The aim of those measures, such as the use of personal identification numbers (PIN codes), filtering systems or labelling, should thus be to ensure an adequate level of protection of the physical, mental and moral development of minors and human dignity, especially with regard to on-demand audiovisual media services". The same premise strongly supports self-regulation through supplying users "with an effective, updatable and easy-to-use filtering system".

For the purposes of this work what is important to point out is that there is no generic reference to immorality or obscenity. The purpose of the provision is to protect minors, and not the general mores of the community. Furthermore they must be protected not from any sexually explicit audiovisual product, but only from those which may "seriously" damage their development.

Considering the high level of regulation, especially of content, in the history of European broadcasting, Directive 2007/65 indicates that pornographic films may be legally offered to the public, within regular on-demand programming, provided some precautions are taken, typically encryption. And the

[8] Discussed in Chapter 2, para. d.

Directive also indicates that explicit sexual scenes may be aired on free-to-view television, provided this is done when minors are not usually in front of the television set.

c. *"Red light" cinemas, night-clubs, privés, sex shops*

A fair number of sexual products and services are supplied in commercial outlets. The activities pursued and the contracts with clients, clearly intended to satisfy their sexual needs, raise the issue of whether these should be considered contrary to morality.

Pornographic films are shown in "red light" cinemas. Purchase of a ticket gives the right to get in and see the film, but the theatre itself is usually used for auto-erotic acts, which can be described as obscene acts in a place open to the public.[9]

At the second level of types of premises described here (omitting from the list those which may serve as meeting places for prostitutes and clients or may themselves be described as brothels[10]) night clubs are places where striptease shows, table and lap dancing are offered, as explained above.

In the *privé* club, behind the legal veil of a private association – and thus the venue cannot be considered a place open to the public – the "members", who pay a sum of money described as a "subscription fee", can watch, put themselves on display or participate in sexual activity of an extremely varied kind – voyeuristic, lesbian, homosexual, sado-masochism and orgies.[11] Thus it is the "members" who supply the service, for which they pay rather than are paid, while the manager ensures the event is organised and that the various tastes are catered to.

---

[9] According to Italian case law such facilities do not constitute obscene displays: "Projecting cinematographic films of intrinsically obscene content in rooms specially set aside for this purpose (so-called 'red light' cinemas) does not amount to an offence under article 528 of the penal code. In today's society it is indeed considered, because of the way ideas in the area of sexual morality have developed, that specific displays can in particular circumstances (such as adequate warnings at the premises and prohibiting entry to certain classes of people) be reconciled to generally held ideas of decency, decorum and modesty" (Cass. pen. 30.11.1986, Benedetti, in *Foro it.* 1987, II, 697).

[10] And therefore fall under criminal prosecution: for an Italian example see Cass. pen. 5.7.2005, n. 33799.

[11] According to Italian case law it does not amount to incitement to prostitution when a person is persuaded to "have sexual relations in an indiscriminate manner with an indeterminate number of persons" where no payment is made (Cass. pen. 20.5.1998, n. 7608, in *Riv. pen.* 1998, 876). Therefore, when consideration is not bilateral, no illegality pertains, for which see the Trib. Milan 1.7.1993 (in *Gius* 1994, 5, 103): "no service contrary to morality is effected when a sum of money is given spontaneously and not by way of consideration after the performance of a homosexual service." But see *R. v. Brown* (HL 2004) when there is the voluntary infliction of harm to others, albeit consenting.

Sex shops, on the other hand, are the last link in the distribution chain for erotic products.[12]

These business operate through a number of contracts, both with their providers (of films, of entertainment services, of goods) and with their clients (who pay for a ticket, an object, a membership fee). What is the inter-relation between such contracts and the admissibility of the company that is a necessary party to them? Simplifying the question: if the contracts are immoral, are the company, its business, its articles of association also immoral and therefore unable to be recognised by the law? One could argue that the systematic nature of contrariety to morality (that is, vitiating the whole complex of contracts) cannot but have repercussions on the entire enterprise and make it illegal, invalidating any existing company agreement.[13] Apart from the direct effects on the company, the collateral effects are easy to imagine, for example on leases, and on employment and finance contracts.

But if the activity is not criminalised[14] one could argue that if it is legal to carry on a type of activity, then contracts concluded to that end are and should

[12] Mostly from a practical point of view see, for the English regulation on the point, Manchester, *Sex Shops and the Law*, Gower, Aldershot, 1986 [in particular chapters 5 (at p. 90ff) and 6 (at p. 103ff) on the legislation on the matter, and chapter 8 (at p. 139ff) on the licence applications].

[13] In the French case decided by Appeals Montpellier 30.4.1992, *Lopez v. Farudjia* (JurisData : 1992-034235), the transfer of the ownership of a *club privé* whose members were married couples could not be declared void as this activity was not against *les bonnes moeurs* and it was not proven that it was in someway similar to prostitution or proxenetism. In another French case (Appeals Paris 21.11.2001, *Franklin v. Calypso*) (JurisData : 2001-159664) the repudiation of the lease by the landlord on the basis that in the scarcely lit café in the Pigalle district in Paris waitresses with little clothing ("tenue légère") encouraged customers to drink was rejected by the court inasmuch there was no evidence that the activity was against *les bonnes moeurs*. However see also the case decided by Appeals Douai 14.6.2007, *GD Concept v. Camif* (JurisData: 2007-347545) (Sub-lease was legitimately repudiated by landlord not only because of non-payment of rent but also because of disparagement of the name of the establishment by organizing male strip-tease evenings). In the jurisdictions where organised prostitution is allowed the transfer of businesses follows ordinary rules: see *Pacific Maxon, Inc. v. Wilson*, 619 *P.2d* 816 (1980) (Nev. S. Ct.) (Respondent bordello seller wished to sell her prostitution business, and she provided her broker with a copy of an appraisal that she altered to reflect an inflated value. Appellant bordello buyers reviewed the brothel's operations, along with the appraisal, and they purchased the business. After learning that the appraisal had been falsified, appellants brought an action against respondent seeking rescission of the contract and damages for fraudulent misrepresentation. The trial court entered judgment in respondent's favour, finding that appellants' reliance upon the appraisal was not established or justified. On appeal, the court reversed the judgment because total reliance upon a misrepresentation was not required to entitle appellants to rescission. In addition, the trial court's conclusion that there had been no actual reliance was not supported by substantial evidence. The court also held that, while a lack of justifiable reliance did bar appellants' recovery on its damage claim for the tort of deceit, even negligent reliance was sufficient to establish an equitable right to rescission of a contract when the misrepresentations were made intentionally by the deceiving party).

[14] As it is in various US states: see *Williams v. Morgan* 478 *F.3d* 1316 (11th Cir. 2007) (Alabama statute prohibiting commercial distribution of devices primarily used for stimulation of human genitals did not violate Fourteenth Amendment privacy rights, inasmuch as public morality

be legal. Or that a finding of contrariety to morality might apply to an individual contract, while leaving other activities associated with the enterprise unaffected, as this does not contravene criminal law.

Confronting these different not easily reconcilable positions raises further queries about the efficacy and efficiency of a general rule (nullity or unenforceability on the basis of immorality) that is so indistinct that it offers no help in the form of reasonable approximate certainty.

d. *Licensing and zoning*

A reply to the questions that have been raised on the admissibility of sex industries could be found in the legislation and administrative by-laws on trade and its licensing.

A first caveat is however necessary: the law on commercial activities is, in all jurisdictions, very complex and often piecemeal. It is extremely difficult to outline a comprehensive framework, especially because, everywhere, ample discretion is left to local authorities. What may be a licit trade practice in one town may not be in another, a few miles away.

From a comparative perspective one has therefore to indicate some possible scenarios and their consequences.

i. In general trade law there is no ban on sex industries, which therefore can be legally established. As any business must operate through

---

provided rational basis for statute; for a Comment, *Substantive Due Process: Sex Toys after* Lawrence, 60 *Fla. L. Rev.* 507 (2008)); *181 South Inc. v. Fischer*, 454 *F.3d* 228 (3rd Cir.2006) (New Jersey regulation prohibiting any lewdness or immoral activity on liquor-licensed premises was not unconstitutionally vague as applied to adult cabaret establishment involving topless dancers; investigators observed a dancer rubbing her breasts and vagina while onstage and straddling a patron while pushing her breasts into patron's face, another dancer was observed straddling a patron and simulating sexual intercourse, and a third dancer was observed rubbing her breasts and massaging her vagina to simulate the act of masturbation, all of which clearly fell within the ambit of conduct the regulation proscribed at liquor-licensed businesses). But in the opposite sense see e.g. *Reliable Consultants Inc. v. Earle*, 517 F.3d 738, 744 (5th Cir.2008) (Texas statute which criminalised the selling, advertising, giving or lending of any device designed or marketed for sexual stimulation, unless defendant could prove that device was sold, advertised, given or lent for statutorily-approved purpose, impermissibly burdened the substantive due process rights of customers of businesses that sold such devices to engage in private intimate conduct of their choosing; neither state's interest in discouraging prurient interests in autonomous sex and the pursuit of sexual gratification unrelated to procreation, nor its interest in protecting children from improper sexual expression or desire to protect "unwilling adults" from exposure to sexual devices, was sufficient to justify its heavy-handed restriction, not only on sale and advertisement, but upon giving or lending of such devices); or *Norfolk 302, LLC v. Vassar*, 524 F. Supp, 2d 728 (E.D.Va., 2007) (Virginia regulation prohibiting "lewd" and "disorderly conduct" by liquor licensee's patrons infringed on substantial amount of speech protected by First Amendment and was not justified by important state interest in regulating fully clothed performances that simulated sex, non-erotic dance, or productions with clear artistic merit, and thus was unconstitutionally overbroad under intermediate scrutiny).

contracts these, necessarily, must be valid. Administrative law, therefore, has the upper hand over private law.[15]

ii. In general trade law there is a ban on (certain[16]) sex industries, which cannot therefore be legally established. One can assume that, as a result of this express prohibition, contracts which are entered into by such businesses are not only immoral but also illegal. Again administrative law determines the fate of a private law transaction.

iii. Sex industries are required to obtain a licence in order to operate lawfully. If they do not, the contracts might be considered invalid on the basis of general rules applied in cases of want of licence.[17]

iv. Local authorities can discretionarily (but not arbitrarily[18]) determine which businesses can be run in their territory on the basis of various criteria, including public policy and morality. Therefore Town A (or county, province, region) might forbid what Town B has instead allowed. In this case one could argue that as contracts may not be valid and enforceable in one part of the country, but not in another, it is private law that prevails over administrative law, as well as on the basis of the principle of hierarchy of the sources of law. Violation of

[15] See the case decided by the German Federal Administrative court BVerwG 23. 3. 2009 (in *NVwZ* 2009, 909): local authorities cannot deny a licence for a bar to be opened in a brothel. Before the 2002 reform (see further Ch. 9, para. 9) the denial could have been legitimate because according to the law there was an explicit ban on immoral activities. The *Prostitutiongesetz* has removed the prohibition and the activity is not against a criminal statute, does not impinge on workers rights and does not present dangers for minors because they are not allowed on the premises. The decision is favourably commented by J.-T. Lehmann, *Prostitution und gaststättenrechtliche Unsittlichkeit im Wandel der Zeit*, in *NVwZ* 2009, 888.

[16] Which? Compare *Dottie's Dress Shop v. Village of Lyons*, 313 *Ill. App. 3d* 70 (2000) (Shop selling sexually oriented gift items was a similar use to adult bookstores, adult movie theatres, and adult cabarets for purposes of falling within a village's zoning ordinance) with *Doctor John's, Inc. v. City of Sioux City*, 389 *F. Supp. 2d* 1096 (2005) (N.D. Ia) (Adult entertainment business owner was entitled to a preliminary injunction enjoining enforcement of a city's ordinance to the extent it defined a sex shop on the basis of a combination of merchandise that included adult media, but issues of fact prevented summary judgment on the provisions related to a combination that included non-media goods).

[17] See for the UK Enonchong, *Illegal Transactions*, London, LLP, 1998, p. 34ff. For the varied solutions in US law see Corbin, *Corbin on Contracts. Illegal Bargains*, LexisNexis, Newark, NJ, 2002, vol 15, p. 623ff (in particular at p. 625 where the principle that the penalty of unenforceability should be expressly included or plainly excluded by statute law is examined; and at p. 627 on the purpose of the licensing statute).

[18] See *Paris Adult Bookstore II v. City of Dallas*, 493 *US* 215 (1990) (The Dallas licensing scheme on "sexually oriented businesses" – inclusive of adult arcades, bookstores, video stores, cabarets, motels, and theatres, as well as escort agencies, nude model studios, and sexual encounter centres – violates the First Amendment, since it constitutes a prior restraint upon protected expression that fails to provide adequate procedural safeguards); *Calderon v. Buffalo* 397 *N.Y.S.2d* 655 (1977) (N.Y. S. Ct) (A city was permanently enjoined from enforcing the sections of an anti-obscenity ordinance because the sections were overbroad and unconstitutional insofar as they banned the display of sexually oriented material that might not have been obscene).

> an administrative order will entail administrative – and not private law – sanctions.[19]

The aspects of licensing sex industries indicate the importance of administrative law in this sector and open the perspective of regulation, which is generally underestimated owing to the general prevalence of criminal law concerns.

One should, at this stage, consider how administrative law is used to promote morality issues. The uncertainties of private law rules, which we have constantly seen in all the various aspects that we have examined here and the fact that they generally operate *ex post facto*, opens the way to more effective legal measures which have a general scope and can be enforced *ex ante*. There is a further, extremely political, advantage in administrative regulations: when it is up to local authorities to decide if, when, and where a sex industry or business can be run they can respond rapidly to what are perceived (or presented) as community concerns.[20]

In this movement towards administrative law there is nothing unusual, for it is simply one of the many facets of the growing activism of public bodies in the field of economic activity which has been gradually encroaching private autonomy and private law.

One of the most typical examples of administrative regulation of sex industries is that of zoning, *i.e.* the practice of establishing where sex-oriented establishments can be set up. Again, it is common procedure for practically all trades and commercial outlets. No restaurants or bars are licensed in residential neighbourhoods. Shopping malls are located where there is adequate access by road and parking space. Noisy and polluting activities are restricted to industrial zones. Behind each of these choices there are rational arguments which are widely used and put into practice in most Western countries. The problem with sex-oriented establishments (typically sex shops, but also 'red-light' cinemas) is that the restrictions are based on public morality arguments, behind which lie other arguments, more economically grounded, such as the (fear of) loss of value of real estate.[21]

---

[19] See – but in the field of licensed health care services – *Chatham Foot Specialist v. Health Care Service*, 837 *N.E.2d* 48 (2005) (registration requirement held merely administrative mechanism).

[20] "In regulating sexual behavior, politicians have used social or moral panic as a means of focusing public attention on degenerate or immoral behaviour" (Cook, *Shaken from Her Pedestal: A Decade of New York City's Sex Industry under Siege*, 9 *N.Y. City L. Rev.* 121 at 156 (2005). The "moral panic" argument is exposed by other authors: Brock, *Making Work, Making Trouble: Prostitution as a Social Problem*, U.Toronto Press, Toronto, 1998 (at p. 31ff); Sanders, *Paying for Pleasure. Men who Buy Sex*, Willan Pub., Cullompton, 2008 (at p. 162ff). And sex crimes are increasingly commercialised by the press: see Greer, *Sex Crime and the Media: Sex Offending and the Press in a Divided Society*, Willan Pub., Cullompton, 2003, pp. 92ff.

[21] See Hennigan, *Property War: Prostitution, Red-Light Districts, and the Transformation of Public Nuisance Law in the Progressive Era*, 16 *Yale J.L. & Human.* 123 (2004). For a German

These decisions appear to be problematic not so much because they violate some fundamental right – this is the typical First Amendment obsession in US legal debate[22] – but because they are not, generally speaking, in line with the principles of equal treatment and proportionality. If there is no explicit ban on sex industries one must justify why they cannot operate in a certain commercial district, and why they cannot obtain a licence; while if it were a shop, a hairdresser or a bookstore licence that was being requested it would be granted.[23]

The very high level of discretion of public authorities reaches its climax when they decide that nowhere in the territory under their control can one run a sex oriented business.[24]

---

approach to the question see Schröer, *Bordellbetriebe und Öffentliches Baurecht*, in *NZBau* 2009, 166.

[22] See *ex multis* Calvert, Richards, *Stripping Away First Amendment Rights: The Legislative Assault on Sexually Oriented Businesses*, 7 *N.Y.U. J. Legis. & Pub. Pol'y* 287 (2003); Cook, *Shaken from Her Pedestal: A Decade of New York City's Sex Industry under Siege*, 9 *N.Y. City L. Rev.* 121 (2005); Comment, *Sex and the City: Zoning "Pornography Peddlers and Live Nude Shows"*, 49 *UCLA L. Rev.* 1139 (2002); Note, *Sex, But Not the City: Adult-Entertainment Zoning, the First Amendment, and Residential and Rural Municipalities*, 46 *Boston College L. Rev.* 625 (2005). And everything falls into the unlimited boundaries of freedom of speech: see *GMC, Inc. v. Chrisofolli*, 381 *N.E.2d* 217 (1978) (Oh. C.A.) (A trial court appropriately balanced adult bookstore owners' economic interests against anti-pornography picketers' First Amendment rights where the trial court limited but did not prohibit anti-pornography picketing in front of the owners' stores).

A different view is taken in European jurisdictions. See the English case *Belfast City Council v. Miss Behavin'* (2007): "If article 10 and article 1 of Protocol 1 are engaged at all, they operate at a very low level. The right to vend pornography is not the most important right of free expression in a democratic society and the licensing system does not prohibit anyone from exercising it" (*per* Lord Hoffmann); "there are far more important human rights in this world than the right to sell pornographic literature and images in the backstreets of Belfast City Centre. Pornography comes well below celebrity gossip in the hierarchy of speech which deserves the protection of the law" (*per* Baroness Hale).

[23] "Subverting an unpopular activity or form of expression does not solve a perceived problem. Rather, it conceals a slice of raw humanity that, if shunned in favor of dominant hegemonies, will surely resurface in another form" (Cook, *Shaken from Her Pedestal: A Decade of New York City's Sex Industry under Siege*, 9 *N.Y. City L. Rev.* 121 at 159 (2005). And discrimination can occur between businesses of the same kind: see *Stratton v. Drumm*, 445 *F. Supp.* 1305 (1978) (Ct.) (An amendment to a town massage parlour ordinance which forbade a massagist from administration of a massage to a person of the opposite sex was in conflict with Title VII and therefore was invalid under the Supremacy Clause).

[24] In the case decided by the House of Lords, *Belfast City Council v. Miss Behavin'* (2007), it would appear that there was a flat denial of a licence anywhere in the town, but the facts are not so clear. See Baroness Hale's opinion ("No-one is suggesting that pornographic literature and images (always supposing that it is lawful) should be inaccessible to those in Belfast who wish to gain access to them. The authors can publish their work in any other medium should they wish to do so, and the public can gain access to them there. Indeed, the City Council has not, as far as we know, refused to license sex establishments elsewhere in the city. There were good reasons for refusing to license establishments in this street and even better ones for refusing this particular company a licence. The suggestion that this is a disproportionate limitation on the company's right to freedom of expression is to my mind completely untenable. The same applies, *a fortiori*, to the complaint under Article 1 of Protocol 1").

Although the decision generally is based on public interest and morality, it is clear that general rules of administrative procedure require not only an appropriate review of the competing reasons, but also that the concerns which lead to the denial of a licence must have substantial grounds and evidence.[25]

e. *Sex tourism*

Sex tourism has become a serious concern over the last twenty years with the increase of mass tourism and low-cost air transport.[26] In particular it has been pointed out that in a great number of cases it is associated with child prostitution and sexual exploitation of children.

This has prompted many jurisdictions – European in the first place[27] – to introduce strict criminal laws that punish all those engaged, at various levels, in this kind of activity. One of the characteristics of the laws enacted is their extra-territorial scope. The crime is punished wherever it is committed, even abroad in a country where it is not considered an offence, and against someone who is not a national.[28]

This vast legislation brings along the obvious consequence that any contract that is somehow instrumental to the offence is void; the monies received are the profit of the crime and must be seized.

But once one has reached the obvious conclusion about the sexual exploitation of children in foreign countries, can the same be said if sex tourism involves only adults in countries where sexual services are not forbidden? The obvious examples are lawful Nevada bordellos in the US, massage

---

[25] But see Lord Neuberger's *dictum* in *Belfast City Council v. Miss Behavin'* (HL 2007) for rejecting concerns over violation of article 10 ECHR: "When it comes to restrictions on the dissemination of pornographic material, the margin of appreciation afforded to member states must, it appears to me, be wide".

[26] Ryan, Hall, *Sex tourism: marginal people and liminalities*, Routledge, London, 2001; Chawla, *Sex tourism and development*, Sonali Pub., New Delhi, 2004; Wonders, Michalowsky, *Bodies, Borders, and Sex Tourism in a Globalized World: A Tale of Two Cities – Amsterdam and Havana*, 48 *Soc. Probs.* 545 (2001).

[27] See the EU Council Framework Decision 2004/68/JHA of 22 December 2003 on combating the sexual exploitation of children and child pornography, to which legislation of the member states conform.

[28] But there is wide criticism that this, often, does not happen: see the Note, *Extraterritorial Accountability: An Assessment of the Effectiveness of Child Sex Tourism Laws*, 28 *Loy. L.A. Int'l & Comp. L. Rev.* 641 (2006); Note, *Child Sex Tourism Legislation under the Protect Act: Does It Really Protect?* 79 *St. John's L. Rev.* 445 (2005); Comment, *U.S. Domestic Prosecution of the American International Sex Tourist: Efforts to Protect Children from Sexual Exploitation*, 94 *J. Crim. L. & Criminology* 415 (2003); Steinman, *Sex Tourism and the Child: Latin America's and the United States' Failure to Prosecute Sex Tourists*, 13 *Hastings Women's L.J.* 53 (2002) But what if the laws of both countries make it crime, but on different basis and with different sentencing consequences? See the Comment, *Justice beyond Borders: A Comparison of Australian and U.S. Child-Sex Tourism Laws*, 13 *Pac. Rim L. & Pol'y J.* 405 (2004).

parlours in South-East Asia,[29] or wide-spread individual prostitution in the Caribbean.[30]

In these cases we are confronted with an activity which is legal and no distinction is made between clients that are nationals and those that are foreigners. One should be reminded that generally sexual services are not prohibited in Western countries, but only their organisation on an industrial basis. This last rule however does not have an extra-territorial scope and therefore the fact that organised prostitution is lawful in one country does not enable the laws of another country to declare it unlawful and sanction those involved in it.

On this basis can one argue that the contracts organising travel, accommodation and sexual services would be valid? The answer cannot be so straightforward. One could claim that the travel organisation is but one of the many moments of a complex prostitution exploitation organisation. The crime is therefore partly committed in the country which punishes organised prostitution and therefore all the contracts are void (and the participants are liable to be sentenced). One could also maintain that the hypothetical possibility of a conflict of laws between countries where prostitution is legal and subject to the private law regime and those where it is illegal or is based on unenforceable contracts is eliminated by the general *ordre public* principle.

For these reasons one could doubt the lawfulness of businesses engaged in sex tourism operating in countries where the organised provision of *corpore corpori* sexual service is unlawful, even when the service is rendered abroad.

This is probably the reason for the fact that most sex tourism is organised on an individual basis. Here, however, a further aspect arises. In the last few years there has been a growing trend for women to become sex tourists in Caribbean and African countries where men are available for sex at low cost and without social stigma.[31] This radically undermines the 'feminist' justification of criminalisation of the prostitute's client (male sexual violence

[29] Lim (ed.),*The sex sector: the economic and social bases of prostitution in Southeast Asia*, ILO, Geneva, 1998; Jeffrey, *Sex and borders: gender, national identity, and prostitution policy in Thailand*, UBC Press, Vancouver, 2002.

[30] Kempadoo (ed) *Sun, Sex, and Gold. Tourism and Sex Work in the Caribbean*, Rowman & Littlefield, Lanham Md,, 1999; Padilla, *Caribbean Pleasure Industry. Tourism, Sexuality, and AIDS in the Dominican Republic*, U. Chicago Press, Chicago 2007. The sex tourism profile is often in a bundle with package tours to transgressive holiday resorts (*e.g.* the Hedonist chain in Jamaica) where it is difficult to distinguish clearly to what extent sex is "swapped" or bought.

[31] On female sex tourism see Ringdal, *Love for Sale. A Global history of Prostitution*, London Atlantic Books, 2004 (at p. 354ff); De Albuquerque, *Sex, Beach Boys, and Female Tourists in the Caribbean*, in Dank (ed), *Sex Work & Sex Workers, Sexuality and Culture*, vol. 2, Transaction, New Brunswick, 1999 (at p. 87ff); O'Connell Davidson, Sanchez Taylor, *Fantasy Islands. Exploring the Demand for Sex Tourism*, in Kempadoo (ed.), *Sun, Sex, and Gold. Tourism and Sex Work in the Caribbean*, Rowman&Littlefield, Lanham, Md, 1999, p. 47 ff

towards women) and the only argument remaining is the ideologically charged but legally marginal one of exploitation of the 'poor' by the 'rich'.[32] And this raises serious doubts as to the reasonableness of legislation against adult sexual services with an extra-territorial scope.[33]

---

[32] "The source of their empowerment is their Whiteness and their wealth" (Hernandez, *"Sex in the [Foreign] City". Commodification and the Female Sex Tourist*, in Ertman, Williams (eds.), *Rethinking Commodification. Cases and Readings in Law and Culture*, NYU Press, New York, 2005, p. 222 (at p. 231). And from a more neutral perspective differences in income are the reason for which "rich Western women demand prostitution services from men in developing countries" (Della Giusta., Di Tommaso, S. Strøm, *Who is watching? The market for prostitution services*, online Journal of Population Economics (2007) at http://www.springerlink.com/content/k2v47x73u2n62604/fulltext.html [and now republished in EAD., *Sex Markets. A Denied Industry*, Routledge, Abingdon 2008]. Which brings us to the treacherous terrain of sex as class struggle, for which see the groundbreaking passages in Calverton, *Sex and Economics*, in *New Masses*, March 1927, p. 32.

[33] And is it prostitution, anyway? According to Cabezas, *Legal Challenges To and By Sex Workers/Prostitutes*, 48 *Clev. St. L. Rev.* 79 at 91 (2000) the answer is negative or, at least, doubtful. Sex tourism brings up a further contradiction: as discrimination against homosexuals is considered unacceptable, "political correctness" openly advocates gay tourism: see Waitt, Markwell, *Gay Tourism. Culture and Context*, Haworth Hospitality Press, New York, 2006; and even promotes it as a factor of economic growth: Guaracino, *Gay and Lesbian Tourism. The Essential Guide for Marketing*, Elsevier, Amsterdam, 2007. No books on management of brothels or marketing of porn videos are available on the market.

CHAPTER SIX

THE PROTECTION OF SEX CONSUMERS

The sex market is clearly consumer-oriented.[1] Services are directly provided to the final client and there are very few intermediary steps. Goods – whether porn materials or material objects – require limited equipment for their production.

If one accepts the view that transactions for sexual goods and services are valid and not merely tolerated, one is faced with the legal issues of sex consumers. If one applies contract law, there is no reason to derogate from its general and specific rules. Therefore, in the absence of some express legislative provision there is no doubt that consumer protection rules should apply.

We shall use the vast EC legislation on consumer contracts as a test field, as it covers practically all the aspects in which we are interested here. Similar analysis can, however, be easily applied to other Western jurisdictions.

a. *The parties*

EC consumer protection Directives, since the first one on contracts negotiated away from business premises (1985/577), has constantly provided a standard definition of consumer and trader. The first "means any natural person who is acting for purposes which are outside his trade, business, craft or profession". The second is "any natural or legal person who is acting for purposes relating to his trade, business, craft or profession and anyone acting in the name of or on behalf of a trader".

Do the parties to a sexual contract fall within these categories? The definition clearly fits the client of sexual services or sexual goods, which one can assume are beyond the scope of his or her profession or employment. Once one has set aside immorality issues, there is no difference between going to a health spa or to a massage parlour (with sex services); between going to the theatre or to a nude entertainment show; and buying a household appliance or a dildo. There may be some exceptions (for example in certain telecoms services) but that is because the whole area is exempted.

---

[1] See Clark, *Desire. A History of European Sexuality*, Routledge, New York, 2008 ("sexual consumerism has defeated sexual utopianism", at p. 220); Hawkes, *A Sociology of Sex and Sexuality*, Open University Press, Philadelphia,1996, p. 117ff.

Is the provider of goods and services a "trader"? Again there is no doubt when the counterpart is a business entity run by a company or another legal person. One might question the case of individually rendered services (typically, prostitution). But since the ECJ Jany decision[2] it appears to be firm EC law that they too fall under the freedom of services provision set out in Article 49 of the Rome Treaty [now Article 56 of the Treaty on the functioning of the European Union – TFEU]. Therefore, to exemplify the most common situation, in those countries where prostitution is a valid and enforceable contract, the prostitute is a professional; and her (or his) client is a consumer.

This may be a field in which consumer issues might rarely arise.[3] However, it is useful in order to point out that the same criteria should apply in transactions in which actual consumer concerns are present, such as sex over the Internet, and sex-enhancing products.

b. *Sale of goods*

From what has been said there should be no doubt that the two-year guarantee set by Directive 1999/44 on the sale of consumer goods and associated guarantees should apply to the sale of all sex products, whether magazines, videos or sex-enhancing objects, together with its various provisions, especially those concerning the expected quality of the product, fitness for purpose, the right to obtain a replacement of the defective item, or reimbursement of expenses.

In the case of sex-enhancing products, and considering that they are generally used in direct contact with the body (or even inside it) of the consumer, the liability rules set by Directive 1985/374 on producer's liability should also apply. The general principles of high level of safety and of reasonable consumer expectations should be observed.

If and when the contract is concluded – as it often is – on-line or by mail the consumer should have the right to withdraw from it within the period of time fixed by Directive 1997/7 on the protection of consumers in respect of distance contracts. General provisions on e-commerce set by Directive 2000/31 are applicable,[4] with the exceptions of aphrodisiacs, which should fall under the very vague provision of Article 3, para. 4, which is generally interpreted as excluding drugs and pharmaceutical products from the scope of the Directive,

[2] Discussed further at Chapter 9, para. d.

[3] Unless – but this is not the case in Europe – brothels are legalised (but see, at Ch. 2, fn. 18 under the legislation which regulated 'closed houses' the argument that the contracts concluded within were not enforceable).

[4] It is interesting to note that Article 1, para. 5, in listing the areas where the Directive shall not apply, includes gambling, but makes no reference to one of the economic 'drivers' of e-commerce, *i.e.* on-line pornography.

and which leaves it to national authorities to establish the rules.[5] However these products would fall under the defective products Directive (1985/374) or the more rigid provisions set by national legislation in this field.[6]

c. *Services*

The area in which sexual services have had an enormous development is on-line erotic services, whether it is on-the-phone sex or Internet web sites.

If one considers that these services are widely offered, and are one of the main sources of income of on-line service providers, there is a clear public interest in bringing them under the control of the law. The ambiguous legal standing of sex-lines encourages fraudulent activities towards consumers to the benefit of off-shore companies of dubious ownership.

The fact that most people consider engaging in on-line sex a distasteful practice does not – from a strictly legal point of view – justify a lessened protection in their contractual relations. Social stigma cannot impose legal sanctions, and especially cannot ensure to one of the parties of the transaction a privileged legal regime.

From a consumer point of view the issue is not so much the content of the service, but the accessibility of the file, the integrity and quality of the copy received, effective length and price, anonymity and personal privacy, as well as safety of payment.

What is surely relevant are the procedures for the formation of contracts set down by Directive 1997/7 and especially the right to correct eventual mistakes in expressing consent. It should be reminded that as these services are immediately provided and "consumed" there is – in accordance with Article 6, para. 3 of the Directive – no right to cancel or withdraw.

A particularly delicate issue is that of personal data which is provided by the sex consumer and which concerns his or her most intimate sphere. Not only should consent for their processing require special forms, in accordance with Directives 1995/46 and 2002/58, but they should be detained only for the time strictly necessary for the rendering of the service. They should not be

[5] For similar issues in the US system, see Terry, *Prescriptions sans Frontières (or How I Stopped Worrying About Viagra on the Web but Grew Concerned About the Future of Healthcare Delivery)*, 4 *Yale J. Health Pol'y L. & Ethics* 183 (2004).

[6] For the US see *Brumley v. Pfizer, Inc.* 149 *F.Supp.2d* 305 (S.D.Tex., 2001) in which the court granted summary judgment for the pharmaceutical company arguing that a) the package insert contained adequate warnings against use of the drug by patients with certain heart conditions; b) the deceased person's physician had had adequate warning about prescribing the drug to patients with heart conditions; c) there was not sufficient evidence to prove causation between use of drug and patient's death.

communicated or used for marketing purposes. There should not be unsolicited offers. Instead, this appears to be an area in which most privacy regulations are disregarded and the use of so-called 'spyware' is extensive.

Consumers should receive detailed information on the service provider, including the address of his business premises. It might also be reasonable to require that the services provided do not include in any way child pornography, which would immediately bring criminal sanctions into action.

Another field in which consumer law might apply is that of sex tourism. Let us assume that the services offered by the tour operator involve only consenting adults. Can one apply Directive 1990/314 on package holidays to these "tourist services not ancillary to transport or accommodation and accounting for a significant proportion of the package" (Article 2, para. 1, letter c)?

Does the "sexual tourist" have the right to cancel his reservation and be refunded? Has he the right to receive all the relevant information and alternative arrangements? Is the tour operator liable for damages that the sexual tourist has received (typically venereal disease)? Can one apply the ECJ ruling in the *Leitner v. TUI* case, which extends damage awards to non-pecuniary losses?[7]

d. *Payment*

Payment for sexual services and goods is traditionally by cash. But with the spread of on-line providers credit/debit cards are increasingly used. This brings to the foreground Directive 2008/48[8] on consumer credit and the protection of consumers when paying through credit schemes. Moreover, in general a consumer should be able to revoke the payment order if there has been no performance, and activate the procedures set by Recommendation 1988/590 on the relationship between cardholder and card issuer in cases of fraudulent misuse of credit cards.

e. *Unfair terms and deceptive practices*

A glance at the general conditions of contract applied to on-line sex services captures the vast amount of unfair terms. One can find practically the whole black list set out in Directive 1993/13. It is, in practice, rather unlikely – for legal and social reasons – that a consumer will bring a claim against sex services providers. However, it is clear that by ignoring unfair terms legislation sex industries have a competitive advantage in respect of other businesses which instead must abide by the law.

---

[7] Case C-168/00 decided 12.3.2002

[8] Which repeals the first Directive 1987/102 on the same subject.

The same may be said for unfair trade practices – forbidden by Directive 2005/29 – which are extremely common in the field, not only through advertising but also by offering services in which the price is concealed or difficult to ascertain.[9]

f. *The applicable law*

The question of applicability of consumer law to consumer transactions is however rather theoretical for a simple, and quite obvious, reason. The serious doubts on the lawfulness of such activity suggests to most businesses – the online ones, in the first place – to establish and run their activities from countries where no such regulations exist. This means that even if one were to solve the problems of private international law in favour of the consumer, it is practically impossible to serve a summons on the defendant company and to enforce a judgment.

From a legal-realist point of view this means that there is substantial equivalence between abstractly including sex transactions within consumer contracts, and refusing to apply contract law and remedies on the basis of immorality, and it opens the road to *ex ante* regulation.

[9] For some French cases of criminal fraud against the consumer see Appeals Paris (crim.div.) 24.1.2000, Laik (JurisData: 2000-111383): The owner of a peep-show parlour is liable for fraud if he attracts his clients through strip-tease artists who promise performances (Thai massages) which are not received by the clients who have paid for them. And Appeals Paris (crim.div.) 18.2.2004 (JurisData 2004-243542): The price paid by a not entirely mentally able adult for ten peep-shows was not exorbitant, and disability of client was not immediately perceivable. For a US case, in which a general statute on fair trading practices was successfully invoked see *Chassman v. People Resources* (573 *N.Y.S.2d* 589) (1991) (cited in detail further at Ch. 8 fn. 46)

CHAPTER SEVEN

SEX AS A PROFESSION

The 'sex industry', in a not too metaphorical a sense, sells human bodies: its services are of necessity provided personally. Even where the products, such as audiovisual items, are goods for sale their manufacture entails use being made of people's bodies.[1]

Regarding certain types of service, of which prostitution is the most typical, these are provided individually and thus require a direct relationship between supplier and user. But as we have seen there are many cases in which the service is organised in a way that implies an employer-employee type of relationship.[2]

What legal rules apply to the 'sex workers' required to carry out these activities? It is assumed for this part of the discussion that the end contract (purchase of a pornographic video, or a ticket to a strip- or lap dancing show, etc.) is legally valid. Does this necessarily imply that the labour relation entailed in the production is equally recognised as valid? It is here that the first problems arise.

a. *Human dignity and the validity of acts of disposal of one's body*

Following the horrors of totalitarian regimes and of World War Two, modern European Constitutions have included among their cornerstones the principle of human dignity.

In particular those countries such as Germany and Italy, which had most suffered – and created suffering for – the violation of basic human rights, gave the principle special importance.

Article 1 of the German *Grundgesetz* states, under the heading "Protection of human dignity", that "The dignity of man is inviolable. To respect and protect it is the duty of all state authority". Article 41 of the Italian Constitution

[1] The topic of sex work is one of the most examined in legal writings, albeit from different angles. Among the many books and articles one can cite Kempadoo, Doezema (eds.), *Global Sex Workers. Rights, Resistance, and Redefinition*, New York, Routledge, 1998; Sanders, *Sex work. A risky business*, Willan Pub., Cullompton 2005 and, by the same author, *Blinded by morality? Prostitution policy in the UK*, in *Capital & Class* n° 86, p. 9 (2005), which is very critical of the report "*Paying the price*" (cited above at Ch. 2, fn 14); Campbell, O'Neill (eds.) *Sex Work Now*, Willan Pub., Cullompton 2006. See also the proceedings of the conference on "*Economic Justice for Sex Workers*" published in 10 *Hastings Women's L.J.* 1–252 (1999).

[2] Dank, Refinetti (eds.), *Sex Work & Sex Workers*, Transaction Pub., New Brunswick 1998.

makes violation of 'human dignity' a limiting factor on the exercise of economic freedom.

More recently the principle of the inviolability of 'human dignity' has been enshrined in Article 1 of the European Charter of Fundamental Rights.

The first question that must of course be posed concerns the validity of the legal act by which a person renounces his or her dignity. Prostitutes, actors in pornographic films, participants in live nude shows are undertaking activities which common morality, "a sense of decency", deems to fall below a minimum level of dignity. Behind this lies the age-old argument about the balance between self-determination and protection of the basic conditions of existence, between the minimal and the paternalistic state.

One view of the problem is that the legal order cannot admit such a radical renunciation of one's own dignity. And it is easy to trace a line of continuity between this position and support for prohibitions on physically disposing of one's own body (selling organs, 'renting out' one's womb, etc.). To a lesser degree it is sufficient to follow the debate on the admissibility of the practice of "dwarf tossing" which has prompted both legislative bans[3] and administrative interventions.[4]

The ban on "sex work" has therefore a solid ideological and legal basis, without even having to enter into thorny discussions about morals. The human body is seen as a whole and, as a whole, it merits protection. Shifting the debate on human dignity avoids the quagmires of prurient interests and of reciprocal accusations between "bigots" and "rakes". Human dignity appears to be a common ground of understanding, which is at the foundations of a modern and civilized state.

Constitutional history – since the US Constitution – demonstrates that general principles are enacted through legislation and the courts. There is no reason why the human dignity principle should not follow the same course and be gradually applied to a variety of cases, including those involving the use of one's body for the sexual gratification of someone else.[5]

---

[3] See the Ontario Dwarf Tossing Ban Act, 2003.

[4] See the November 21, 1991 circular of the French Minister of Interior suggesting that mayors should ban dwarf tossing within the municipal boundaries on the basis of Article 3 of the ECHR. The legitimacy of the circular was challenged by a dwarf who made his living in discos, but the request was declared irreceivable by the European Court of Human Rights (Petition n. 29961/96 *Wackenheim v. France*, rejected October 16, 1996). For a comment of this and other cases see Resta, *La disponibilità dei diritti fondamentali e i limiti della dignità*, in *Rivista diritto civile* 2002, II, 801. Previously see McGee, *If Dwarf Tossing Is Outlawed, Only Outlaws Will Toss Dwarfs: Is Dwarf Tossing a Victimless Crime?*, 38 *Am. J. Juris.* 335 (1993)

[5] This raises the question of the admissibility of a free choice of a prostitute or a porn actor/actress: Cornell, *At The Heart of Freedom. Feminism, Sex, & Equality*, Princeton U.P., Princeton, 1998, at p. 47 "What kind of regulation, if any, is appropriate when a woman insists she is involved in the self-representation of her sexuate being by becoming a porn worker and/or a prostitute?". And provides social motivation for her work? See Decker, *Prostitution: Regulation and Control*, Littleton, Co., Rothman, 1979 ("Their [the prostitutes'] feeling [is] that they are providing a needed service to society", at p. 453).

From a general standpoint the objection that the principle encroaches on individual freedom and autonomy does not appear to be irresistible. There are many other cases in which such freedom and autonomy are limited in the name of general or higher interests. And this not only in the field of economic freedoms, but also of fundamental human rights: freedom of expression is curtailed by anti-hate laws; freedom to circulate by anti-pollution measures; freedom of association and assembly by public order exigencies. It is not therefore implausible that sex work may be proscribed.

At any rate a ban based on the human dignity principle appears to be much more coherent and non-discriminatory than if it were posited in immorality and indecency. There is no distinction (and discrimination) of the gender of the sex worker (male, female, transgender) and therefore one skirts the pitfalls of the feminist approach.[6] The intentions of the parties (health, lust, procreation, wealth) are irrelevant, because what is at stake is the sanctity of the human body. What is protected is not the interest of a minority (children's rights to be brought up in a protected sphere) but a basic rule of a civilised society.

The human dignity principle, furthermore, can easily be used as a foundation of the vast amount of national and international legislation aimed at contrasting the unacceptable phenomenon of human trafficking and other modern forms of slavery, of which sex workers are often the main victims.[7]

The consequences of this approach – which, as has been illustrated, has many arguments in its favour – are that all contracts in which a person renounces his or her dignity are invalid. And that includes, obviously, employment contracts, shutting down any discussion on the point that is not founded in criminal law.

b. *The disposability of one's sexual features*

What renders the human dignity principle unattractive is that – as with all broad and idealistic principles – it is extremely difficult to set its boundaries. And, from a methodological point of view, once one starts finding exceptions to mitigate the harshness of a generalised application these can rapidly swallow up the rule.[8]

---

[6] see further in Chapter 9, para. b.

[7] See *ex multis* Lim (ed.),*The sex sector: the economic and social bases of prostitution in Southeast Asia*, ILO, Geneva, 1998; Brown, *Sex slaves: the trafficking of women in Asia*, Virago, London, 2001; Guinn Steglich (eds.), *In Modern Bondage: Sex Trafficking in the Americas*, Transnational Pub., Ardsley, N.Y., (c2003); Matter, *Trafficking in Persons: An Annotated Legal Bibliography*, 96 *Law Libr. J.* 669 (2004).

[8] Therefore the rule would be: "We should begin from the realization that there is nothing per se wrong with taking money for the use of one's body" Nussbaum, *Taking Money for Bodily Services*, in Ertman, Williams (eds.), *Rethinking Commodification. Cases and Readings in Law and Culture*, NYU Press, New York 2005, p. 243 (at p. 246).

Let us start with some examples where sexual features are extremely important but are not considered, by general standards, obscene. Waitresses, hostesses, salesgirls, barmaids chosen on the basis of their physical appearance and on whom a dress code is imposed by their employers requiring they dress in such a way that their femininity is better exposed.[9] The reasons are quite obvious and are not only related to stereotyped ideas men have of women; an attractive girl also "attracts" other girls, transmitting a feeling of reassurance.[10]

These contractual provisions have been attacked in some common law jurisdictions as contrary to anti-discrimination laws, but the claims have been rejected.[11] In a European context, however, it is possible that they might be upheld on the basis of the human dignity principle.

In these cases we are faced with the validity of only one or a few clauses in a contract of employment which otherwise is valid, but the innuendo is clear. The human dignity principle is a very slippery tool to handle, especially by the judiciary, and may result in rendering unpredictable the regulation of labour relations in a way that is not very different from the more traditional immorality rule, which is left to the subjective view of each judge, in his seat and in his time.

---

[9] These occupations are amply examined by Avery, Craine, *Branded: Corporate Image, Sexual Stereotyping, and the New Face of Capitalism*, 14 *Duke J. Gender L. & Pol'y* 13 (2007); and by McGinley, *Harassment of Sex(y) Workers: Applying Title VII to Sexualized Industries*, 18 *Yale J.L. & Feminism* 65 (2006) (especially on sexual harassment against these kinds of workers). But see also Williams, *Sexual Harassment in Organizations: A Critique of Current Research and Policy*, in Dank, Refinetti (eds.), *Sexual Harassment & Sexual Consent*, Transaction Pub., New Brunswick 1998, p. 19ff.

[10] Is the contract of employment with a model who poses in the nude for paying clients immoral and therefore void? According to Appeals Orleans 4.6.1998 (*Hameon v. Niamke*) (JurisData: 1998-045327) the answer is no. An erotic performance is not necessarily considered pornographic.

[11] See the US case *Jespersen v. Harrah's Operating Co.* (444 *F.3d* 1104 (9th Cir. 2006)) (amply commented by Avery, Craine *Branded: Corporate Image, Sexual Stereotyping, and the New Face of Capitalism*, 14 *Duke J. Gender L. & Pol'y* 13 (2007)); and the Australian case *Zhang v Kanellos* [2005] *FMCA* 111. The plaintiff claimed that having been required to wear a mini skirt as bar attendant in the gaming room of a hotel she had been treated as a sex object. The claim was rejected (see the critical comment by Hunyor, *Short Skirts and the Sex Discrimination Act: 'What's Wrong With Being Sexy?'*, 31 *Alternative L.J.* 15 (2005)). But if the worker has been employed with an ordinary (*i.e.* non-sexual) task and during her employment she is asked to engage in sexual activities with clients, her refusal is no legitimate reason for dismissal and opens the road for a claim for damages: see the French case decided by Appeals Rennes 26.6.2007, *Leclerc v. Quilfen* (JurisData: 2007-342165). Obviously if one shares the opinion that there *is* something wrong "with being sexy" there are no limits to shame: see the article by Bergin, *Sexualized Advocacy: The Ascendant Backlash against Female Lawyers*, 18 *Yale J.L. & Feminism* 191 (2006) ("sexualized advocacy" "is a familiar, yet played out, strategy for forestalling the professional advancement of women", at p. 222); following the leading opinion of MacKinnon, *Sexual Harassment of Working Women A Case of Sex Discrimination*, Yale U.P., New Haven, Ct., 1979, p. 159: "A great many instances of sexual harassment in essence amount to solicitation for prostitution".

But if it is a matter of contention that one can dispose of the way in which one dresses and appears, it is even more doubtful that one can dispose of one's sexual attitudes.[12] There are, however, some significant differences from other cases in which one disposes of one's body. In the case of organs there is a permanent impairment (typically, kidney transplant). In the case of surrogate motherhood there are *ordre public* concerns related to ensuring that the child may know exactly who his parents are. But in the case of sexual services we are confronted with activities that normal people do in their normal lives.[13] In the bedroom, between consenting adults, there is no human dignity obligation. And even outside ordinary domestic relations it is difficult to imagine that the human dignity principle applies to "wife swapping" or other forms of non-traditional sex.

So what is under discussion is – once again – sex for a consideration. Human dignity is offended not because of base, lewd and obscene behaviour but because of the money that is involved, which brings us back to the dilemma at the origin of this book: what really is the devil's pay? Sex or money? Or the combination of the two?[14]

It is difficult to find a reply to the question arguing on the basis of Article 3, para. 2 of the European Charter of Fundamental Rights, which introduces "the prohibition on making the human body and its parts as such a source of financial gain". This is not only because the provision is related to "the fields of medicine and biology", but also because its expanded interpretation would quite legitimately bring a prohibition to any form of manual labour, from bricklaying to professional football, not forgetting the work of the baker and the mime artist.[15]

---

[12] "We might claim that one's sexual services, like one's blood, are inalienable rights which should not be traded" (Cameron, *The Economics of Sin. Rational Choice or No Choice At All?*, Edward Elgar, Cheltenham 2002, at p. 183).

[13] Some authors – both of the past and of the present – see a relation between sex within marriage and sex for money: *e.g.* "The wife, who obviously is aware that her loveless sex relations with her husband might be regarded as a kind of prostitution, will vigorously defend herself against that charge on the basis that no cash changes hands specifically for the sexual act" (Benjamin, Masters, *Prostitution and Morality*, Julian Press, New York, 1964, at p. 275); "The crucial distinction between the prostitution contract and other contracts to which women are a party thus rest on the guarantee of access to sex" (Carpenter, *Re-Thinking Prostitution. Feminism, Sex, and the Self*, Peter Lang, New York, 2000 (at p. 110). And Cameron, *The Economics of Sin. Rational Choice or No Choice At All?*, Edward Elgar, Cheltenham 2002, reminds us (at p. 184) the "Marxist-Feminist position that marriage has been, in many times and many places, a form of prostitution hidden behind a veil of respectability".

[14] Over 70 years ago, in one of the first sociological investigation on the subject, it was noted that "since prostitution is a contractual relation in which services are traded (usually in terms of an exchange medium) and sex is placed in an economic context, it is strange that modern writers have made so much of the fact that the 'social evil' has economic causes" (Davis, *The Sociology of Prostitution*, 2 *American Sociological Review* 744 (1937) (at p. 749).

[15] Article 3, para 2, is indicated in the draft opinion of the European Parliament dated 30.6.2006 as the first suggestion for opposing the legality of paid sexual services.

By contrast one might reasonably argue, construing the above cited provision, that the fact that the prohibition refers to medical and biological aspects does not warrant its extension to other fields, in which there is, and must be, much more freedom.

c. *The 'commodification debate'*

Many of the arguments which have been presented in the previous paragraphs are condensed into what may be called the 'commodification debate'. Its birthplace is feminist theory,[16] which, applied to the use of one's body for sexual activity, challenges the trends towards a market approach inasmuch as this simply means transforming women's bodies, and their sexual features into something you can sell and buy on the market, *i.e.* a commodity like any other. Women therefore are not considered as integral human beings but simply as object of pleasure in the hands, and in the wallets, of men.

The 'commodification of sex' is therefore an unacceptable stance for its intrinsic content and extrinsic consequences. Practically all the goods and services which have been described in the previous chapters are meant to perpetuate sexual dominance of men over women and a relationship which is based on the satisfaction of men's sexual urges.

The opposition to 'commodification' has therefore become a *mot d'ordre* of the feminist approach to sexual services and goods; the term itself is, if not an insult, surely disparaging towards positions which suggest that a contractual/regulatory approach would be preferable compared to the present state of affairs.

With regard to the limited scope of this work, which is mainly focused on the legal issues of the sex market, the first thing that should be noted is that the trend towards commodification is typical of our age of extraordinary developments in science and technology. Whether we are talking about computer science, information, knowledge, or bio- and nanotechnologies, all the new elements which have changed – and are changing – our lives over the last three decades are tightly bound in a circular relationship: discovery/legal protection/commodification. Obviously there is a profound and stimulating debate of the various opinions as to the amount of legal protection, and rather wide criticism towards the excesses of intellectual property protection. However, it is quite clear that commodification is one of the economic drivers and goals of advancement in new fields of scientific research.

In this general context, commodification is not a dirty word, and its antithesis, ultimately, is the so-called 'commons perspective', in which everybody is

[16] *Ex multis* see Pateman, *The Sexual Contract*, Polity, Cambridge 1988; O'Connell Davidson, *Prostitution, Power and Freedom*, Polity, Cambridge, 1998.

entitled to benefit from progress without having to pay revenue to the holder of IP rights.

It is very clear to a lawyer (especially if he comes from a common law background) that commodification implies the existence of property rights and of entitlement. It points towards a market – mostly a consumer market – in which modern forms of wealth are exchanged for a consideration.

One of the most critical aspects of commodification is that of the human body, and most of the bioethical aspects of the new life sciences (cells, DNA, genoma, organs *et caetera*) have to do with ownership and allocation of rare and precious resources.

The debate on the 'commodification of sex' however has little to do with this. Sexual services have always – *i.e.* since antiquity – been "commodified".[17] There is nothing scientific or technologic in most sexual services or goods (with the exception of sex-enhancing drugs). There is very little novelty in the market, apart from being able to use digital technologies and telecommunication networks to transfer and access pornographic materials or to participate in discussions with a sexual content.

On the other hand, one cannot forget that human bodily features have always been commodified through work. Provided there is no permanent and negative alteration of one's body, the differences between sexual organs and other parts of the body is cultural, intellectual and moral. It is perfectly legitimate to follows the tracks of early Marxist theory on the appropriation by capitalists of the sweat of the brow of the working class, but this involves any kind of physical work, not only sex work.

The final result of the opposition to commodification would therefore be the withdrawal from the market of an entity which has always been available,[18] and an extremely difficult operation of distinguishing "sexual features" (which therefore cannot be available on the market) from non-sexual features.[19]

Ultimately, the 'commodification of sex' theories – however well argued – give the impression of being highly ideological nominalism, which finds its justification within a closed debate where everybody agrees on its premises. But if one (legitimately) sees things from a different perspective – in this work

[17] The most radical critique to the feminist "commodification theory" comes from a different feminist perspective: Nussbaum, *"Whether from Reason or Prejudice": Taking Money for Bodily Services*, 27 *J. Legal Stud.* 693 (1998). It is followed by Della Giusta, Di Tommaso, Strøm, *Sex Markets. A Denied Industry*, Routledge, Abingdon 2008.

[18] "Sex is currently commodified, fully or partially, through legal products and services including film, Internet, and print pornography, strip clubs and peep shows, telephone sex services, sex therapy and sexual surrogacy, bathhouses, sex clubs, and sexuality workshops" (Lucas, *The Currency of Sex. Prostitution, Law, and Commodification*, in Ertman, Williams (eds.), *Rethinking Commodification. Cases and Readings in Law and Culture*, NYU Press, New York 2005, p. 248 (at p. 259).

[19] See above at para. b) the heated feminist debate over "sexy" dress codes.

from a legal point of view[20] – the "commodification debate" is simply a different and gendered version of the immorality question (which has its own long list of strong arguments). Certain contracts are not allowed (or have limited legal effects) because they are immoral, not because their object is non-commodifiable.[21]

d. *The reality of sex workers*

A further reason which renders the – theoretically appealing – human dignity principle somewhat undesirable is that once one has reached the inescapable conclusion that sex work contracts are void because they are quite obviously contrary to human dignity, the consequences are extremely severe and mostly sanction the weaker part of the bargain, that is, the sex workers.[22]

Their employer could legitimately refuse to pay them any wages or other benefits. All collateral rights and obligations would be swept away: amongst others, accumulated end-of-contract bonuses, maternity leave, insurance and benefit contributions, and so on.[23] Such claims would necessarily have to be rejected by the courts on the basis of the immemorial and wide-spread rule *Nemo auditur*.[24]

---

[20] In a civil law context there is a further technical-systematic difficulty in accepting the 'commodification' perspective: as one does not have 'property rights' over one's body (Ulpian: *Dominus nemo videtur membrorum suorum*) sexual services are not, from a legal point of view, 'commodities' but simply a prestation which falls under the law of obligations, and not property law. The issue is extensively examined by Calabresi, *An Introduction to Legal Thought: Four Approaches to Law and to the Allocation of Body Parts*, in 55 *Stanford L. Rev.* 2113 (2003) (at p. 2132ff)

[21] The relativity of the conclusion appears to be accepted also by some feminist writers: "Perhaps the best policy solution, for now, is a regime of regulation expressing incomplete commodification. The issue becomes how to structure an incomplete commodification that takes into account of our non ideal world yet does not foreclose progress to a better world of more nearly equal power"(Radin, *Contested Commodities*, in Ertman, Williams (eds.), *Rethinking Commodification. Cases and Readings in Law and Culture*, NYU Press, New York 2005, p. 81 (at p. 90)

[22] In this sense see Lemoncheck, *Loose Women, Lecherous Men*, OUP, New York 1997 ("I contend that viewing sex work as degrading tends to universalize questions of degradation that are context-sensitive and precludes ascriptions of agency or autonomy to sex workers with which many may resist or transcend their subordinate status as dehumanized sexual commodities", at p. 117).

[23] For a typical example see the French case decided by Appeals Paris 16.5.2003, *URSSAF v. Tremblay* (JurisData: 2003-212888). In first instance the court had excluded that a prostitute should pay social security dues because that would have meant legalising the trade of a human body. The court of appeal rejected the argument: the fact that the activity was against *bonos mores* did not prevent the enforcement of the welfare provisions and the social security bodies could not be considered as "pimps" for receiving part of the prostitute's profits.

[24] See below Chapter 9, para. a). This is not always true: see the French case decided by Appeals Paris 27.4.2006, *Sylvialize v. Ramarolahy* (in *JurisData*: 2006-299897) in which a worker who had been hired as a sales-girl in a sex-shop (but was actually engaged in prostitution) was fired for purported redundancy. The court rejected the defence of the former employer who argued that the contract was void. He was perfectly aware of the nature of the employment and could not take any advantage from it being contrary to *les bonnes moeurs*. For a different

And neither would there be any obligation to apply any safety or other protective measures to the 'base trade' in which they are engaged.[25] The state could – indeed should – deny them access to the welfare system that provides benefits to other workers in cases of accident or illness.[26]

If one considers the development of the sex industry, well beyond that of traditional prostitution, one can easily understand that the number of people involved is far from small.

Illegality of work brings with it the impossibility of organising trade unions[27] and other forms of collective and mutual assistance. Standard employment contracts and all the remaining achievements that the workers' movement has obtained over the last century and a half cannot be applied and extended to sex workers.[28]

So sex workers operate illegally.[29] The sanctions imposed by law inevitably consign them to a 'black' if not outright criminal market. The businesses that operate in it have a competitive advantage from not being burdened by heavy

---

outcome of an Irish case see *Coral Leisure Group v. Barnett* [1981] I.C.R. 503 (in which the employee had undertaken to procure prostitutes for the employer's clients).

[25] In this regard see the generic references to "fighting trafficking in human beings" in the draft opinion of the European Parliament of 30.6.2006, which contains instructions, also in the form of proposed new criminal offences, on the need to protect the health of 'sex workers'.

[26] See the case decided by the European Court of Human Rights *Tremblay v. France* (11.9.2007) concerning payment of social security fees by a former prostitute (and the critical comment by Marguenaud *Les droits de la femme prostituée à l'épreuve du proxènetisme de l'Etat*, in *Revue Trimestrielle Droit Civil* 2007, 730). Or another French case decided by the Cour de cassation (chambre sociale) 6.4.1995, *Galdéano v. CRAMIF*: here the social security was asking the former prostitute to disgorge the pension she had received, purporting that her (high) income did not entitle her to receive it. The defendant argued that her profits came from an immoral activity but the French judges were not convinced: "le droit de l'assuré au bénéfice de la pension d'invalidité et de l'allocation supplémentaire est apprécié en fonction de ses salaires ou gains pour la pension, et de ses ressources pour l'allocation, peu important le caractère professionnel ou non de ces gains ou ressources".

[27] See the copious 'trade union' documentation published on the www.sexworkeurope.org site including a "Declaration of the rights of sex workers in Europe". For an example of the difficulty to "unionise" sex workers even in a state where prostitution is legal see Murray, *Labour Regulation in the Legal Sex Industry in Victoria*, 16 *Austr. J. Labour L.* 321 at 333f (2003). And similar difficulties are met by sex workers in joining a union in the US: see the Comment, *We'd Better Treat Them Right: A Proposal for Occupational Cooperative Bargaining Associations of Sex Workers*, 9 *U. Pa. J. Lab. & Emp. L.* 679 at 692f (2007). From a sociological perspective see Jeness, *Making It Work. The Prostitutes' Rights Movement in Perspective*, De Gruyter, New York, 1993; Gall *Sex Worker Union Organising: An International Study*, Palgrave, Basingstoke, 2006. At any rate "State prohibition of prostitution and the move for vigilant criminal enforcement rob women who are porn workers and prostitutes of the most effective weapon against the abuses that have been graphically described – unionization" (Cornell, *At The Heart of Freedom. Feminism, Sex, & Equality*, Princeton U.P., Princeton, 1998, at p. 47).

[28] See Jeffrey, MacDonald, *Sex Workers in the Maritimes Talk Back*, UBC Press, Vancouver 2006 (mostly devoted to interviews to prostitute workers): "Viewing sex work as work rather than sexual exploitation or moral debauchery enables political approaches that recognize and support sex workers as rights-bearing political and social agents rather than objects of intervention and control" (at p. 11).

[29] Hence the urge that "sex workers" regain their "consensual capacity": Sullivan, *Prostitution and Consent: Beyond the Liberal Dichotomy of 'Free or Forced'*, in Cowling, Reynolds (eds.), *Making Sense of Sexual Consent*, Ashgate, Burlington Vt, 2004, p. 127 (at p. 138).

welfare dues. And obviously taxes remain unpaid for one of the most lucrative activities in the market.[30]

From this overview it is clear that the human dignity principle – or the illegality of contracts of employment for sex workers – leads to the most *laissez faire* result. No constraints upon businesses, except the risk of criminal proceedings, and no protection for the workers.[31] The latter therefore are permanently bound to their employer and to his will. They have lost their dignity and have gained little more than some additional money.

e. *The quest for respectability*

Sex workers are clearly the weakest element of the chain in the sex market.[32] Although many of them are self-employed and for others their exploitation by their employer is not much different from other professions, a great number of them have been engaged through fraud, blackmail or violence and are held in conditions of segregation. Often they have been smuggled illegally into a country and live in constant fear of being expelled.[33]

The boundary between self-employment and employees can be very slim, and is one of the many ways through which flexibility of the labour market is

---

[30] This one of the most debated issues in the various jurisdictions. The ECJ, in the *Coffeeshop Siberie* case (C-158/98 decided 29.6.1999: the case concerned the sale of cannabis in a Dutch cafe) expressed the view that "Renting out a place intended for commercial activities is, in principle, an economic activity and therefore falls within the scope of the Sixth Directive. The fact that the activities pursued there constitute a criminal offence, which may make the renting unlawful, does not alter the economic character of the renting and does not prevent competition in the sector, including that between lawful and unlawful activities." In the same sense see the French decision by Cass. soc. 19.12.1996, *URSSAF v. Tremblay* (JurisData: 1996–005145) (decision of lower court not to enforce payment of taxes due by prostitute because her activity is immoral, is quashed: taxes are due for any income from self-employment). But the opposite view is held, for prostitution services, in other national jurisdictions: see the Italian cases decided by Cass. 1.8.1986, n. 4927; and by Commissione Tributaria Milan 22.12.2005, n. 272 in *Giur. merito* 2006, 1795.

[31] "Attacking the industry from a moral standpoint, an approach shared by criminalisation and a 'social control' licensing system, does nothing to improve the lot of workers" (Crofts, Summerfield *The Licensing of Sex Work: Regulating an Industry or Enforcing Public Morality*, 33 *UWAL Rev* 289 at 306 (2007)). Similarly Marella, *Bocca di Rosa, Roxanne e le altre: considerazioni in tema di sesso, mercato e autonomia privata*, in 2 *Polemos*, issue 2/2008, p. 35.

[32] See Murray, *Labour Regulation in the Legal Sex Industry in Victoria*, 16 *Austr. J. Labour L.* 321 (2003): "A focus on the sex work industry also contributes to the growing discourse surrounding 'decent work' and the extension of basic legal protections to all workers. The sex industry presents significant challenges to a more inclusive system of labour law because there is no agreement that the 'thing' of sex work – namely, the commercial exchange of a sexual service – warrants legal protection as it is often considered debasing and corrupting to those who engage in it" (at p. 322).

[33] Walker, *Damned Whores and the Border Police: Sex Workers and Refugee Status in Australia*, 31 *Melb. U. L. Rev.* 938 (2007).

ensured, reducing significantly the contractual power of the sex worker.[34] In some jurisdictions, such as Nevada, the prostitute is self-employed but can work only in licensed establishments to which most of their earnings go.[35]

For all sex workers there is a stigma of immorality and indecency.[36] Prostitution is the main term of reference, even if the activity they actually do is different.[37] Prostitute (and all its synonyms: call girl, harlot, streetwalker or whore) is a term which itself impresses a mark of infamy on the person.[38]

---

[34] See Murray, *Labour Regulation in the Legal Sex Industry in Victoria*, 16 *Austr. J. Labour L.* 321 at 327 (2003): "Working conditions in the legal sex industry are therefore characterised by a schism between the ascribed relationship of contractor/contractee, which suggests that the sex workers are powerful, autonomous agents who do not need the law's protection, and the workers' actual economic dependence on venue operators." (and in more detail p. 337ff). Bingham, *Nevada Sex Trade: A Gamble for the Workers*, 10 *Yale J.L. & Feminism* 69, at 93f (1998) points out that qualifying prostitutes as "independent contractors" is a way to deprive them of "health care, vacation pay, retirement benefits, or any of the other rights and benefits many other workers have". One should however note that this is common tendency in all labour markets (see Law, *Commercial Sex: Beyond Decriminalization*, 73 *S. Cal. L. Rev.* 523 at 591(2000). The problem with sex workers is that they are weak from an organizational point of view and suffer from their social stigma. As the same Author admits (at p. 96) "the majority of the workers, whether they work in the sex industry or not, are exploited".

[35] See Bingham, *Nevada Sex Trade: A Gamble for the Workers*, 10 *Yale J.L. & Feminism* 69, at 93f (1998) ("While the prostitute may be able to make a decent income if there is a steady flow of customers, it is clear that the county and the brothel benefit far more than the individual prostitute").

[36] Balos, Fellows, *A Matter of Prostitution: Becoming Respectable*, 74 *N.Y.U. L. Rev. 1220* (1999); Dalla, *Exposing the 'Pretty Woman' Myth. A Qualitative Investigation of Street-Level Prostituted Women*, Lexington Books, Lanham, Md. 2006 ("The stigma associated with prostitution is felt, not by the buyers of sex, but by the suppliers. The sexual double-standard is alive and well, indeed. The demand for commercial sex, one could reasonably argue, drives the industry; if the demand did not exist, there would be no need for suppliers", at p. 205). See however the different opinion of Sanders *Paying for Pleasure. Men who Buy Sex*, Willan Pub., Cullompton, 2008, at p. 112 ff. The effects go well beyond contractual and labour relations: see *e.g.* the Italian case decided by Cass. 13.7.1982, no. 4107 on entrusting the care of minors to a mother who is a prostitute.

[37] A good example is that of women or men involved in sex tourism: "In the analysis of sex tourism, the notion of work needs to be broadened to encompass the shifting, flexible structures between leisure and labor, paid work and unpaid work, the private and the public are sometimes difficult to discern" (Cabezas, *Legal Challenges To and By Sex Workers/Prostitutes*, 48 *Clev. St. L. Rev.* 79 at 91 (2000)). And despite ideological generalizations, pornography is different from prostitution: Abbott, *Motivations for Pursuing an Acting Career in Pornography*, in Weitzer (ed.) *Sex for Sale: Prostitution, Pornography, and the Sex Industry*, Routledge, New York, 2000, p. 49.

[38] Quite appropriately Law, *Commercial Sex: Beyond Decriminalization*, 73 *S. Cal. L. Rev.* 523 at 523(2000) points out that 'The word 'prostitution' both describes and condemns. The primary meaning of the word has a sexual connotation, historically describing women who offer sexual services on an indiscriminate basis, whether or not for money, and more recently, the offer of sex for money. But a common secondary meaning of 'prostitution' is any service to 'an unworthy cause'. " In a similar sense Sullivan *The Politics of Sex. Prostitution and Pornography in Australia Since 1945*, Cambridge U.P., Cambridge, 1997 ("Legal definitions of prostitution are extrapolated from deliberations which seek to fix the meaning of normal sexuality and gender relations." The same Author adds: "Debates about what should count as normal and appropriate sexual practice have often been advantageous for women." (at p. 241) See also Murray, *Labour Regulation in the Legal Sex Industry in Victoria*, 16 *Austr. J. Labour L.* 321 at 335 (2003).

One should add that one of the negative side-effects of the feminist absolutist approach to female sex work is that it is rarely studied in its practical legal aspects.[39] Starting from the assumption that there can be no improvement of working conditions but only a complete ban, it is extremely difficult to set into an ordinary labour law framework practices that in other 'respectable' professions are regulated by law or through general bargaining agreements.[40]

A different perspective would instead lead to examining the nature of the service, the parties' interests, mutual rights and obligations, the specific precautions to be taken,[41] soliciting the opinions of the parties involved, together with considering the many aspects of general interest, in a manner no different from the way in which one would react to the emergence of any new field of work in a changing society.[42]

The main way through which it is reasonable to expect that the rights granted to other workers will be recognised for 'sex workers' is – without prejudging the nature of the work contract, which is the judge's prerogative – to remove the stigma of 'contrariety to morality' from certain activities and bring a "dishonest and illegal trade" within the ordered scope of the market[43] while taking into account its peculiarities.[44]

---

[39] Lewis, Maticka-Tyndale, *Licensing Sex Work: Public Policy and Women's Lives*, 26 *Canadian Public Policy / Analyse de Politiques*, 437 (2000); Geadah, *La prostitution: un métier comme un autre?*, VLB, Montreal, 2003 (arguing that with reference to prostitution of adults and child prostitution "il ne s'agit pas d'éléments sépares, mais des multiples facette de l'énorme iceberg" (at p. 136)).

[40] Murray, *Labour Regulation in the Legal Sex Industry in Victoria*, 16 *Austr. J. Labour L.* 321 at 341 (2003); Brewis, Linstead *Sex, Work and Sex Work. Eroticizing Organization*, Routledge London 2000 (see in particular chapter 10 at p. 241 on material variations in sex work; at p. 259 on market segmentation; and Chapter 11 at p. 272 on the temporal organization of sex work.

[41] See the volume *Hustling for Health. Developing services for sex workers in Europe*, edited by the *European* N*etwork for HIV/STD Prevention in Prostitution*, published in 1998 and available online at www.europap.net.

[42] "Moralistic resolutions and the concomitant lack of any true representation of the prostitute's women constituency are the key factor crippling law reform workshops on the issue of prostitution" (Kotiswaran, *Preparing for Civil Disobedience: Indian Sex Workers and the Law*, 21 *Boston Coll. Third World L. J.* 161 at 233 (2001)).

[43] See Murray, *Labour Regulation in the Legal Sex Industry in Victoria*, 16 *Austr. J. Labour L.* 321 at 342(2003) ("The challenge that sex work presents to labour law scholarship and practice is how to overcome an ingrained cultural view that sex work is not 'decent work' and how to challenge dominant legal paradigms to achieve a more comprehensive system of protection for all workers"). For a similar French view see Corbin, *Les filles de noce. Misère sexuelle et prostitution*, Aubier Montaigne, Paris 1978 ("Le retour des prostituées dans le droit commun impliquerait encore l'abandon du mépris qui les écrase et, du même coup, l'atténuation puis la disparition du sentiment de culpabilité et des mécanismes d'autopunition qu'il engendre"; "le retour au droit commun entraînerait probablement une distension des liens que les prostituées entretiennent encore avec le 'milieu' ", at p. 9).

[44] First of all the "gender asymmetry" of the market: see Crofts, Summerfield, *The Licensing of Sex Work: Regulating an Industry or Enforcing Public Morality?*, 33 *UWAL Rev.* 289 at 291 (2007). For regional specificities see Kempadoo, *Sexing the Caribbean. Gender Race, and Sexual Labor*, Routledge, New York, 2004: "Putting sexuality, as defined through everyday Caribbean practice, on the public agenda, as the sex worker organizations and initiatives do, makes not

One of the most obvious fields in which this practical approach could be applied is that of the self-employed/employee distinction. As has been seen the former qualification is one of the typical legal ways of denying a worker's rights. If one applies the substantive[45] continental European labour law approach,[46] which disregards the form of the contract, one is immediately brought to analyse a number of features which are extremely relevant in any labour relationship. The simple questions are: where is the work done? Who owns the premises? Who establishes the working hours? Does the worker have a direct commercial relation with the client? Who pays who? On what basis? How are the sums calculated? What is the organization of the business and how much of it is within the control of the business entity, and how much instead of the worker? Is the worker bound by an exclusive relation with the business? Is it a stable relationship, which normally has a more than yearly span? The replies to these questions[47] are those that enable any court or industrial tribunal to establish if a house-maid or a secretary are – rather improbably – autonomous workers or instead parties to a typical master/servant stable relationship.[48] Once one has reached this point one has to move on to

---

just prostitution, but broader sexual-economic relations in the region visible, for it speaks not only about overt transactions but also about the ways in which sexualities have been fashioned and refashioned through very particular social, political, and cultural histories that began with the emergence of global capitalism" (at p. 201).

[45] *i.e.* what in US labour law is called the "economic realities test".

[46] The differences between European labour law and US labour law appear to be a main source of incomprehension on the subject. One of the strongest arguments used in the very broad and detailed article by Law, *Commercial Sex: Beyond Decriminalization*, 73 *S. Cal. L. Rev.* 523 (2000) to challenge the "sex for money" approach is the very poor working conditions of would-be self-employed sex workers would be forced to work in. But if labour law is different, the argument fails. To put the question squarely: if sex workers received, in the US, exactly the same benefits as any other full-time regular employee, would "commercial sex" be an acceptable practice? The Author's reply on the point (at p. 599) appears a good starting point: "In short, treating commercial sex 'like any other profession' is not likely to offer commercial sex workers much assurance of unionization, access to health insurance, or decent working conditions. Rather, commercial sex workers, like other part-time, self-employed, and contingent workers, confront problems of economic and social insecurity that are particularly acute in fields, like commercial sex, where most of the workers are women. It seems more likely that such problems would be addressed through measures applicable to all workers, and extended to commercial sex workers if commercial sex were legal, rather than through special programs for commercial sex workers."

[47] For some social data from Australia see Boyle, Glennon, Najman, Turrell, Western, Wood, *The Sex Industry: A Survey of Sex Workers in Queensland, Australia*, Ashgate, Aldershot, 1997.

[48] Some of the questions are used by the French Cour de cassation (3.4.2003, *Copper communications v. URSSAF*) (JurisData: 2003-018666) to quash a decision of the Paris Cour d'appel which had rejected the defence of a publisher who did not want to pay social security dues in favour of authors of pornographic texts (according to the court of appeals "ces textes, consultables sur Minitel, ne sont pas accompagnés de commentaires personnels, qu'ils doivent être de nature érotique ou pornographique, que les lecteurs en ignorent l'auteur, qu'ils sont fongibles, et qu'ils ne sont consultables qu'après validation par l'éditeur, de sorte que les auteurs qui ne disposent pas d'une liberté d'action exclusive du salariat, ne travaillent pas de façon indépendante, et que, quel que soit le mode de leur rémunération, ils doivent être affiliés au régime général;

the following step: minimum pay, holidays, sick-leave, overtime, maternity leave, *et caetera*. Without having necessarily to write down *ex novo* collective bargaining agreements, one could easily apply by analogy those existing in other sectors, *e.g.* for masseuses in regular health spas; for secondary actors in the film industry; for employees in call centres; and for dancers and ballerinas in the entertainment business.

From this particular perspective it is not surprising that, at least in the European Union, free movement of workers issues arise. Not only are there countries where sexual services are better paid than others (and that naturally encourages migration from one member state to another)[49] or countries where sexual services cost less (encouraging sex tourism)[50] but there are also countries where the social environment and the disrepute of professions associated with sex are different.[51] Furthermore, being able to work outside one's original community and far away from domestic relations allows a person to lead a double life, of which at least one can be considered 'normal' and not despised.[52]

The topic has already been addressed by the European Court of Justice in its decision in the Jany case,[53] observing pragmatically, in regard to Dutch rules aimed at curbing the activities of Czech and Polish prostitutes, that any measures directed at foreign sex workers are illegal if directed at "conduct which, when attributable to the former state's own nationals" is not repressed in the same manner.

---

but the Cour de Cassation required evidence of subordination between the authors and the publisher). Obviously, if one applies the general rules of labour law the employee who is aware of the nature of the activity before being hired cannot justify his misgivings (slow and sloppy work) alleging religious objections to the pornographic trade (see the French case *Perez v. Societé Marc Dorel* Appeals Paris 27.11.2001) (JurisData: 2001-163440)

[49] Thorbek, Pattanaik (eds.), *Transnational Prostitution. Changing Global Patterns*, Zed Books, London 2002; Monzini, *Sex traffic: prostitution, crime, and exploitation*, Zed Books, London, 2005 (especially p. 58ff.); Agustin, *Sex at the margins: migration, labour markets and the rescue industry*, Zed Books, London, 2007.

[50] Ryan, Hall, *Sex Tourism. Marginal People and Liminalities*, Routledge, London 2001: "Within the global tourism economy of pleasure sex workers need to be recognized as professional providers of sex services in order to ensure that they are not exploited. Such a recognition implies that global measures such as trading and labour agreements therefore provide a significant base with which to improve the conditions of sex workers. However, it also implies that prostitution must be recognized as work" (at p. 149).

[51] The request for de-criminalizing prostitution as a first step towards the protection of "sex workers" is common not only to developed countries: see Kotiswaran, *Preparing for Civil Disobedience: Indian Sex Workers and the Law*, 21 *Boston College Third World L. J.* 161 (2001).

[52] See for the example the Italian case decided by App. Roma 29.11.1993 (in *Diritto informazione e informatica* 1994, 299) (violation of privacy of prostitute through a TV programme which made known her activity among an extremely vast number of people, including those living in her home town).

[53] Cited and commented further at Chapter 9, para. d.

CHAPTER EIGHT

OF SEX AND OF LOVE

A contractual analysis of sexual relations inevitably brings one to discuss something that is, apparently, together with faith, the most removed element of legal interest, and that is love.

It is commonly said that one cannot "buy" love or affection. And therefore no contract can bind a person to love another one. One could therefore conclude that whenever a relation of love includes one of sex, both elements cannot form part of a contractual relationship. The statement, however, appears to be a truism. If one looks at the state of the law the conclusions are quite different.

On the one hand, love and affection are an obligation which is generated by marriage, family relations (mostly between parents and children), donor and donee. Even if one cannot obtain specific performance of these obligations, the violation of the duty has numerous legal sanctions: spouses can be divorced; children removed from their families; deeds of gift revoked.

On the other hand, sentimental relations between adults quite often involve sexual desire and practices. People are attracted to each other by sex. Sexual well-being has a stabilizing effect on personal relations. And the end of a sexual *entente* often marks the end of a relationship. These aspects are quite indistinguishable from other aspects of a sentimental relationship and it makes little sense – at least from a legal point of view – to separate the platonic love sphere from the carnal love sphere.[1]

This is not without legal consequences. Among the duties that spring from marriage, that of conjugal fidelity has an obvious corollary in a spouse's duty of physical consummation owed to the other. Even though the law and decided cases are extremely cautious when it comes to laying down how and in what degree the duty is to be fulfilled,[2] it seems a well established principle that an

[1] The argument, it must be noted, has also been used by those opposing the enforceability of cohabitation agreements: "It would seem more candid to acknowledge the return of varying forms of common law marriage than to continue displaying the naiveté we believe involved in the assertion that there are involved in these relationships contracts separate and independent from the sexual activity, and the assumption that those contracts would have been entered into or would continue without that activity" (*Hewitt v. Hewitt*, 394 *N.E.2d* 1204) (1979) (Ill. S. Ct.)

[2] See Honoré, *Sex Law in England*, Archon Books, Hamden, Ct., 1978, p. 23 ff ("This duty, which I shall call the mutual duty, was hardly recognised until recently and even now is nowhere set out in so many words"). For some Italian cases see those decided by Cass. civ. 7.3.2006, n. 4876; and Cass.civ. 20.1.2006, n. 1202 (in *Foro it.* 2006, 1406).

absolute refusal to do so is grounds for separation and dissolution of the bonds of marriage.[3]

The fact that the law is expressed in very broad language opens the way to private agreements which fill in the gaps and specify the content of what can be called the sexual obligations of the parties.

a. *Cohabitation, premarital, marital, and post-marital agreements*

Most Western legal systems have, for a long time, declared cohabitation agreements invalid. The reasons given are a mixture of public policy and public morality.[4] The only recognised form of union – and only between a man and a woman – was marriage. Other unions were considered as instrumental to circumventing all the procedures, consequences and legal remedies surrounding marriage. To recognise cohabitation agreements meant granting the protection of the law to people who could have not entered into a proper marriage because of a previous marital bond, or because of a blood relationship between themselves.[5] As to property rights, while general law established the way in which the assets between the spouses were to be allocated and divided, with cohabitation the conferral, on a daily basis, of property rights between the parties clashed against one of the taboos of Western private law, and that is gratuitous promises.

---

[3] The opinion is shared in both common law and civil law jurisdictions: compare the Canadian case *Lewis v. Lewis* (1983) (44 *N.B. Rep.(2d)* 268) ("refusal to have sexual relations, starting in the first year, progressively increasing refusals and refusing to explain or even to discuss any reason" considered "mental cruelty", irreparable injury to the husband's deep religious feelings and, therefore, grounds for divorce) with the Italian ones, Cass. civ. 10.5.2005, n. 9801 (in *Giust. civ.* 2006, 93); Cass. civ. 23.3.2005 n. 6276 ("The persistent refusal to engage in affective and sexual relations with one's spouse is a serious violation of the dignity and personality of the partner"). One would be mistaken to think that non-performance is only on the wife's side: see the Canadian case *Hock v. Hock* (1971) 3 *Rep. Fam. L.* 353 (B.C. C.A.) ("The persistent and strong advances made by the wife for the sexual act could not(…)amount to cruelty. (…) I am unable to find that she had other than a healthy appetite for sex" (Branca J.)).

[4] For a long list of English cases see Barton, *Cohabitation Contracts*, Gower, Aldershot, 1985, p.38ff. French case law has been for nearly two centuries poised on a rigid position of defence of the legitimate family. Therefore any gift between non-married persons living together was supposed to have had a sexual consideration and therefore was immoral. Only recently has there been a *revirement* by the Cour de Cassation (Cass. 1re civ., 3.2.1999, in *JCP G* 1999, I, 143) and confirmed by its plenary session (Cass. ass. plén., 29.10.2004, n. 519 P, *Galopin v. Floréal*, in *JCP G* 2005, II, 10011).

[5] *Hewitt v. Hewitt*, 394 *N.E.2d* 1204 (1979) ("Will the fact that legal rights closely resembling those arising from conventional marriages can be acquired by those who deliberately choose to enter into what have heretofore been commonly referred to as "illicit" or "meretricious" relationships encourage formation of such relationships and weaken marriage as the foundation of our family-based society?" The answer given the court is "yes"). For English law see the cases cited by Freeman, Lyon, *Cohabitation without Marriage. An Essay in Law and Social Policy*, Gower, Aldershot, 1983, p.184ff.

Furthermore, in the background lurked the doubt – if not the certainty – that the promise had sex as a consideration. Giving validity to such an agreement was akin to recognising prostitution.[6]

This was even more unacceptable if one of the parties – or both – was bound by a previous and undissolved marriage. The agreement had an adulterous dimension and undermined the sanctity of marriage and the obligations underlying it.[7]

These arguments, widely expounded by the courts, clearly reflect 19th century moral standards for which sex was mostly considered a distasteful practice, and not to be spoken of.[8] It was allowed, and mainly for reproductive purposes, between married couples. Outside a legalised union it was nothing other than fornication,[9] and had a venomous effect on legal relations, in a way not dissimilar to those venereal diseases which were so common in those times and had devastating consequences for health and life.[10]

---

[6] According to Lord Mansfield the bond by the deceased in favour of his former cohabitant was "the price of prostitution, *praemium prostitutionis*" (*Walker v. Perkins*, 97 *Eng. Rep.* 985) (1764). The idea that cohabitation among unmarried couples was a "meretricious relationship" has lived long through the 20th century: see for some US cases *Rehak v. Mathis*, 238 *S.E.2d* 81 (1977); *Samples v. Monroe* (358 *S.E.2d* 273) (1987) (A contract in which the parties agreed to cohabit is void because sexual intercourse outside of marriage is a criminal offence, and contracts to do immoral or illegal things are void); *Long v. Marino*, 441 S.E.2d 475 (1994) ("Meretricious sexual relationships are by nature repugnant to social stability, and our courts have on sound public policy declined to reward them by allowing a money recovery therefore"). For a survey of the long lasting Swiss cantonal attitude opposing cohabitation see Guillaume, Arn (eds) *Cohabitation non maritale: Evolution récente en droit suisse et étranger. Actes du colloque de Lausanne du 23 février 2000*, Droz, Geneva, 2000, p.110ff.

[7] In *The Lady Cox's case*, 3 *P. Wms.*339 (1734) the bond in favour of the mistress was declared void because it rested upon "a wicked consideration, that of her living in adultery with Sir Charles [Cox]". It is doubted that the long line of jurisprudence which confirms the principle is still applicable in English law (see Parry, *The Law Relating to Cohabitation*, 3rd ed., Sweet& Maxwell, London, 1993, p. 235ff). Another author however points out that the argument has never been tested in the courts (Barlow, *Cohabitants and the Law*, 3rd ed., Butterworths, London, 2001, p.18.

[8] On sex in the Victorian age see Hawkes *A Sociology of Sex and Sexuality*, Open University Press, Philadelphia,1996, p.40f.

[9] See Darling's J. *dictum* in *Uphill v. Wright* (1 *KB* 506) (1911): "The flat was let to the defendant for the purpose of enabling her to receive the visits of the man whose mistress she was and to commit fornication with him there. I do not think that it makes any difference whether the defendant is a common prostitute or whether she is merely the mistress of one man, if the house is let to her for the purpose of committing the sin of fornication there. That fornication is sinful and immoral is clear. The Litany speaks of "fornication and all other deadly sin," and the Litany is contained in the Book of Common Prayer which is in use in the Church of England under the authority of an Act of Parliament. Further, fornication is immoral, so that Courts of law take cognizance of the fact that it is immoral". These ideas were hard to die in the common law: see the Note, *Fornication, Cohabitation, and the Constitution*, 77 *Mich. L. Rev.* 255 (1978)

[10] See Honoré, *Sex Law in England*, Archon Books, Hamden, Ct., 1978, p. 42 ff. Not surprisingly one of the many hundreds of pages long treatises on prostitution published in those years is mostly devoted to the relation with the spread of venereal diseases: Jeannel, *De la prostitution dans les grandes villes au dix-neuvième siècle*, Baillière, Paris 1874.

Things have considerably changed – not only the way of thinking, but also demography, health standards, mobility - and these changes are dramatically reflected in the evolution of family law.[11] There is no longer, for the law, one and only one model of the family which lasts, in most cases, for the lifespan of the spouses, but there is a multitude of family relations which succeed one to another and create an intricate pattern of connections between present and former spouses or partners, brothers, sisters, step-children, and children born in and out of wedlock. Inheritance law plays a minor role in the transfer of estates from one generation to another.[12]

In part these relationships are governed through legislation. But once the social and legal stigma has been eliminated,[13] contract law moves in, supporting individual choices and needs. One could suggest that the thrust towards contract – *i.e.* self-determination and risk-avoiding procedures – is largely dependent on the failure of the general legislative framework to provide a satisfactory balance between competing interests.

One of the ways in which contract law is introduced into personal relations is through the fiction of the *société de fait* (in French law)[14] or the *Lebensgemeinschaft* (in German law).[15] The sexual implications of the relations are therefore sterilised and hidden behind the patrimoniality of the partnership.[16]

---

[11] The first reference is necessarily to the clear presentation of the many facets of the problem in Glendon, *The Transformation of Family Law. State, Law, and Family in the United States and Western Europe*, U.Chicago Press, Chicago, 1989, p. 252ff. For some statistics referring to England see Barlow, Duncan, James, Park, *Cohabitation, Marriage and the Law. Social Change and Legal Reform in the 21st Century*, Hart, Oxford, 2005, p. 15ff.

[12] "Adultery, especially when committed by women, once seemed to be the weak link in a social system that attempted to ensure the transmission of family land within the male line. But with the attenuation of the connection between sexual intercourse and procreation and the decreasing role of inheritance in modern society, laws penalizing private sexual acts between consenting adults have tended to fall in desuetude" (Glendon, *The Transformation of Family Law. State, Law, and Family in the United States and Western Europe*, U. Chicago Press, Chicago, 1989, p. 286). For the parallel evolution of family and inheritance law see Zoppini, *Le successioni in diritto comparato*, UTET, Turin 2002, p. 11 ff.

[13] "But as the idea of marriage as a vehicle for self-fulfilment gained prominence in the twentieth century, consensus about the morality of extra-marital sexual relations weakened; situation ethics and psychotherapy stepped in, and the law retreated in confusion" (Glendon, *The Transformation of Family Law. State, Law, and Family in the United States and Western Europe*, U.Chicago Press, Chicago, 1989, p. 287).

[14] One can easily understand the evolution of the law in French-influenced jurisdictions comparing the various reports presented at the 1957 *Journées Lilloises* of the Association Henri Capitant (and published in vol. XI of its *Travaux*, Dalloz, Paris, 1960) with J. Rubellin-Devichi, *Des concubinages. Droit interne - Droit international - Droit comparé*, Litec, Paris, 2002.

[15] See Frank, *The Status of Cohabitation in the Legal Systems of West Germany and Other West European Countries*, 33 *Am. J. Comp. L.* 185 (1985); Hausmann, Hochloch, *Das Recht der nichtehelichen Lebensgemeinschaft*, Schmidt, Berlin, 1999.

[16] See for an analysis of the French and German experiences as compared with common law ones Glendon, *The Transformation of Family Law. State, Law, and Family in the United States and Western Europe*, U. Chicago Press, Chicago, 1989, p. 255ff.

Later on sex is no longer considered an obscene feature, to be hidden and ignored, but enters, in its full right, into the agreement of the parties.[17] Quite often it is concealed in fidelity (or infidelity) clauses. And when no fidelity is required from the partner the whole agreement is at risk of collapsing.[18]

Premarital ("prenup"), marital and post-marital agreements are widely adopted, mostly in the United States, and not only amongst celebrities and wealthy persons. Twenty six states have enacted the 1983 Uniform Premarital Agreement Act which does not contain any reference to sexual relations, but at Section 3, n. 8 includes "any other matter, including their personal rights and obligations, not in violation of public policy or a statute imposing a criminal penalty". The contractual approach inevitably sees sexual activity as an obligation owed to the other partner. Refusal of performance or violation of exclusivity is therefore grounds for claiming breach of contract with all its consequences.[19]

One could express some doubts as to whether these agreements bring about a commodification of sex. It would seem, rather, that the main intent of the parties is that of regulating their patrimonial interests. Sexual fidelity would appear to be an ancillary provision more useful as a *casus belli* than as a valuable asset in the economy of the agreement. One could also distinguish between an action in which sexual obligations are brandished as a sword, and cases in which they are used as a shield.

At any rate, what deserves to be noted is that immorality is no longer used to reject claims in (quasi) family law. It can no longer be presumed but it needs

---

[17] The turning point in US law is generally indicated in the landmark case *Marvin v. Marvin* (557 *P. 2d* 106)(1976). Although Glendon (*The Transformation of Family Law. State, Law, and Family in the United States and Western Europe*, U.Chicago Press, Chicago, 1989) carefully points out (p. 278ff) that the practical result in that case was nil (the cohabitant of actor Lee Marvin ended up by obtaining nothing), the impact on subsequent jurisprudence is vast and long lasting: see Bruch, *Cohabitation in the Common Law Countries a Decade after Marvin: Settled in or Moving Ahead*, 22 *U.C. Davis L. Rev.* 717 (1989) (at fn 19 a host of US cases following Marvin).

[18] See the French case (amply commented by Glendon, *The Transformation of Family Law. State, Law, and Family in the United States and Western Europe*, U.Chicago Press, Chicago, 1989, p. 257f.) decided by the Appeals Montpellier 8.6.1982 (in *D.* 1983 Jur. 607, Note Dhavernas) according to which "l'union libre n'est susceptible de produire certains effets juridiques que lorsque la situation des concubins est empreinte d'une certaine stabilité imitée du mariage, cette stabilité dépendant, en partie, en raison des mœurs monogamiques qui sont, actuellement, celles de la majorité de la population, de la condamnation, au moins de principe, des rapports sexuels en dehors du couple pendant la durée de l'union". Therefore no protection can be granted to a relationship in which a man and a woman "sont d'accord pour que chacun ait, en même temps, les maitresses ou les amants qui lui plaisent". The comment points out (p. 609) that in such a way the court has, questionably, excluded the existence of an *affectio societatis* on the basis of the life style chosen by the parties.

[19] For other jurisdictions see Fehlberg, Smyth, *Binding Prenuptial Agreements in Australia: The First Year*, in Mulcahy, Wheeler (eds.), *Feminist Perspectives on Contract Law*, Glasshouse, London 2005 (at p.125).

to be proven. The mere fact of sexual relations between the parties no longer vitiates consideration,[20] and on some occasions it is considered an important indicia of what might be called "seriousness of intent" in establishing a near-to-family relationship.

Where the question of immorality returns is with homosexual partnerships, which have only received a limited support from legislature and courts in Western legal systems. But also in this case contract law is seen as a way to avoid troublesome discussions on what happens in the bedroom and which the crude language of some US states squarely epitomises as "sodomy" and "buggery".

The issue of homosexual rights puts a further strain on the general ban of extra-marital relationships based on sex. Their distinctive feature – which clearly singles them out from friendships – is that two people of the same sex regularly have sexual intercourse. And if there were no sex the relationship would be on a completely different legal basis. It is interesting to note that, at least in Europe, the constitutional principle of equality and non-discrimination among sexes is currently interpreted – whatever the contrary arguments may be – in the sense that one cannot be discriminated against on the basis of sexual orientation. The many decisions by national and transnational courts in this sense[21] are clear indicia of a general attitude which renders the traditional opposition towards non-marital cohabitation untenable.

b. *Marriage brokerage*

The function of matrimonial agencies was formerly to introduce persons to one another with marriage in mind, where lack of information or social inhibitions made it difficult to meet suitable people. Even though the motivation

---

[20] Frank, *The Status of Cohabitation in the Legal Systems of West Germany and Other West European Countries*, 33 *Am. J. Comp. L.* 185, at 186 (1985). But the contrary may apply if they are expressed: see *Whorton v. Dillingham*, 248 *Cal.Rptr.* 405 (1988) ("The parties' sexual relationship was an express, rather than implied, part of the consideration for their contract. The contract cannot be enforced to the extent it is dependent on sexual services for consideration, and the complaint does not state a cause of action to the extent it asks for damages from the termination of the sexual relationship. The issue here is whether the sexual component of the consideration is severable from the remaining portions of the contract". The California court decided that it was).

[21] *Ex multis* see the English case *Ghaidan v. Godin-Mendoza* (HL, 2004) (lease transferred by the court to surviving homosexual partner). In front of the ECJ see C- 117/01 (decided 7.1.2004) (*K.B. v. National Health Service*) ("Article 141 EC, in principle, precludes legislation, such as that at issue before the national court, which, in breach of the European Convention for the Protection of Human Rights and Fundamental Freedoms, signed in Rome on 4 November 1950, prevents a couple such as K.B. and R. from fulfilling the marriage requirement which must be met for one of them to be able to benefit from part of the pay of the other. It is for the national court to determine whether in a case such as that in the main proceedings a person in K.B.'s situation can rely on Article 141 EC in order to gain recognition of her right to nominate her

of satisfying sexual needs may have been present, the act (ratified generally by a religious ceremony) of marriage, with its role as a "remedy for concupiscence", covered whatever moral objections could have been raised.

This contract has widely been considered, in common law jurisdictions, as immoral from the mid 18th century,[22] and well into the 21st.[23] The reasons that are given are mostly connected to the fact that the service rendered is related to an unenforceable promise, such as marriage.[24] Moreover

partner as the beneficiary of a survivor's pension"). In front of the ECHR see *Dudgeon v. UK* (22.10.1981) (criminal laws against homosexual acts between consenting adults); *Lustig-Prean and Beckett v. UK*; *Smith and Grady v. UK* (both of 27.9.1999); *Beck, Copp and Bazeley* (22.10.2002) (all concerning discrimination in the armed forces).

[22] See *Wallis v. Duke of Portland*, 3 *Vesey Junior* 494, 30 *ER* 1123 (1797) "Marriage-brokerage bonds, &c. are not void upon acts of Parliament; nor were they till very lately considered as bad at law: *Collins v Blantern*, 2 *Wils*. 341 [1767], and another case before Lord Mansfield are the first cases, in which such bonds were held bad at law." The precedent quoted, however, is not related to a brokerage agreement but to the payment of monies in order to avoid prosecution. Lord Justice Wilmot draws strong support for his decision in Roman law: "we are all of opinion that the bond is void *ab initio*, by the common law, by the civil law, moral law, and all laws whatever; and it is so held by all writers whatsoever upon this subject, except in one passage in Grotius, lib. 2, cap. II, sect. 9, where I think he is greatly mistaken, and differs from Puffendorf, lib. 3, cap. 8, sect. 8, who, in my opinion, convicts the doctrine of Grotius. In Justin. Instit lib. 3. tit, 20, De Turpi Causa, sect. 23, *Quod turpi ex causa promissum est, veluti si quis homicidium vel sacrilegium se facturum promittat, non valet.* And Vinnius, in his Commentary, carries it so far as to say, you shall not stipulate or promise to pay money to a man not to do a crime, *Si quis pecuniam promiserit, ne furtum aut cædem faceret, aut sub conditiones si non fecerit, adhuc dicendum, stipulationem nullius esse momenti; cum hoc ipsum fiat vitiosum est, pecunium pacisci quo flagitio abstineas.* Dig lib. 1, tit. 5. Code, lib. 4, tit. 7, to the same point."

[23] "Bargains to bring about a marriage – so-called marriage brokerage contracts – are opposed to public policy and are invalid" (Williston, *A Treatise on the Law of Contracts*, (4th edition by Lord), Lawyers Coop., Rochester, N.Y., 1997, at p.. 435); "The business of a marriage broker is illegal and no action will lie in favour of such a person for the collection of his promised fee for procuring a wife or a husband" (Corbin, *Corbin on Contracts. Illegal Bargains*, LexisNexis, Newark, N.J.,2002, vol 15, p. 546). For recent US case-law see *Muflahi v. Musaad*, 522 *N.W.2d* 136(1994) (Mich. App.) in which action by plaintiffs seeking the return of a gift to defendants in dowry, was dismissed because a marriage brokerage contract was an unenforceable, illegal contract; *Rainbow Int'l Marriage Serv. v. Ping Cui* (2002 Mass. App. Div. 34) ("The question presented is whether an international matchmaking services agreement providing for the payment of $7,500 following the marriage of the defendant, Ping Cui, to a person introduced to her by Rainbow International Marriage Service Incorporated (Rainbow), is enforceable. We conclude that the agreement is a marriage brokerage contract void and unenforceable as a matter of public policy"). Exceptions to the rule appear to be limited: see *Duval v. Wellman*, 26 *N.E.* 343 (1891) in which the lower court's decision was quashed having denied a widow's petition for equitable relief from an illegal marriage brokerage contract when the facts showed that she was the victim of imposition by the other party and not equally responsible for the illegal bargain.

[24] See Gooderson, *Turpitude and Title in England and India*, 1958 *Cambridge LJ* 199 according to whom "It was equity that introduced the rule that all marriage brokerage agreements are illegal and void" (p. 202). However it would seem that the notion of marriage brokerage is not a settled one: see *e.g.* the early 20th century English case *Hermann v. Charlesworth* [1905] 1 *KB* 24 ("However distasteful to most persons may be the search for a spouse amongst persons introduced by a paid advertising agent, and however foolish and reckless the agent may appear to

public policy is against any agreement that imposes or is in restraint of marriage.[25]

In civil law countries case-law has evolved. In France after being considered illegal throughout the 19th century,[26] the Cour de Cassation changed the law in the mid-20th century.[27]

More recently marriage brokerage has been seen as instrumental to marriages of convenience between nationals of the European Union and third-country nationals in order to circumvent the rules on entry and residence in the EU and the acquisition of citizenship rights. One of the elements pointing in this direction is when a sum of money has been handed over in order for the marriage to be contracted.[28]

Similar legislation has been introduced in the US through the International Marriage Broker Regulation Act of 2005 ("IMBRA"),[29] which imposes strict regulation on the activity of those engaged in marriage brokerage. The reasons are mainly two: on the one hand they are seen as favouring illegal immigration into the US, with negative consequences on stable family relations and social structure.[30] This argument is not immune from criticism. In particular its consistency with general immigration rules is challenged and its distorting effects are pointed out.[31]

---

be if he promises a lady that her search shall be successful (and the facts cannot be put more favourably for the plaintiff than this), the transaction is, in our judgment, not one of marriage brokage. (...) We are not prepared to extend the application of the doctrine of the illegality of marriage brokage contracts, as it has been established in the reported decisions, to the circumstances of the present case" (*per* Kennedy J.)) According to Buckley, *Illegality and Public Policy*, Sweet & Maxwell, London, 2002, p. 90 "perhaps preferably, it might be held that *Hermann v. Charlesworth* does not reflect contemporary public policy".

[25] For an ancient US case see *Bartle v. Nutt*, 4 *Pet.* 45 (1830).

[26] Cass. civ., 1.5.1855, in *DP* 1855, 1, p. 147.

[27] Cass. req., 27.12 1944, in *D.* 1945, p. 121; and in *S.* 1945, 1, p. 32. See also Dorat Des Monts, *La cause immorale*, Rousseau, Paris, 1956, n° 38 s. Brokerage in view of adoption remains, however, illicit: see Cass. 1re civ., 22.7.1987, in *D.* 1988, jurispr. p. 172, with Note by Massip*).* For a view from Italy see Rescigno, "*In pari causa turpitudinis*", in *Riv. dir. civ.* 1966, 1, at pp. 34f.

[28] Council Resolution of 4 December 1997 on measures to be adopted on the combating of marriages of convenience (97/C 382/01).

[29] 119 Stat. 2960 (2006).

[30] See Abrams, *Immigration Law and the Regulation of Marriage*, 91 *Minn. L. Rev.* 1625 at 1653ff (2007); Ezer, *The Intersection of Immigration Law and Family Law*, 40 *Fam. L.Q.* 339 at 347f.(2006).

[31] "IMBRA, however, turns the usual structure of immigration regulation on its head. Rather than regulating the immigrant, IMBRA regulates the citizen-sponsor." (Abrams, *Immigration Law and the Regulation of Marriage*, 91 *Minn. L. Rev.* 1625 at 1659 (2007). The same author adds (at p. 1661): "this provision is striking because it requires a U.S. citizen to disclose extensive information in the immigration process for the benefit of the immigrant fiancée. Usually, the person the government is most interested in is the immigrant: Does she have a record of criminal convictions that would make her inadmissible? Are her papers fraudulent? Has she been vaccinated, and does she have any communicable diseases?".

The second argument, which is much more related to the core subject of this book, is that "mail-order brides" are seen as a modern form of human trafficking, selling easy sex in exchange for the illusion of a new family and a new country.[32] The perspective is clearly feminist[33] and points out that there is no similar experience in which men are offered (or offer themselves) as would-be-grooms from distant and exotic countries.[34] The aim is that of preventing domestic abuse[35] and the perpetuation of relationships in which women are subjugated to men's will. This reflects the movement towards not only equal rights but also equal roles in society and family relations, which is very strong in North America and other Western countries.[36] At the same time there are strong ties between marriage brokerage and other forms of exploitation of female sex.[37]

---

[32] Newsome, *Mail Dominance: A Critical Look at the International Marriage Broker Regulation Act and Its Sufficiency in Curtailing Mail-order Bride Domestic Abuse*, 29 *Campbell L. Rev.* 291 at 296f (2007).

[33] See Jackson, *Marriages of Convenience: International Marriage Brokers, Mail-Order Brides, and Domestic Servitude*, 38 *U. Tol. L. Rev.* 895 (2007); Buckwalter, Perinetti, Pollet, Salvaggio, *Modern Day Slavery in Our Own Backyard*, 12 *Wm. & Mary J. Women & L.* 403 (2006). As soon as one changes perspective, the analysis, however, differs widely: see the Note, *The International Marriage Broker Regulation Act: Protecting Foreign Women or Punishing American Men?*, 29 *Campbell L. Rev.* 317 (2007).

[34] See Jackson, *Marriages of Convenience: International Marriage Brokers, Mail-Order Brides, and Domestic Servitude*, 38 *U. Tol. L. Rev.* 895 at fn1 (2007).

[35] "The women not only become American citizens, but they become American wives, sisters, daughters, and mothers who, because of their situations, may not have a strong voice. Therefore, they need the thundering voice of strong legislation to protect them from domestic abuse" (Newsome, *Mail Dominance: A Critical Look at the International Marriage Broker Regulation Act and Its Sufficiency in Curtailing Mail-order Bride Domestic Abuse*, 29 *Campbell L. Rev.* 291 at 309 (2007)); "Considering the issues surrounding commodification, consent, the consumer husband's sexual and domestic expectations, and criminal organizations' and sex industries' connections to the IMB industry, all of which are compounded by INS immigration procedures, the IMB problem may be primarily one of trafficking. Indeed, the IMB industry may be a trafficking industry. As a result, domestic violence may be conceived of as a subset of the trafficking problem." (Lindee, *Love, Honor, or Control: Domestic Violence, Trafficking, and the Questions of How to Regulate the Mail-Order Bride Industry*, 16 *Colum. J. Gender & L.* 551 at 568 (2007)).

[36] But one can find also (female) voices opposing this view: "Heightened review of mail-order bride marriages may result in the rejection of marriages solely because they conform to traditional gender roles for men and women. Individuals must have the freedom to uniquely define marriage and their roles within it" (Kelly, *Marriage for Sale: The Mail-Order Bride Industry and the Changing Value of Marriage*, 5 *J. Gender Race & Just.* 175 at 191 (2001) (footnotes omitted)).

[37] "Like the IMB industry abroad, the IMB industry operating in the United States has close ties to Internet pornography, sex tourism, and prostitution: IMB websites often have links to sites specializing in "Internet porn, sex tourism, and escort services," and often advertise on adult websites and in magazines like Penthouse. Moreover, IMB "romance tours," during which men travel abroad to meet hundreds of would-be-mail-order brides, often closely resemble sex tours" (footnotes omitted) (Lindee, *Love, Honor, or Control: Domestic Violence, Trafficking, and the Questions of How to Regulate the Mail-Order Bride Industry*, 16 *Colum. J. Gender & L.* 551 at 565 (2007).

This brings us to the regulation of a market: on the one side are men asking for a kind of person they believe they cannot find at home and for whom they are willing to offer wealth and status in exchange. On the other side are women who want to change their social position which they feel unsatisfactory in their home country and can offer in exchange (mostly) good looks and (probably) sex. The two adverbs ("mostly" and "probably") have been added because it is not unlikely that in what is a typical two-sided market, the broker is underlining to the parties what each of them is expecting from the bargain. Apart from the obvious language differences, it is rather unlikely that foreign would-be-brides will be told that they are being "sold" as "sex-machines", and that national would-be-grooms will be told that the only reason that someone is willing to have intercourse with them is to leave their own country and, possibly, get rich.

From a contract theory point of view one might question whether the parties reach a *consensus in idem* or whether both are wilfully misrepresenting their intent, or whether the liability must be put on the broker.[38] But at the same time one should ask if the motives that bring the parties together may be of any legal relevance and can influence the contract that binds them to the marriage broker. Setting aside complex issues of private international law and consumer protection law, the question one could ask is whether the final legal affair which the parties are pursuing is valid or not. If the aim, on both sides, is a marriage of convenience, one could argue that brokerage to that effect is invalid. But if instead the parties are seriously intending to get married and set up a family, it is difficult to understand why, from a strictly contractual point of view (and setting aside the impact of legislation on human trafficking), the agreement with the intermediary should be voided.[39] The problem is that this approach requires a case-to-case enquiry into intent and this will mostly be analysed with hindsight.

One can brush away these objections with the strength of public law instruments contrasting human trafficking and illegal immigration. However when it comes to fundamental individual choices, one could have reservations on the broad impact that legislation might have.[40] It would seem that sex cannot

[38] For this last solution see *Fox v. Encounters International*, 318 *F. Supp 2d* 279, affirmed in an unpublished decision by the 4th Circuit in 2006 (Lexis 9269): Broker owes fiduciary duty to victim of violent husband found via international marriage brokerage agency and is liable for fraud, unfair and deceptive trade practices, wilful and wanton negligence, unauthorized appropriation of the victim's name and likeness, and defamation.

[39] The "combination of existing safeguards and the lack of statistical evidence indicating heightened fraud in the mail-order bride industry suggest that there is no need to infringe further upon the fundamental right of marriage simply because the couple was introduced pursuant to the mail-order industry" (Kelly, *Marriage for Sale: The Mail-Order Bride Industry and the Changing Value of Marriage*, 5 *J. Gender Race & Just.* 175 at 192 (2001)

[40] "In short, because of immigration policy's family unification goals, immigration law intrudes much more extensively into courtship than does state family law. Much of this

licitly live in the world of law without love. Defining the latter however, is quite impossible even for a Parliament of poets, novelists, painters and musicians.

Similar issues arise with so-called escort services, in which young women (and sometimes also young men) are paid to accompany professionals who find themselves on business in a different city or foreign country.[41]

It is assumed, *ex hypothesi*, that these businesses are not a concealed way of organising prostitution; otherwise they would immediately be committing an offence.[42]

There is, at first sight, no element of illegality or immorality in the service rendered. The sexual motive is usually implicit and alluded to, and only on rare occasions is made explicit.

If sexual relations do take place between the parties, this is as a result of individual choice and unconnected with the enterprise's main activity.[43] In the European context the contractual terms are carefully drafted to use abstract expressions such as 'friendship' and 'company' to describe the relations involved. If there is any departure from this profile it is merely contingent and

intrusion results directly from the fact that marriage is one of our society's fundamental organizing principles, and we use it to test whether a couple is a "family." But some of these laws go far beyond effecting a policy of family unification, attempting instead to change the balance of power, based on gender, race, or citizenship, in relationships involving citizens and immigrants. When federal immigration law does this, it may be regulating the family much more than it is regulating immigration" (Abrams, *Immigration Law and the Regulation of Marriage*, 91 *Minn. L. Rev.* 1625 at 1664 (2007)).

[41] Note, *A Guide for Municipalities on the Validity of Licensing and Regulating Oriental-Style Hostess Bars as Escort*, 14 *Whittier L. Rev.* 249 (1993).

[42] The term "escort" has different meanings: in the US it would appear that "The escort agency is essentially like a bordello with added flexibility on the matter of the site transaction" (p.194) (Cameron, *The Economics of Sin. Rational Choice or No Choice At All?*, Edward Elgar, Cheltenham 2002, at p. 194). Therefore, often, escort services lumped together with other illegal ones: see Zelizer, *Money, Power, and Sex*, 18 *Yale J.L. & Feminism* 303 at 308 (2006) ("telephone and cyber-sex, production of pornography, live sex shows, erotic massage, escort services, and a wide variety of prostitution"); Note, *Jobs and Borders*, 118 *Harv. L. Rev.* 2171 (2005) ("The commercial sex industry usually operates in brothels, strip clubs, bars, massage parlors, or escort services"). In a US State where prostitution is legal, the opposite may turn out to be true: "the other main mode of illegal prostitution in Nevada takes the form of escort services, which usually involve customers calling the service by telephone and arranging for the escorts to meet them in a private residence or hotel room" (Note, *The Best Little Whorehouse Is Not in Texas: How Nevada's Prostitution Laws Serve Public Policy, and How Those Laws May Be Improved*, 6 *Nev. L.J.* 217 at 234 (2005). In the Australian state of Victoria an escort agency is defined as a (legal) "business of providing prostitution services to persons at premises") (See Murray, *Labour Regulation in the Legal Sex Industry in Victoria*, 16 *Austr. J. Labour L.* 321 at 324 (2003).

[43] Or, to put it the other way round, "This form of prostitution is disguised as something it may not actually represent. The escort agency offers men the opportunity to enjoy the company of women for a specific period while they attend various social gatherings and events. For one night, the escort business provides men with female companionship without the awkwardness of a first date. In addition to the benefit of companionship, some escorts services offer their clients some type of sexual gratification that is exchanged sometime during the course of the 'date.'" (Thompson, *Prostitution - A Choice Ignored*, 21 *Women's Rts. L. Rep.* 217 at 227 (2000).

extraneous to the contract and is only legally relevant, if at all, as a criminal offence.

We encounter here, therefore, dealings that resemble those connected with sexual purposes bound up with others to which no censure can attach. However, while sex is bought and sold, friendship and companionship are 'beyond commerce' and not susceptible to evaluation in terms of morality.

c. *On-line dating services*

The analysis of the preceding paragraphs is confirmed by the myriad of online sites dedicated to putting people with common sexual interests in touch with one another. Using a range of technical devices (especially pseudonyms) the parties can be assured of anonymity while they gradually get acquainted.[44] The filter of anonymity is however quickly abandoned when parties avail themselves of webcams and can see and speak to each other directly. While the relations between the parties, not having an economic element, appear to be extra-contractual and protected by secrecy of communication as recognised by most Western constitutions and Human Rights conventions, the position of those who organise the sites may be different. Firstly, use of these chat facilities is generally paid for. Secondly, the various security measures are adopted with the purpose, studiously left unspecified, of facilitating sexual activities, which in fact do become explicit in the profiles submitted by individual site users. Both organisers and users of the sites are well aware that the purpose served by 'chatting' is to increase one's chances of a sexual encounter, albeit virtual.[45] But this circumstance in itself does not seem to distinguish the organisers legally from those who set up a romantic bulletin board for 'lonely hearts' to exchange messages. While the former is well aware of what occurs, the principle of secrecy of communication not only protects users, but also places the organisers of chat rooms in a state of deemed ignorance by which they escape the liability they would otherwise incur.[46]

---

[44] Note, *Anonymity and International Law Enforcement in Cyberspace*, 7 *Fordham Intell. Prop. Media & Ent. L.J.* 231 at 248 (1996).

[45] See Waskul, *Self-Games and Body-Play. Personhood in Online Chat and Cybersex*, Peter Lang, New York, 2003.

[46] This is not always true: in *Chassman v. People Resources* (573 *N.Y.S.2d* 589) (1991) the contract between a woman looking for her twin soul the organizer of the web-site was voided on the basis of a consumer protection N.Y. law: "The clear intent of the services provided by Defendant is to arrange for unattached persons of the opposite sex to meet each other socially. Defendant advertises and holds itself out as "an oasis of social opportunity" and as a "cost effective method to select and meet 'quality singles'." This is precisely the kind of activity which the statute seeks to regulate. Defendant cannot avoid the reach of the statute simply because it does not provide computer matches. Since General Business Law 394-c was designed to protect consumers, *see* L.1971. ch. 559, p. 96 (Memorandum of the N.Y. Attorney General), the agreement between the parties hereto is void and unenforceable. Further, despite the statute's silence as to the penalty for non-compliance, public policy demands that in order to insure public

If one were to try and extract a rule, it would seem that it is possible to sell sexual services legally under a different name, or to disguise them in a way that renders them indistinguishable from other perfectly valid transactions. It is a question of form not of substance. Or to go back to critical studies of bourgeois 19th century private law, of hypocrisy. Law's good name is saved. A coherent system of governance of sexual interests is, however, a long way off.

compliance with the statute, non-complying contracts be deemed void and unenforceable. If such contracts were to be enforced either in whole or in part, it is certain that social referral services would continue to violate the statute with impunity, secure in the knowledge that the only penalty they face will be a reduction in their fee to the statutory limit. It cannot be presumed that contracts barred by the statute should be accompanied by no other consequence than the reduction of the fee".

CHAPTER NINE

A COMPARATIVE VIEW

a. *The* In pari causa turpitudinis *and* Ex turpi causa non oritur actio *rules*

Sexual contracts are of many kinds. If it were not for the mesmerising attraction/repulsion of sex, there would be little to keep them together.

We would hardly develop a coherent legal system for all the transactions that have to do with food or beverages, from their production to wholesale distribution, sale and consumption.

One could therefore reasonably argue that in many cases ordinary rules (contracts for goods, services, labour, or partnership) apply.

However if the principle of immorality should continue to exist – and it is difficult to exclude the notion from the Western lawyer's dictionary – comparative experience indicates various approaches which, it should be underlined, are not necessarily mutually exclusive, but could instead apply variably to different sets of contracts.

The fascination with Latin maxims still lcontinues in the Western legal tradition.[1]

In pari causa turpitudinis, Ex turpi causa non oritur actio, Nemo auditur suam turpitudinem allegans, however, are not only brightly polished phrases that shine with the light of antiquity and transmit a millenary wisdom. They reflect very well a notion of morality that was absolutely coherent with 19th century social standards.[2] In that century civil law systems produced their highest achievement, from which they took their name, that is civil codes. On the other hand English common law reflected the mores of a country which

[1] The list of legal writings is endless. One should start by referring to one of most thoughtful, but also ice-breaking (over 40 years ago), articles, full of historical, comparative and cultural references: Rescigno, "*In pari causa turpitudinis*", in *Riv. dir. civ.* 1966, 1. For a comparison between Scottish and South African law see MacQueen, Cockrell, *Illegal Contracts*, in Zimmermann, Visser, Reid, *Mixed Legal Systems in Comparative Perspective. Property and Obligations n Scotland and South Africa*, OUP, Oxford, 2004, p. 143 ff. For the traditional views in French legal doctrine see Ripert, *La règle morale dans les obligations civiles*, LGDJ, Paris, 1949, Dorat Des Monts, *La cause immorale*, (th. Paris), Librairie Rousseau, Paris, 1956; Le Tourneau, *La regle "nemo auditur"*, (th. Paris), LGDJ, Paris 1970.

[2] But not always in previous ages: Rescigno, "*In pari causa turpitudinis*", in *Riv. dir. civ.* 1966, 1, at p. 56, reminds us of the different opinions of Christian moralists on the subject of the legitimacy of paying prostitutes. And in the famous judgment of Solomon the king-judge did not refuse to hear the case of the two prostitutes on the basis of some *Nemo auditur* principle. Nor was the child assigned in accordance to the *In pari causa turpitudinis* rule.

was already ahead of all others in its industrial revolution and was establishing itself as the new world power. Freedom of contract, *laissez faire*, and private autonomy were the key words of a society that slowly but finally was seeing the way out of poverty, famine, epidemics and ignorance.

There was a very high price to pay – mostly by those who provided the man (and woman)power of the change. But capitalism was – and is not – unprincipled. And amongst these principles was the fact that sex was to be hidden. One can more easily understand the morality of the 19th century, and the end of pre-industrial, libertine mores of the previous age, comparing *Les liaisons dangereuses* with *Madame Bovary* and *Don Giovanni* with *La Traviata*.[3]

The *In pari causa turpitudinis* rule perfectly reflects these morals. The urge of the flesh – obviously only a man's – could be satisfied through infamous commerce, but was not to be brought to light. Prostitutes, mistresses and illegitimate children were not criminalised but tolerated – words are revealing: a brothel is a "house of tolerance".[4] The law therefore is not indifferent.

To a civil lawyer the distinction between illegal contracts and immoral contracts is quite clear. The former are invalid *because* they are prohibited. The parties should know that they cannot conclude them. Only if one party was unaware of the illegality may he find a remedy in restitution.

Immoral contracts, instead, are not prohibited. If the parties perform them the law will not intervene. The courts will not use their *ex officio* powers to invalidate them. Illegality produces its effects *ab initio* in the sense that the contract could – and should – never have risen. An immoral contract is valid; the performance has a *causa* (or, as common lawyers would say, a consideration). What is barred is specific performance, damages, and restitution. From a common law perspective, for which remedies precede rights, case-law offers similar situations, such as those of past consideration.[5]

But if one shifts the point of view from rights to liberties, one can conclude that there can be sexual freedom without sexual rights. The bourgeois rule – which many might judge as hypocritical – presents many aspects of efficiency.

Citizens – male citizens, quite clearly, those that pay taxes and vote – feel free to unleash their desires. Provided this is done in a discreet way the state is

---

[3] From a Law and Humanities perspective see Markesinis, *Good and Evil in Art and Law: An Extended Essay*, Spinger, Vienna, 2007 (at p. 41ff a detailed analysis of Don Giovanni's character).

[4] And the term "prostitution" (and its related verb) in many languages means much more than the sale of sexual services: "We commonly hear of people 'prostituting' their morals or their talent in the sense that they are exploiting something, of intrinsically higher moral worth, for the mere pursuit of income for its own sake" (Cameron, *The Economics of Sin. Rational Choice or No Choice At All?*, Edward Elgar, Cheltenham 2002, at p. 183)

[5] Grubb (ed.), *The Law of Restitutions*, Butterworths, London, 2002, p. 311: no restitution for contracts prejudicial to sexual morality ("modern society continues to draw a line at a certain level of sexual morality, and the cases on prostitution will no doubt still apply").

not encumbered with difficult, and often embarrassing, tasks of repression and adjudication.

The social costs will be taken care of by private endeavour, through charitable associations for the redemption of "lost women"; or by the growing organised and welfare state, through medical control of prostitutes and through orphanages.

Although according to today's standards 19th century morality may appear rather outdated, one should consider that the *In pari causa turpitudinis* rule reflects an important step towards secularisation of society. Religious aspects are further divided from legal ones. A sin may not necessarily be a crime or an illegal transaction. As with many other bourgeois achievements this may have been an involuntary result, but it has had lasting effects on the juridical notion of morality, which is not divorced from ethics and religion, but is quite clearly distinct.[6]

One could also express an evaluation as to the efficiency of the rule considering how few reported cases there are, in the various jurisdictions, over the last two centuries. This is not – one could venture – because society has had firm sexual morals, but simply because the ancillary rule *Nemo auditur suam turpitudinem allegans* has kept litigants away from the courts, leaving the damage to remain where it fell and keeping the clean waters of justice unpolluted.[7]

If one looks at things from the unabashed and disillusioned point of view of a 21st century lawyer, this means that in the last two centuries considerable administrative and litigation costs have been saved by the state and by the parties, avoiding controversies with a highly uncertain outcome and which would have probably divided the courts and public opinion.

Operating the *In pari causa turpitudinis* principle as a default rule, the parties to a sexual transactions have steered away from litigation. They have learned through experience, without having to be taught publicly in court, a lesson by the guardians of morality who would have exposed their weaknesses and sent both parties back home, reprimanded and empty-handed.

Admittedly the rule was forged – and had to operate – in a rather limited sex market, that of prostitution services. Once these were expanded the rule entered into the crisis, which has been illustrated in the previous pages, and

---

[6] Albeit shrouded in truisms: "Immorality then, for the purpose of the law, is what every right-minded person is presumed to consider to be immoral" (Devlin, *The Enforcement of Morals*, OUP, London, 1959, at p. 16). And more recently, in other jurisdictions, legal doctrine is not much more enlightening when it suggests adopting "a rigid, objective concept of immorality as *the intention to offer services commercially of a kind that the law does not recognise as within the logic of exchange*" (italics in the original) established through the "incremental process of interpretation" (Carusi, *Contratto illecito e* soluti retentio, Jovene, Naples, 1995, at p. 199.

[7] "No polluted hand shall touch the pure fountains of justice" [*Collins v. Blantern* (1767) 2 Wilson KB 341 at 350]. But the idea is still lingering: see the UK Law Commission *Illegal Transactions: The Effect of Illegality on Contracts and Trust. A Consultation Paper* (no. 154), HMSO, London 1999, suggesting the need of "upholding the dignity of the courts" (at. p. 87).

was at odds with the role of sex in modern society and life – free, explicit, and even ostentatious.

But the history of the rule also has to be viewed from a critical point of view. As with many other general principles it has been used by the courts in an expansive way. But when it has been transferred from sex markets to family relations the results have been disappointing, if not disastrous even.

The courts were looking for sex where, most of the time there was love. They were using the rule not to control and hide sexual misconduct, but to keep the lawful family, that based on marriage, united. The many transactions that occur in an adulterous relation were challenged not by the parties themselves, but most frequently by the heirs of the unfaithful husband. The rule was invoked first of all to square accounts with the former mistress. It was easy – and more comforting – to argue that the betrayal was due to the sexual snares of a person who was considered not any different from a harlot. Again literature expresses the idea, vividly, in one line, as in the famous "*Pagata ti ho*" *aria* from Verdi's Traviata. The courts, quite unprepared to settle matters of love, were much more at ease with morality.

On the other hand, it was difficult to ask the betrayed person to perform a promise that had arisen *Ob turpe causa*. To see things even more cynically one could say that the unenforceability rule was used not to keep a family united – love had died long before, the lover too – but to ensure that the estate of the deceased was kept within the legitimate family.

From a civil law perspective the issue was related with property, rather than with contracts, the validity of which was incidentally challenged in order to protect the former.

Equally unsuccessful has been the use of the *In pari causa turpitudinis* rule outside sexual and family matters in cases concerning agreements to divert the ordinary course of justice, or trade of public offices, or transactions in the black market.[8]

Having become a *portmanteau* expression it is used as one of the many tools that the judge has at his disposal to mend (or set aside) a bargain: good faith, lack of consideration, change of circumstances.[9]

[8] Beale, Hartkamp, Kotz, Tallon, *Cases, Materials and Text on Contract Law*, Hart, Oxford, 2002 note (at p. 297) that "writers who try to put the cases into some sort of order invariably add that the categories they adopt are neither exhaustive nor mutually exclusive. Among the contracts potentially invalid as illegal or immoral are bargains harmful to the administration of justice, contracts intended to defraud third parties, agreements inducing a party to breach its contract with another or to commit an unlawful act, and many others".

[9] The UK Law Commission in its *Illegal Transactions: The Effect of Illegality on Contracts and Trust. A Consultation Paper* (no. 154), HMSO, London 1999, at p. 81 expresses criticism of what it calls "crude and draconian nature" of the *nemo auditur* and *in pari causa* principles. This however appears a misunderstanding – quite common among common lawyers (see the following fn. 10) – between the legal consequences of illegality and of immorality. The analysis of case law from all the diverse jurisdictions in sex matters appears far from "draconian".

But turning sex into a matter of public policy (or, to put things the other way round, by considering public policy as a question of morality) the *In pari causa turpidinis* rule has been deprived of any pre-definable ambit.[10] It has moved into new territories but has lost its barycentre, leaving those to whom it should be addressed disoriented.

It continues to be used it in sexual transactions, in the sense that 'wisdom of the blood' suggests to those operating in sex markets to avoid resorting to the law. Applying an ancient common law metaphor, the *In pari causa turpitudinis* rule may well be in its grave but it still governs firmly, sparing the courts from having to embark on the difficult task of re-examining its actual thrust.

b. *The prohibitionist/ feminist approach*

The *In pari causa turpitudinis* rule expresses disapproval and refusal to support. It is hypocritical because it turns the eyes of the law away from lewdness. It reflects the moral ambiguity of a half-measure that does not dare to require complete respect.

One can understand therefore that it may be criticised by those who (a considerable number in the past, but still representing a significant voice in the community today) are deeply convinced that the morality of the law requires equal morality from men and women. If sex outside the sanctity of marriage has detrimental effects on the stability of the foundations of society, it simply must be forbidden. Violations must be sanctioned, first of all through criminal law.

There cannot be a contract for sexual goods[11] or services, any more than there can be a contract for the sale of drugs or for the murder of a person. There is no need to report here all the arguments in favour of this approach, or to question their foundation. Views about sex widely differ even in modern

---

[10] A comparatist notes that in common law jurisdictions there is a tendency to consider together illegality and immorality, two aspects which, instead, in a civilian's mind, are quite distinct: see *e.g.* Law Commission *Illegal Transactions: The Effect of Illegality on Contracts and Trust. A Consultation Paper* (no. 154), HMSO, London 1999: the L.C. does not address directly the issue of immoral contracts, although some 19th century precedents are cited such as *Taylor v. Chester* [1869] LR 4 QB 309 (half bank-note left as security for payment of food consumed in a brothel). See also Birks, *Recovering Value Transferred Under an Illegal Contract*, 1 *Theoretical Inq. L.* 155 (2000) where the *In pari causa turpitudinis* rule is analyzed in detail but always with reference to illegal transactions. Authors with a civilian background clearly distinguish between immoral and illegal transactions Grodecki, *In pari delicto potior est conditio defendentis*, 71 *L. Quarterly R.* 254 (1955) (at p. 258).

[11] "The work of personal redemption and the work of social redemption would be significantly advanced in an environment purged of pornography. I find that it is hard enough anyhow for men and women to rise to the levels of decency and unselfishness without the handicaps of drinking and gambling and immorality" (Rev. Soper in Rolph (ed.) *Does Pornography Matter?*, Routledge, London, 1961, p. 53

societies and are part of the rich pluralism of opinions. What we are interested in pointing out here is that, in a comparative perspective, they are found in all Western societies and have a common logical development: there are moral principles; these principles must be respected; if they are not respected the damage is great both for the individual soul and for the body politic; the law must intervene to prevent, repress and punish sexual misconduct.

This task is generally entrusted on criminal law, leaving no room for private transactions. Private autonomy cannot be lawfully used to commit a crime. Consent between the participants of a sexual act is no justification because it is tantamount to the agreement between accomplices.

Nor can there be a defence when irregular sex has been carried out in private. The criticism that can easily be made against the *In pari causa turpitudinis* rule is that it reflects a double morality, one in public, and one in private. But this is quite unacceptable as a point of principle.

Moral corruption starts within the household and then expands to the whole community.[12] Anticipating a *mot d'ordre* of the feminist movement, nothing is more public than private life.

The bedroom is the place where a family is started, grows and multiplies: if moral values have to be preserved it must start from there, and move outwards into the city: pornography, nude entertainment, sex shops and the like are aspects of infamous commerce that must be fought. Local authorities – first of all elected officials who represent the community – must uphold morality with coherent administrative decisions. If they do not they will be attacked and lose their position.[13] Even worse if they themselves contravene the rules and indulge in sexual misconduct for they will be chased from the Garden of Eden.

What has been depicted here is not a distant, pre-industrial 19th century society. One has simply to turn to day-to-day politics in the US and in the UK to realise the weight that private sexual behaviour has in these systems as compared with other Western countries where similar conduct is considered nothing more than an inevitable frailty of the flesh, with no significant consequences.[14]

---

[12] *Ex multis* see Devlin, *The Enforcement of Morals*, OUP, London, 1959: "All sexual immorality involves the exploitation of human weaknesses. The prostitute exploits the lust of her customers and the customer the moral weakness of the prostitute. If the exploitation of human weaknesses is considered to create a special circumstance, there is virtually no field of morality which can be defined in such a way to exclude the law"; "An established morality is as necessary as good government to the welfare of society" (at p. 14)

[13] At a risk: see Hubbard, *Sex and the City. Geographies of Prostitution in the Urban West*, Ashgate, Aldershot 1999 (especially Ch. 5 devoted to "Community protest, citizenship and the paranoid public" and – at p. 148ff – to the Nimby syndrome).

[14] *Ab uno disce omnes*: the Clinton-Lewinsky affair could have become a matter of constitutional importance only in the US. To mention a contemporary head of state no longer in life, nobody in France ever dreamed of impeaching President Mitterand for his well known extramarital relations and his out-of-wedlock issue.

Turning to the more legal aspects, these principles are well embodied in the laws of many US states which still – and notwithstanding multiple interventions by the Supreme Court – attempt to close the flood-gates of rampaging sex.

This prohibitionist system entered into a crisis well before the "sexual revolution" of the sixties and the age of globalisation. Railways, world wars, Hollywood, rock stars, and television, made it extremely difficult to keep unified (or at least dominant) moral standards which form the basis of the (self) enforcement of the law.

While the *In pari causa turpitudinis* rule exploded in trying to become the guiding principle in new territories, the prohibitionist rule imploded because sex was and is everywhere. Public sexual behaviour (in how women dress and how young couples kiss and embrace each other, in language and conversation topics) made it extremely difficult to keep the principles of morality coherent and respected. Its credibility was undermined, like a nun in a bikini or in a mini-skirt.

But just as the prohibitionist approach was moving towards what appeared to be an irresistible decline, new and unexpected vigour came to it from the expansion of feminist doctrines on sex.[15]

No doubt its foundations are profoundly different.

They rest not on morality but on an undeniable fact: women have been discriminated against socially, politically and legally since antiquity. Their sexuality was controlled and owned by men, either as fathers and husbands, or as lovers and clients. The border between rape and domestic violence was practically non-existent.

The first step towards complete emancipation therefore passes through control of one's own sexuality, fertility and pleasure.

Feminist theory joins with traditional morality to oppose the slippery slope of the market approach. Commodification is the shape of the new oppression of women because, put very crudely, it means selling women's bodies. Whether in real life, as in prostitution, or through their image, as in pornography, men are buying sex and perpetuating oppression.[16]

---

[15] The literature on the point is far too vast to be listed in a footnote. The following are some among those which better express feminist views and offer a rich list of further readings, starting from the most referred to: MacKinnon, *Only Words*, Harvard U.P., 1993; Smith (ed.), *Feminist Jurisprudence*, OUP, New York, 1993 [in particular the essays of Radin, *Market Inalienability*, at p. 389; Wolgast, *Pornography and the Tiranny of the Majority*, at p. 431; Dworkin, *Against the Male Flood: Censorship, Pornography and Equality*, at p. 449]; Becker, Bowman, Torrey, *Cases and Materials on Feminist Jurisprudence. Taking Women Seriously*, West, St. Paul, 1994 (on prostitution p. 291ff; on pornography p. 313ff.); MacKinnon, *Pornography as Trafficking*, 26 *Mich. J. Intern. Law* 993 (2005). For a rich selection of MacKinnon's writings on these topics see her *Women's Lives – Men's Laws*, Belknap Press, Cambridge, Ma., 2005.

[16] *Ex multis* Estes, *Prostitution: A Subjective Position*, in Soble, Power (eds.), *The Philosophy of Sex. Contemporary readings*, V ed., Rowman &Littlefield, Lanham, Md. 2008:

The trade is in the hands of criminal organisations, specialised in human trafficking and in sex slavery.

There cannot be any room for contract – which presupposes freedom, equality and consent – all elements that are lacking in the sex trade. Contract mystifies reality, endeavouring to legalise violence, both physical and psychological.

On the contrary, the law must intervene actively to strike down any move towards commodification: whether domestic violence and sex roles within the family; sexual harassment and exploitation of female appearance in the workplace; the use of female bodies in advertising[17] as the threshold of pornography; pornography as prostitution; or prostitution and sex work as modern slavery.

The strength of the feminist theory is in the historical repetition of acts of sexual violence by men against women, that is without reciprocity. A man raped by a woman is rarer than the proverbial dog bitten by man.

Organised crime that provides new bodies for sexual consumption is not a creation of feminist fears.

The weakness of feminist theories, however, is not in the facts and the figures, but rather in their very strong ideological structure and in their difficult relationship with the law. Clearly this is not an exclusive feature of feminist theory and history offers us a host of similar cases. If one concentrates one's attention on conformity to a certain creed one loses the perception that legal rules are the expression of social conduct. Ideological laws are unable to promote the values they purport to express, just as socialist laws were unable to promote equality in the Soviet Union.[18]

Not only, from a sociological point of view, is it difficult for this kind of approach to find the support of those against whom the feminist rules are meant to operate. But one should also add that it is not shared by a considerable number of women who openly criticise the approach or, more simply, disregard it in their daily conduct.[19] An *avant-garde* mentality may be productive in art movements but much less in law reform.[20]

"prostitution is morally wrong, socially destructive, and personally harmful, because it proffers a monetary substitute for mutual desire and concern and thereby defies the myths of respectful sexual relations" (at p. 353).

[17] See e.g. Rosewarne, *Sex in Public. Women, Outdoor Advertising and Public Policy*, Cambridge Scholars Pub., Newcastle 2007 (advertising as sexual harassment is inappropriate for public space, at p. 61ff; and therefore suggests ban on sexist advertisements similar to ban on tobacco advertising, at p. 224).

[18] Sanders, *Paying for Pleasure. Men who Buy Sex*, Willan Pub., Cullompton, 2008, titles the paragraph at p. 203 "Pursuing eradication: futile, simplistic and failing".

[19] See for a head-on critique of the MacKinnon and Dworkin stances, Strossen, *Defending Pornography. Free Speech, Sex, and the Fight for Women's Rights*, Doubleday, New York, 1995. Or Cornell, *At The Heart of Freedom. Feminism, Sex, & Equality*, Princeton U.P., Princeton, 1998.

[20] Incidentally one should note that although both start from a 'sexual liberation' perspective, feminist and homosexual theories widely differ in their conclusions, the former mostly promoting a prohibitionist approach, the latter a libertarian 'free sex' one.

If one looks at laws from an efficiency point of view it is easy to see that the degree of efficiency is inversely proportional to its ideological purity.

A good example is that of pornography. According to the feminist approach using women to produce it cannot be anything other than a crime which promotes further crimes (violence against women).[21] The response of the pornographer is to move to countries where it is a lawful activity or an unprosecuted offence. The counter-reply is to extend criminal sanctions to those who import, distribute and sell pornographic materials.

The trade will then move on-line. The only possible reaction is that of punishing possession of pornographic images – whether physical or digital – following a pattern experimented with criminal legislation against child pornography.

Ultimately, the sex life of all citizens is under constant scrutiny, and the difference with the US laws punishing buggery and fornication even between husband and wife is only a matter of degrees of repression.[22]

There is a further aspect which the traditional prohibitionist theory and most feminist ones have in common.[23] Those whose opinions differ and who suggest different approaches are rapidly labelled as promoting lewdness, debauchery, violence and crime.[24] This makes it rather difficult to find balanced solutions which take into account not only the variety of positions, but also the significant differences between factual situations. Sex work is not all the same; sex workers are not all in the same situation. Criminalisation is not necessarily the only response by the law. One should be able to ask, oneself and others, if contract law might be a more reasonable and protective response and if it is possible to consider that sexual services might be the object of a bargain. Although this approach may appear like as second-best, it is preferable to the radical but ineffective best choice.

These arguments, however, have to take into account the fact that in at least one country – Sweden – feminist theories have been embraced and put into

---

[21] But see the introductory pages *Does Pornography Cause Violence? The Search for Evidence*, in Church Gibson, Gibson (eds.), *Dirty Looks. Women, Pornography, Power*, British Film Institute, London, 1993, p. 5ff.

[22] "What does it mean for a feminist to advocate that the state should save a woman from herself?" (Cornell, *At The Heart of Freedom. Feminism, Sex, & Equality*, Princeton U.P., Princeton, 1998, at p. 47)

[23] Strossen, *Defending Pornography. Free Speech, Sex, and the Fight for Women's Rights*, Doubleday, New York, 1995, p. 13: "The pornophobic feminists [*disparagingly named "MacDworkinites"*] have forged frighteningly effective alliances with traditional political and religious conservatives who staunchly oppose women's rights, but who also seek to suppress pornography".

[24] "The debate about experimental research into pornography has, at times, been unnecessarily vitriolic. Scholarly debate should be conducted in a civilised manner and focus on objective, impersonal analysis of the scientific evidence. Veiled and unfounded accusations of researchers being driven by political agendas are irrelevant and unhelpful" (Gunther, *Media Sex. What Are the Issues*, Lawrence Erlbaum, Mahwah, N.J., 2002, at p. 264).

law.[25] And Sweden – it should be remembered – is one of the countries which in the mid 20th Century opened the way to the so-called "sexual revolution" of the Sixties, and where the role of women in society and in government is one of the most important in the whole Western world.[26]

In Sweden, since 1999, it has been an offence to pay for sexual services, including those obtained abroad.[27] The reasons for this legislation are those typical of feminist writings: prostitution is a form of violence by men against women and is directly related to heinous crimes such as human trafficking.

Although Swedish representatives have tried to export their legislation, especially to European Union institutions, their attempts have not brought any significant results.

The most obvious objection[28] is that – retorting the ideological starting point of the law – the rule which punishes male clients of female prostitutes is gender discriminatory,[29] inasmuch as it leaves out male or transgender prostitution, together with female sex tourism (or, seen from a different perspective,

---

[25] Ekberg, *The Swedish Law That Prohibits the Purchase of Sexual Services*, in 10 *Violence Against Women* 1187 (2004); Bindel, Kelly, *A Critical Examination of Responses to Prostitution in Four Countries: Victoria, Australia, Ireland, the Netherlands, and Sweden*, London Metropolitan University 2003, available at www.endviolenceagainstwomen.org.uk; Outshoorn *Comparative prostitution politics and the case for state feminism*, in Outshoorn (ed.), *The Politics of Prostitution. Women Movements, Democratic States and the Globalisation of Sex Commerce*, Cambridge U.P., Cambridge 2004, at p. 265.

[26] However other Northern European countries, equally advanced in equality among sexes have not taken the same road: see *e.g.* van Doorninck, *A Business Like any Other? Managing the Sex Industry in the Netherlands*, in Thorbek, Pattanaik (eds.), *Transnational Prostitution. Changing Global Patterns*, Zed Books, London 2002 (at p. 193); or Reinicke, *La prostituzione in Danimarca*, in Carchedi, Stridbeck, Tola, *Lo zoning possibile. Governance della prostituzione e della tratta delle donne. Il caso di Venezia, Sottocolma ed Amsterdam*, Franco Angeli, Milan 2008 (at p. 156).

[27] Svanstrom, *Prostitution in Sweden: debates and policies 1980–2004*, in Gangoli, Westmarland, *International Approaches to Prostitution. Law and Policy in Europe and Asia*, Policy Press, Bristol 2006, at p. 67ff.

[28] There is a considerable amount of critical comments – much larger than those supportive – on the Swedish prostitution legislation: see *inter alia* Gould *The Criminalisation of Buying Sex: the Politics of Prostitution in Sweden*, 30 *Journal of Social Policy* 437 (2001) ("Better ways need to be found to protect women in the sex trade" p. 454); Sanders, *Paying for Pleasure. Men who Buy Sex*, Willan Pub., Cullompton, 2008: "The [Swedish] prohibition law has brought with it other negative consequences" (at p. 177); "Northern European states taking an abolitionist line by criminalizing the purchasing of sex symbolize a backlash against other European liberal states that have traditionally opted for a legalized or decriminalized system whereby safety, regulation and employment rights are at the heart of the law" (at p. 178). According to Collins, Judge, *Client Participation and the Regulatory Environment*, in Munro, Della Giusta (eds.), *Demanding Sex: Critical Reflections on the Regulation of Prostitution*, Ashgate, Burlington, Vt, 2008 (at p. 145) "it should be noted that the Swedish policy does not seem to address the root problem of sex trafficking at all, as was heralded, since the experience so far appears to indicate that migrant workers are merely being deported".

[29] Svanstrom, *Criminalising the John – a Swedish Gender Model?*, in Outshoorn (ed.) *The Politics of Prostitution. Women Movements, Democratic States and the Globalisation ox Sex Commerce*, Cambridge U.P., Cambridge, 2004 (at p. 225); Leander, *Reflections on Sweden's Measures against Men's Violence against Women*, 5 *Social Policy and Society* 115 (2006).

it extends to completely different sexual practices a prohibition with has its own specific, and exclusively, feminist rationale).[30] Women and male homosexuals can therefore buy sexual services. Ordinary men, instead, are committing a criminal offence.

On the other hand one, should consider that as female prostitution covers the vast majority of the market, the practical consequence of the law is mostly of an administrative nature, keeping the streets "clean", and avoiding the development of "red light" districts.[31]

This suggests legal rules should be read from a functional, rather than an ideological point of view, to try to ascertain and evaluate significant data which could guide both legislatures and regulators.[32]

c. *The market approach*

At the opposite end of the spectrum – in respect of the prohibitionist/feminist approach – is the market approach. Sex relates to pleasure, and is one of the many ways in which we find pleasure together with food, drink, entertainment, travel and relaxation. Why be astonished if people also strive to reach sexual pleasure, by themselves or with someone else? Sex is no longer a mere function to the perpetuation of the human species. Sex is an essential part of our life and is associated with physical and mental health. Deprivation of sex is a serious limitation to a basic human need. One does not need to share libertarian views to reach these conclusions which are common place in psychology and physiology. Sexual repression is harmful for individuals and for society, and the first to have benefited from an open approach are women who freely and unabashedly take pleasure from sex.

Female sexual tourism to the Caribbean is not the expression of some sort of perversion but simply the evidence of a common nature that unites mankind. Women, just like men, like sex for sex without any sentimental complications, and without having to risk social stigmatisation.

From this simple fact one can easily build a coherent contract system, in which the relationship between the parties is no different from that of any purveyance of consumer goods and services.

---

[30] Kulick, *Four Hundred Thousand Swedish Perverts*, 11 *GLQ- J. Lesbian & Gay Studies*, 205 (2005).

[31] From a strictly economic point of view, and without reference to a specific country, Cameron, Collins, *Estimates of a Model of Male Participation in the Market for Female Heterosexual Prostitution Services*, 16 *EJL&E* 271 (2003) note that "it would seem that shifting the burden of risk and punishment cost on to the man may prove an efficient strategy in reducing the level of prostitution" (at p. 286).

[32] For a comparison of policies in Sweden and in the Netherlands see Stridbeck, *La compravendita di prestazioni sessuali in Svezia e Olanda. Regolamentazione ed esperienze locali*, in Carchedi, Stridbeck, Tola, *Lo zoning possibile. Governance della prostituzione e della tratta delle donne. Il caso di Venezia, Stoccolma ed Amsterdam*, Franco Angeli, Milan 2008, p. 84 ff.

It is, however, clear that private law rules are not neutral or ideologically empty. Applying contract law to sex markets requires a preliminary decision on the legality of the trade: in the simplest of cases it means setting aside the *In pari causa turpitudinis* rule or significantly reducing its scope.

Private law in contemporary societies plays a governance role which is difficult to ignore. It would be altogether simplistic to imagine contract as a sort of magic broom that cleans up the filth of sex markets.

And although modern economies are largely based on contractual relations, they are, at the same time, shaped by regulation.

Advocating that contract law should govern the provision of sex implies not only more room for private autonomy but also a significant role for public choices and decisions. The latter are clearly difficult not only because of ideological objections that can easily be anticipated, but also because there is a significant lack of experience. The cases in which regulation has been introduced (in the US or in Australia, in Germany or in the Netherlands) do not yet offer us – or a legislative body – sufficient comparative data which allow informed decisions.

To this first difficulty one must add that regulation and contract law present a very limited appeal when it comes to combating criminal organisation such as those engaged in human trafficking. One can easily draw a parallel with similar problems encountered in attempting to regulate light drugs. De-criminalising personal use has not brought to an end the grip of organised crime over the wholesale market.[33]

Not withstanding these quite obvious limits, the market approach presents several advantages: it conforms to the generally more relaxed moral standards of modern society, in which men and women strive to enhance their sexual features. They will not necessarily put themselves on any market, but surely will use them to seduce, please, attract, tease or play. It is rather difficult to imagine that those who are unable to do so will simply sit back and put their minds (and their bodily instincts) at peace, without trying to search on the market for what nature, character or age has denied them.[34]

Secondly, it favours a careful process of distinguishing. A sex market is made up of many submarkets (for example, those which have been analysed in the previous chapters) each with its distinctive features, and not necessarily requiring the same kind of regulation.

---

[33] "The mere presence of careful regulation does not eliminate the illegal market" (Cameron, *The Economics of Sin. Rational Choice or No Choice At All?*, Edward Elgar, Cheltenham 2002, at p. 200).

[34] "The best thing about prostitution is that it allows a sexual outlet for some people who otherwise would be precluded from the type of sexual interaction they wish to have" Reynolds *The Economics of Prostitution*, C.C.Thomas, Springfield, Ill., 1986, at p. 189.

What may appear morally indistinct is instead very clearly differentiated by its components of capital, organisation, and labour. Each submarket has its own economic dynamics: studying it helps understand how it operates. Whatever the aim of the observation it is surely more useful than simply turning one's head away in disgust.[35]

Segmenting the markets enables one to see their distance from, or their contiguity with other markets which are completely legal, albeit regulated, such as, *e.g.*, that of medical aphrodisiacs. The relations between these different markets may be appropriately examined and, if there is no outright ban on them, one can imagine public and private law incentives to shift offer and demand from one market to another, which is considered preferable from a public policy point of view.

One may obviously criticise this "permissibility rule" as morally nihilist and indifferent to what really happens – violence, privation of freedom and human rights, and exploitation – in sex markets. But if one cannot reach a consensus on what measures should be taken this is the way things will go. And for a legal realist that is, *per se*, an appropriate reply. To study reality is better than fretting about it, urging some improbable and illusory reform.

d. *European perspectives: Towards a "common market"?*

In the previous pages it has briefly been illustrated how some of the feminist theories have been enacted by Swedish legislation.

The rest of Europe does not, however, seem to follow the same direction. Most European countries, whether of civil law or common law tradition, are still strongly tied to the *In pari causa turpitudinis* rule, which, we have seen, allows a certain amount of individual autonomy, albeit without the protection of the courts. The legislation on legal brothels was abolished decades ago, and administrative regulation is mostly at local authority level, and is concerned with zoning and policing street prostitution.

There is one noticeable exception, and that is Germany, which in 2002 abandoned the *In pari causa turpitudinis* principle and introduced a *Prostitutiongesetz*.[36] The main provision of this law recognizes full binding effects to contracts for sexual services, and therefore renders the obligation of payment

[35] According to Baruch Spinosa "*Non ridere, non lugere, neque detestari; sed intelligere*" [I am grateful for this quote to Giovanni Sartor's comments to an earlier version of this work].

[36] Law n. of 20.12.2002 (*Prostitutiongesetz)*. For a lengthy comment of the law and its private law implications see Ambruster, in the *Münchener Kommentar zum BGB*, 5th ed., Beck, Munich, 2006. See also Wendtland, in the Bamberger, Roth (eds.), *Online-Kommentar zum BGB*, Beck, Munich (updated to 1.5.2009); Marcks, in Landmann, Rohmer (eds.), *Gewerbeordnung und Erganzende Vorschriften*, Beck, Munich, 2009, § 14.

of sums due enforceable in front of the courts.[37] Although there is a provision which does not allow assignment of credits arising from sexual contracts, the new law opens a host of typical private law issues, such as exact performance, warranties and implied conditions, damages for non-performance, *et caetera*.[38]

On the whole, the law seems to be grounded in a realistic approach to sex markets which exist and cannot be ignored. It is preferable to regulate them rather than apply the hypocritical policy of the ostrich.

But the most important feature of the German law is that it openly creates a significant variation between legal regimes within European Union member states. And Germany is not only one of the founding members but also the most populated and one of the most influential (together with France and the UK). Its legislation on this point cannot be simply set aside as a matter of national sovereignty. One is therefore confronted with three competing systems within the EU: the traditional one, which is followed by the majority of its 27 member states, with the Swedish solution at one extreme and the German one at the other.

If one considers the economic importance of sex industries, the amount of financial capital and people involved at various levels of production and consumption, it is hardly surprising that differences in legislation between member states can lead to inefficiencies and discrimination, which is exactly what the common market for goods, services, capital and labour force – enshrined in the "four liberties" of the EU – wants to avoid.

From this perspective the indications that come from the European Court of Justice (ECJ) are particularly important from a general policy point of view.

Three decisions by the ECJ, all on preliminary questions of interpretation of EU law, should be mentioned.

i. In Case C-34/79 (*R. v. Henn and Darby*)[39] the case was referred to the ECJ by the House of Lords. Henn and Darby had been convicted because they had knowingly imported into the UK "indecent or obscene articles" contrary to various provisions of Customs Acts of

[37] see Ambruster, in the *Münchener Kommentar zum BGB*, 5th ed., Beck, Munich, 2006, § 18.

[38] The feminist critique to this outcome is very clear: "In this context both specific performance and damages seem to go all the way to complete commodification. Thus, we should continue to make prostitution contracts unenforceable, denying the most important factor of commodification – enforceable free contract. We could either provide for restitution if the woman reneges or let losses lie. If we let losses lie, we preclude any increased domino effect that that official governmental (court) pronouncements about commodified sexuality might cause" (Radin, *Contested Commodities*, in Ertman, Williams (eds.), *Rethinking Commodification. Cases and Readings in Law and Culture*, NYU Press, New York 2005, p. 81 (at p. 91).

[39] Decision of 14.12. 1979.

1876 and 1952. The articles consisted in "several boxes of obscene films and magazines" imported from Denmark.

The question put to the ECJ was whether these provisions were contrary to the free movement of goods principle set out by Article 30 (now 28) of the Rome Treaty and if the prohibition of import was consistent with the exception "on the grounds of public morality" set out by Article 36 (now 30).[40]

The Court's decision was taken in the sense that if there was no lawful trade in such goods in the UK, the prohibition of import, however strict, could not be regarded "as amounting to a measure designed to give indirect protection to some national product or aimed at creating arbitrary discrimination between goods".[41]

The ECJ added that observance by the UK of the 1923 Geneva Convention on the suppression of traffic in obscene publications was not precluded by the provision relating to public morality contained in article 36 of the Rome Treaty.[42]

ii. In Case C-121/85[43] (*Conegate v. HM Customs & Excise*) the ECJ was again requested for an interpretative decision raised by the Queen's Bench Division in a similar case involving the import into the UK of inflatable dolls and other erotic articles that were considered by the customs authorities as "indecent and obscene" and were therefore seized.

The facts of the case were different from those of case C-34/79 as the seized materials were not publications or videos but objects. The Court, which in its *Henn* decision had somehow anticipated its opinion, however applied a similar principle, having ascertained that apart from certain limitations (prohibition of sale by post, public display, age of purchasers) no prohibition on manufacture or marketing of such objects existed in the UK.

Therefore the provisions in the 1876 Customs Act were incompatible with Article 30 of the Rome Treaty because they created

[40] "The first sentence of Article 36 upon its true construction means that a member state may, in principle, lawfully impose prohibitions of the importation from any other member state of articles which are of an indecent or obscene character as understood by its domestic law and that such prohibition may be lawfully applied to the whole of its national territory even if, in regard to the field in question, variations exist between the laws in force in the different constituent parts of the member state concerned" (at para. 17).

[41] At paras 21 and 22 ("If a prohibition on the importation of goods is justifiable on grounds of public morality and if it is imposed with that purpose the enforcement of that prohibition cannot, in the absence, within the member state concerned of a lawful trade in the same goods, constitute a means of arbitrary discrimination or a disguised restriction on trade contrary to article 36").

[42] At para. 27.

[43] Decision of 11.3.1986.

discrimination between national products – which could be legitimately manufactured and sold –and products from other EC countries which were not allowed to enter the country on the grounds of public morality.[44]

iii. In Case C-268/99[45] (*Jany v. Netherlands Secretary of Justice*)[46] the principle that public morality arguments cannot be used for discriminatory purposes is stated again by the ECJ in a case concerning the offer of prostitution services by Polish and Czech women in the Netherlands. The women were denied residence permits on the grounds of public morality.

The ECJ stated that "the activity of prostitution pursued in a self-employed capacity can be regarded as a service provided for remuneration" and therefore fell within the EC Treaty provisions concerning the free rendering of services.[47]

Furthermore the Court, in noting that prostitution was permitted in the Netherlands, added that "although Community law does not impose on Member States a uniform scale of values as regards the assessment of conduct which may be considered to be contrary to public policy, conduct may not be considered to be of a sufficiently serious nature to justify restrictions on entry to, or residence within, the territory of a Member State of a national of another Member State where the former Member State does not adopt, with respect to the same conduct on the part of its own nationals, repressive measures or other genuine and effective measures intended to combat such conduct".[48] "Consequently, a conduct which a Member State accepts on the part of its own nationals cannot be regarded as constituting a genuine threat to public order".[49] Therefore Member States may put limitations on those "wishing to pursue the activity of prostitution within the territory of the host Member State" with "the condition that that State has adopted effective measures to monitor and repress activities of that kind when they are also pursued by its own nationals."[50]

These decisions must be analysed taking into account the specific surrounding legislation: the ECJ is primarily interested in applying, and defining the

---

[44] "A member state may not rely on grounds of public morality within the meaning of article 36 of the Treaty in order to prohibit the importation of certain goods on the grounds that they are indecent or obscene, where the same goods may be manufactured freely on its territory and marketed on its territory subject only to an absolute prohibition on their transmission by post, a restriction on their public display and, in certain regions, a system of licensing of premises for the sale of those goods to customers aged 18 and over" (at para. 20).

[45] Decision of 20.11.2001.

[46] For some comments see Luciani, *Il lavoro autonomo della prostituta*, in *Quad. cost.* 2002, 398.

[47] Fourth ruling of the decision.

[48] Para 60.

[49] Para 61.

[50] Para 61.

boundaries of, the free movement principle. The questions pertaining to illegality fall into second place. This shows how the position of a court in deciding matters concerning sex is extremely important for the outcome of the decision. A criminal division will probably take a different stance from a family division; and a taxation court will view things differently from an ordinary court which has been asked to enforce a contract.

From this perspective the ECJ decisions show that in a neutral area, such as interpretation of general principles of trade, it is difficult to use moral standards as the only yardstick. Furthermore the boundaries that separate what are considered immoral transactions from all other legal commercial activities are blurred.

Obviously one is still very far away from establishing a common European market for sexual goods and services,[51] but surely the ECJ decisions clearly favour what has been called the market approach, rather than the traditional, and blunt, *In pari causa turpitudinis* rule.

This appears to be confirmed by the Audiovisual media services Directive (2007/65)[52] which explicitly allows adult entertainment channels albeit with some content and technical restrictions, rejecting the idea, voiced in some European Parliament draft documents, that pornography should be considered as a blatant violation of women's dignity and should be banned or at least restricted.[53]

e. *International trade issues*

As previously shown one of the main concerns related to sex markets is their international dimension.[54] Long before any market approach, it was necessary to face the dramatic challenges posed by trafficking of human beings and by paedophile tourism.[55] A vast set of special criminal provisions have been enacted, often at international level. These crimes, which are categorised at an extremely high level together with drug trafficking and money laundering, generally require transborder investigation and prosecution.

---

[51] Collins, Judge, *Client Participation and the Regulatory Environment*, in Munro, Della Giusta (eds.), *Demanding Sex: Critical Reflections on the Regulation of Prostitution*, Ashgate, Burlington, Vt, 2008 suggest (at p. 145) that owing to the ease with which transborder sex can be acquired in Europe "markedly divergent rates of offending behaviour, including that related to the consumption of prostitution services, are not intrinsically desirable".

[52] For its analysis see Chapter 5, para. b).

[53] See Ch. 5, fn. 3.

[54] Altman, *Global Sex*, U. Chicago Press, Chicago, 2001; Thorbek, Pattanaik (eds.), *Transnational Prostitution. Changing Global Patterns*, Zed Books, London 2002; Outshoorn (ed.), *The Politics of Prostitution. Women Movements, Democratic States and the Globalisation of Sex Commerce*, Cambridge U.P., Cambridge 2004; Abrams, *Immigration Law and the Regulation of Marriage*, 91 *Minn. L. Rev.* 1625 (2007).

[55] Comment, *U.S. Domestic Prosecution of the American International Sex Tourist: Efforts to Protect Children from Sexual Exploitation*, 94 *J. Crim. L. & Criminology* 415 (2003); Comment, *Justice beyond Borders: A Comparison of Australian and U.S. Child-Sex Tourism Laws*, 13 *Pac.*

This, however, does not belittle the importance of recognising that the pornographic trade is widely legal and internationally accepted, particularly since it has moved on-line and there are no longer the limits once set by custom laws to the import of obscene materials.

The result is that the dissemination of pornographic services is considered, *de facto*, as any other on-line service for which no special regulations are required,[56] apart from taxation issues which appear to be extremely difficult to solve in every field. Technology therefore has a much stronger impact in creating a single market than international agreements.

In the other great sex market, that of prostitution, the European experience indicates that the legal framework is evolving towards a competition between legal systems to allowing it on a more open basis. Although prostitution services must be rendered within one jurisdiction and therefore do not, in theory, pose international trade issues, differences between national legislations may create, especially in neighbouring countries, a constant flow of sex tourists.

What should be considered carefully – not taking any options for granted – is the enormous flow of capital related to this trade and the benefits that might derive from its public control. Because the international dimension, in particular, is so intertwined with criminal law issues, a broader view that comprises all the different aspects, including market ones, could be useful.[57] Although quite different, similar problems, albeit at a much higher level, arise in the international trade of arms and military equipment, which does not prevent developed countries from considering both ethical and foreign policy issues.

This approach would allow an open discussion of the similarities and differences in the various legal systems, with the aim not so much as to enhance the trade but rather to put it under control. A second, but not secondary, result of this approach would be to gradually draw attention to the normative aspects of conditions of sex workers and to start requiring "social clauses" in this sector.[58] As previously shown, the dejected conditions of most sex workers is one of the points on which most organizations and authors agree and share common views as to minimum guarantees.[59]

Rim L. & Pol'y J. 405 (2004); Poulin, *La mondialisation des industries du sexe. Prostitution, pornographie, traite des femmes et des enfants*, Interligne, Ottawa 2004.

[56] Note, *Anonymity and International Law Enforcement in Cyberspace*, 7 *Fordham Intell. Prop. Media & Ent. L.J.* 231 (1996).

[57] Chawla, *Sex Tourism and Development*, Sonali Pub., New Delhi, 2004; Gangoli, Westmarland, *International Approaches to Prostitution. Law and Policy in Europe and Asia*, Policy Press, Bristol 2006.

[58] Kempadoo, Doezema (eds.), *Global Sex Workers. Rights, Resistance, and Redefinition*, New York, Routledge, 1998; Gall *Sex Worker Union Organising: An International Study*, Palgrave, Basingstoke, 2006.

[59] European Network for HIV/STD Prevention in Prostitution, *Hustling for Health. Developing services for sex workers in Europe*, (1998), online at www.europap.net; Lin Lean Lim

f. *Regulation and reform*

"Reform" is one of the overused words in the vocabulary of lawyers and social scientists. Dissatisfaction with the present state of things prompts debates, proposals, committees, enquiries, bills. It is therefore no wonder that in such a controversial field as that of sexual services and goods, most authors who have tackled the issue suggest some kind of new solution.

Obviously all ideas need to be taken into account, without prejudice. But what is essential, first of all, is reliable data that is both factual and social. From a methodological point of view there are a few firm *caveats*.

i. Sex markets need to be carefully distinguished. Prostitution and pornography, which represent the biggest share of the whole market are quite different from each other, involve different businesses, different workers and, mostly, different consumers. The former is strongly dependant on the physical element, starting with the site where the service is rendered, and requires the contemporaneous presence of the prostitute and the client. The latter is increasingly de-materialised through digitalisation and telecommunications networks. What may be appropriate – in one sense or the other – for one market may be useless, or even counterproductive, in another. Generalisations here – as in many other fields – are of little use. The main problem is that if one wishes to provide, moral principles through the law, these necessarily are general, and therefore there is an inevitable collision between what is and what should be.[60]

ii. Although in this work the attempt has been that of comparing various national experiences, pointing out similarities and differences, it should always be borne in mind that, ultimately, Savigny's two-centuries old lesson on the importance of *Volkgeist* in fashioning law remains valid. As with all social studies, when one discusses proposals for reform one has to take into account the different realities, which means different data, which implies different solutions. And although Western countries share many common values, these, especially when seen in action, do not cover the entire spectrum of social behaviour.

(ed.), *The Sex Sector: The Economic and Social Bases of Prostitution in Southeast Asia*, ILO, Geneva, 1998; Dank (ed.), *Sex Work & Sex Workers, Sexuality and Culture*, vol. 2, Transaction, New Brunswick, 1999; Brown, *Sex slaves: the trafficking of women in Asia*, Virago, London, 2001; Doais, *Travailleurs du sexe*, VLB, Montreal, 2003.

[60] From a different perspective the same conclusion is reached by Albert, Gomez, Gutierrez Franco, *Regulating Prostitution: A Comparative Law and Economics Approach*, [2007] published online at http://www.fedea.es/pub/Papers/2007/dt2007-30.pdf (at p. 5f).

If one tries to summarise some of the most frequent tendencies, which can be more neutrally defined as changes rather than as reforms (a term which implies a political evaluation), these are:

- A widespread movement towards de-criminalization of prostitution as the first step for recognition of the social identity of the prostitute. This movement has been extremely gradual[61] and from its original humanitarian motivations[62] has moved towards a much more feminist-oriented approach, to the point that the tables have turned: prostitution is not a crime, but availing oneself of its services is (this is the Swedish outcome).[63]
- The recognition of a category of workers – sex workers – who should receive similar treatment as other workers and whose rights need to be promoted openly. This is the field of the most obvious "contractualisation" of sexual services, and, at the same time, of legitimisation by public law, through the extension to these workers of social security benefits.
- The growing importance of regulation of sex industries, which implies legality but at the same time limits.[64] For the time being the approach is still piecemeal, and involves decisions by local authorities (mostly on zoning and on trade licences),[65] national and trans-national legislators on the protection of minors from pornography (implicitly admitting that adults may freely acquire these goods), and tax authorities. What has yet to be established are the public interest goals which are common to all forms of regulation.[66] While in the past these have been the

[61] See already Sanger, *The History of Prostitution: Its Extent, Causes and Effects Throughout the World*, The Medical Pub., New York 1910: "In the special matter of prostitution, the opinion is expressed elsewhere that prohibitory laws are worse than useless" (at p. 26). See also Benjamin, Masters, *Prostitution and Morality*, Julian Press, New York, 1964, at p. 439: "Prostitution is destined to survive. That being the case, it should survive in the form of sex as service".

[62] Decker, *Prostitution: Regulation and Control*, Littleton, Co., Rothman, 1979 at p. 456 ff.

[63] For a critique of the "abolitionist vision: one which understands prostitution as paradigmatic of a system of male power and seeks its elimination by removing both the supply and the demand of sexual services" see Scoular, O'Neill, *Legal Incursions into Supply/Demand: Criminalising and Responsabilising the Buyers and Sellers of Sex in the UK*, in Munro, Della Giusta (eds.), *Demanding Sex: Critical Reflections on the Regulation of Prostitution*, Ashgate, Burlington, Vt, 2008 (at p. 13)

[64] For an interdisciplinary approach to the diverse issues concerning the regulation of prostitution see the *Introduction* by the editors to Munro, Della Giusta (eds.), *Demanding Sex: Critical Reflections on the Regulation of Prostitution*, Ashgate, Burlington, Vt, 2008.

[65] See Hubbard, *Sex and the City. Geographies of Prostitution in the Urban West*, Ashgate, Aldershot 1999 (Ch. 4 on "Space, law and public order: policing the spaces of prostitution", p. 103 ff). For an economic analysis of the effect local decisions may have on neighbouring communities see Collins, Judge, *Client Participation and the Regulatory Environment*, in Munro, Della Giusta (eds.), *Demanding Sex: Critical Reflections on the Regulation of Prostitution*, Ashgate, Burlington, Vt, 2008 (at p. 143f.).

[66] For some indications see the various essays published in Part III ("Politics, Policing, and the Sex Industry") of Weitzer (ed.) *Sex for Sale: Prostitution, Pornography, and the Sex,*

protection of *les bonnes moeurs*, now it would seem more in line with present day priorities to be the safeguard of the physical health of both workers and clients (an extremely important aspect in view of widespread venereal diseases which have a very high social – not only individual – cost) in bodily sexual services. Together with the safeguard of consumers' health and economic interests in the provision of sexual goods and on-line sexual services. Quite clearly these indications are the expression of policies.[67] However, if one considers the dimension of these markets, the option of leaving them in a regulatory "no-man's-lands" equally and clearly expresses a different policy.

g. *Social norms*

Lawyers study and create norms. When they are in a position of command they impose and enforce rules. From a lawyer's viewpoint a world without legal rules is empty, and this void needs to be filled.

Whether it be relations within a family or gentleman's agreements; scuba diving or satellites in outer space; pets or fur skins, there are always good reasons to set rules in the general interest. Practising lawyers earn their daily bread advising, applying rules, and litigating. The academic lawyer may criticise but, ultimately, he has found a new topic of enquiry.

Regulating sex markets, whether it is in one direction (*i.e.* complete prohibition) or in the opposite (*i.e.* legalisation) appears a normal approach to the problem. One should however take the time to stop and ask oneself if sex markets – or at least some of the sub-markets of which it is composed – really need to be regulated by legal norms, and if this is not a typical case in which social norms are much more effective.[68]

Sexual mores are complex and fragmented. It is extremely difficult to find one rule which will fit all, and widespread criticism inevitably will undermine

---

Routledge, New York, 2000, and in particular the works by Weitzer, *The Politics of Prostitution in America* (at p. 159); Chapkis, *Power and Control in the Commercial Sex Trade* (at p. 181); Lewis, *Controlling Lap Dancing: Law, Morality, and Sex Work* (at p. 203); Hausbeck, Brents, *Inside Nevada's Brothel Industry* (at p. 217).

[67] "In a regulated market, prospective clients also know they can report any complaints to the regulating and licensing agency, so that they will feel more secure about using the services of a regulated and licensed prostitute than one in an unregulated market": Reynolds *The Economics of Prostitution*, C.C.Thomas, Springfield, Ill., 1986, at p. 44. See also the policy recommendations in favour of regulated markets in Kuo, *Prostitution Policy. Revolutionizing Practice through a Gendered Perspective*, NYU Press, New York, 2002, at p. 153ff. An ample analysis of the kind of regulation which could be introduced in the different segments of the bodily sexual services market is presented by Albert, Gomez, Gutierrez Franco, *Regulating Prostitution: A Comparative Law and Economics Approach*,[2007] published online at http://www.fedea.es/pub/Papers/2007/dt2007-30.pdf (at p. 29ff).

[68] The reference is to the main work on the subject: Posner *Law and Social Norms*, Harvard U.P., Cambridge, 2000.

its enforcement. The array of solutions which have been presented in the previous pages, with their inevitable drawbacks, suggests that a very cautious approach is preferable. Law makers and public authorities are unable to understand and tackle certain social phenomena. Each community is better equipped to solve the problems that arise, and in any event no rule is better than a bad rule.[69]

Sexual behaviour has been a long time – and still is – governed by social norms. If one looks at the other side of the coin of the *In pari causa turpidinis* rule it shows that citizens are well aware of the fact that when they venture into the sex market – not much differently from a tourist in a flea market or a *suq* – they will not have the assistance of the law. They will be careful, and if they have been driven by enthusiasm they will learn a sobering lesson.

As empirical research has illustrated, where individual and collective conduct is governed by social norms there is no need for a contract, which entails promise, exactness of fulfilment of obligations, punctuality in payment, conditions and warranties, and remedies. Sex – starting from that between husband and wife – is no matter for contractual relations.[70] Even if money moves from one party to another, this is not enough to justify the birth of reciprocal obligations.

A time may come in which this might be necessary and desirable. But in the early 21st century we are still far away from such a solution, and – apart from the lawyer's anxiety to occupy new territories – there is no need for haste.

---

[69] A typical example is pornography: see Sullivan *The Politics of Sex. Prostitution and Pornography in Australia Since 1945*, Cambridge U.P., Cambridge, 1997 "pornography has no universal or fixed meaning and becomes meaningful only in particular political contexts"(at p. 243).

[70] "There is a low expectation of trust for both parties in the prostitution game, yet they need to cooperate to achieve their desired deal" (Sanders, *Sex Workers. A Risky Business*, Willan Pub., Cullompton, 2005, p. 53).

CONCLUDING REMARKS

Sex markets are still, in their many guises, mainly uncharted waters. Certain aspects – mostly those that have to do with criminal activities – are relatively well studied.

Others, such as those concerning sex transactions, are widely hypothetical. Sex is central to the life of modern women and men, and one cannot only look at it through law's lense. It has to do with primary biological needs and with sophisticated cultural rituals. It is both explicitly of the body and hidden in the depths of one's mind. In the Western mentality the idea of sex is inextricably bound with that of transgression. To put things in an extreme way, between sex and morality there is an intimate contradiction which no law can eliminate.[1] And at the same time, when mankind (especially in developed countries) has reached general levels of wealth and longevity quite unimaginable only fifty years ago, sex is one of the main components of a hedonist society.[2]

It is no wonder, therefore, that the task of fitting sex into the, albeit very big, box of contract law is a difficult one. This research has chosen a starting point – that of a market approach – which is quite novel in legal literature on sex. As often is the case the results are not univocal.

a. *Interdisciplinarity and plurality of legal approaches*

New subjects require examination from many different angles. Lawyers are still unaccustomed to this. Public law and private law are still a strong divide, intellectually and professionally. It is even more so when one has to tackle economic, social, psychological and physiological data and theories. Lawyers – but also specialists of other fields – are not equipped for this venture.[3] Teamwork would probably be more fruitful but it requires leaving one's comfort

---

[1] Scrutton, *Sexual Desire. A Philosophical Investigation*, Weidenfeld&Nicholson, London, 1986: "There could be neither arousal, nor desire, nor the pleasures that pertain to them, without the presence, in the very heart of these responses, of the moral scruples which limit them" (at p. 362).

[2] See Sanders, *Paying for Pleasure. Men who Buy Sex*, Willan Pub., Cullompton, 2008, at p. 196: "Sex is [presented as] an intrinsic part of capitalism and culture, supported by the principles of hedonism, pleasure and fulfilment". See also McNair, *Striptease Culture. Sex, Media and the Democratization of Desire*, Routledge, London 2002 who analyses the "sexualization of culture" and the "democratization and diversification of sexual discourse" (at p. 205).

[3] Honoré, *Sex Law in England*, Hamden, Ct., Archon Books 1978, in the introduction to his work (at p. 5), felt it necessary to state that: " If that makes an unusual sort of law book my defence is that the subject demands it and that lawyers should be readier than they are to cut across the bounds of conventions".

zone and question the validity of one's methods. Are peep-shows and dildos worth the endeavour?

Lawyers, especially with a continental European background, feel their role being imperilled by other professions and other methodological approaches.

However open-minded, they are uneasy with the widespread sociological attitude of US scholars. A European lawyer is not interested in being a social scientist, and a century after the Brandeis briefs he still mistrusts this kind of approach.

When it comes to sex markets willingly or not he is forced to take into account the considerable amount of literature produced by US scholars, but he has difficulties with pinpointing its relevance. What John Merryman called 'differences of style' are even more striking when it comes to a prurient argument. And while in other markets globalisation imposes the quest for common rules, this happens with much less intensity for sex, and generally only in the field of criminal law. Transatlantic comparisons are not easy and it is doubtful that they can bring significant results.

A few examples will suffice: in the US, sex law is the main field of influence of legal feminism. A dozen or more law reviews fuel the debate, which is mostly political in a broad sense, rather than about legal techniques.[4] Very little of all this arrives on the European continent, and surely not for want of intellectual ability and of sensitivity, especially on behalf of women lawyers. The reasons are more profound but essentially rest in a perplexed attitude towards strongly postured policies dressed up in legal scholarship robes.[5]

A further example is that of criminal law response. While this is considered quite normal in the US, there is widespread scepticism in Europe on whether sex markets should – and can – be regulated through penal law.

Obviously one's own standpoint can be that of only one jurisdiction, considering irrelevant what happens in others.[6] However the analysis that has been conducted through this research points out at numerous existing similarities, first of all the recourse to century old Latin maxims as guiding principles of law.

[4] Non-feminist authors are influenced by it and, for reasons related to "political correctness" or simply because the perspective is mostly one-sided, avoid the topic. It is significant that one of the founders of the Law and Economics theory, Richard Posner, in his vast book on "*Sex and reason*" hardly considers sex markets and their structure and dynamics. Is it because "in the United States (and increasingly in Europe) political correctness has forced us all to express our lifetime beliefs and values in bland and thus uninteresting terms"? (Markesinis, Fedtke, *Engaging with Foreign Law*, Hart, Oxford 2009, at p. 51).

[5] And not only in Europe: see Kotiswaran, *Preparing for Civil Disobedience: Indian Sex Workers and the Law*, 21 *Boston Coll. Third World L. J.* 161 at 231 (2001)): "Reinforcing the stereotypes that Western feminist writings create leaves the West firmly in command over feminist discourse in India".

[6] This attitude is extensively examined by Markesinis, Fedtke, *Engaging with Foreign Law*, Hart, Oxford 2009, at p. 195ff).

This reminds us that the shaping of a new legal system is a very lengthy process and although we feel we are living in times of fast and rapid changes, the speed of the clock always remains the same, and to assess significant variations one must wait one, if not two, generations.

b. *Non-market sex*

Sex markets are contiguous to a non-market, in which individuals offer, seek and exchange sex with other individuals, or indulge in solitary pleasure.[7] It is not easy to find parallels: if one does not want to buy the services of a restaurant one must go to the market anyway and buy some food; if one does not want to go to market one must at least own a vegetable garden and buy the seeds; one can paint one's house without hiring a decorator, but one must buy paint and brushes and spend considerable time doing the work. The only possible similar example is that of walking instead of paying for the bus or a taxi. But that does not bring us very far. We must instead assume that, in terms of pleasure, paid sex is more or less equivalent to exchanged sex, and that solitary sex can often be a valid alternative to the two.

Although there has been an attempt in some US literature to construct personal sexual and emotional relations as a contract, the comparison appears rather strained.[8] Obviously one can reconstruct relations within a primitive tribe in terms of contract, or use legal stereotypes to describe the functioning of a mafia family. But the recourse to analogy or to metaphors – widely used by lawyers since antiquity – has its limits in law's rigid ontology: a contract is a contract[9]; and what is not a contract has a different name.[10]

---

[7] However see Laumann, Ellinson, Mahay, Paik, Youm, *The Sexual Organization of the City*, U. Chicago Press, Chicago, 2004, at p. 32 who include non-monetary exchange in the market: "Sexual expression is organized like a market and shares many of the same features of traditional matching markets (*e.g.* transaction costs, search behaviors, exchanges of one sort or another)".

[8] see for the first comprehensive presentation of the theory Pateman, *The Sexual Contract*, Polity, Cambridge 1988; see also the debate between Feaver, Kling, Plofchan Jr., *Sex as Contract: Abortion and Expanded Choice*, 4 *Stan. L. & Pol'y Rev.* 212 (1992); and Fineman, *A Legal (And Otherwise) Realist Response to Sex as Contract*, 4 *Colum. J. Gender & L.* 128 (1994).

[9] And contract requires consent, but how does one express consent in sexual transactions? The vast amount of literature on the subject demonstrates how opinions, quite reasonably, differ and it is extremely difficult to find a common reply: Archard, *Sexual Consent*, Westview Press, Boulder Co. 1998; Dank, Refinetti (eds.), *Sexual Harassment & Sexual Consent*, Transaction Pub., New Brunswick 1998; Wertheimer, *Consent to Sexual Relations*, Cambridge U.P., Cambridge, 2003; Cowling, Reynolds (eds.), *Making Sense of Sexual Consent*, Ashgate, Burlington Vt, 2004.

[10] The warning issued by Vassalli, *Del* Ius in corpus, *del* debitum coniugale *e della servitù d'amore, ovverosia la dogmatica ludicra*, Bardi (Roma 1944), is still appropriate. In a comment on a neighbouring area, legal intervention in sexual relations between married couples, he described as a "waste of midnight oil" the attempt to force these into the mould of property law or the law of obligations, a process which does "no favours to the law or to people's perception of its proper function" (p. 143). This is not, however, the view of some legal feminists: for some

The question therefore is: what are the connections between non-market sex and sex markets?[11] One can imagine a few models.

i. *Mutual exclusion*

The more satisfactory the sex life of an individual, the less likely one can expect him or her to go to the market for sexual services. In fairy tale love – somehow similar to a perfect competition model – there are no prostitutes or porn shops. Everybody lives happily with one's soulmate and is satisfied with life's plenty.[12] One can also imagine the opposite situation in which a person's provision of sex comes only from the market and there is no interest in exchange of sexual experiences (the most obvious reasons being age, physical aspect, mental disposition *et caetera*).[13] From a theoretical point of view one could evaluate the impact of public policies which enhance individual sexual capabilities (psychological counselling, "schools of seduction", aphrodisiacs) and therefore reduce the demand for paid sexual services. This might have a positive effect on the amount of prostitute sex being sold on the market. A simulation might be carried out between two different age groups, *e.g.* 18–30 and 40–52, investigating empirically the amount of 'sex consumption', verifying how much is free, and how much is paid for, and motivations (economical? psychological?) for the choice. Following a rather simplified *cliché*, one would suppose that the first age group rarely resorts to prostitution; the second much more frequently.

Is it possible to reduce such a propensity to market sex, and how? Would there be an unwelcome side effect consisting of the search for a partner different from one's spouse and the consequent breaking-up of families?[14]

---

remarks see Calabresi, *An Introduction to Legal Thought: Four Approaches to Law and to the Allocation of Body Parts*, in 55 *Stanford L. Rev.* 2113 (2003) (at p. 2148f)

[11] Archard, *Sexual Consent*, Westview Press, Boulder Co. 1998: "the fact that prostitution is the explicit sale of unloving sex may serve to mark the distinction between this kind of sex and the valued sexual intimacy that cannot be bought or sold" (at p. 105).

[12] And one should not forget that in matters of sex men and women – thanks heaven! – are different and do not necessarily share the same views. See the experiment reported by Wertheimer, *Consent to Sexual Relations*, Cambridge U.P., Cambridge, 2003 (at p. 42): 100 girls/ 100 boys on a campus were asked by a good-looking student of the opposite sex the simple question "Would you come to bed with me?". The results were widely different.

[13] "Paid sex markets, in general, may form the primary sexual release market for some individuals who are unwilling or unable to have a non-paid sexual partner. Likewise some individuals may have a partner who is totally unwilling or unable to meet the volume or nature of their sexual demands" (Cameron, *The Economics of Sin. Rational Choice or No Choice At All?*, Edward Elgar, Cheltenham 2002, p. 191).

[14] Sex practices can be bizarre, but economic theories sometimes have nothing to envy: see Liu, *An effective punishment scheme to reduce extramarital affairs: an economic approach*, 25 *EJL&E* 167 (2008) (extramarital affairs can be effectively reduced if the legal punishment scheme is designed in the way that makes the adulterer's expected loss increase with the level of adultery at an increasing or constant rate).

It is quite clear from this hypothetical that sex markets depend, much more than from law, from education, culture, style of life.[15]

ii. *Complementarity*

There are other instances in which non-market sex and sex markets are in a relationship of complementarity. This is generally the case with sex-enhancing products and aphrodisiacs which one can assume are used in non-market sexual relations. They are meant (and are bought) to increase physical and emotional pleasure. A moralist would see in them instruments of perversion. A realist, however, perceives a useful function which, from a different point of view, implies having an alternative in respect of sex services which are on the market.

iii. *Substitutability*

In other cases the relation is one of substitutability.[16] Solitary sex is second best compared with exchanged sex.[17] A pornographic film is second best compared with direct physical sex services. Prostitute sex is less time-consuming than dating, courting and seducing.[18]

One could chart the preferences of a certain group of individuals and establish in what order the many variables would be placed. What one is willing to do in order to obtain sexual pleasure; how much is one disposed to pay.

---

[15] T. Honoré's remark appears to hit the point: "One of the pluses to be expected from getting married is precisely that one escapes from the market in sexual and economic attractiveness in which the unmarried perforce move. The married opt for a closed shop. For them the cost of making a change, the adjustment cost, is generally speaking too high. Only if the marriage has ceased to be viable does the cost of making a change become an important consideration. The mere fact that a better alternative appears to be available is not in itself enough to put the continuance of the marriage bond at issue" (Honoré, *The Quest for Security: Employees, Tenants, Wives* (Hamlyn Lecture 1982), Stevens, London, 1982, at p. 105).

[16] "The primary market (marriage and 'ongoing' serially monogamous relationships) may fail due to constraints on meeting the needs of the male partner for variety/unusual practices" and therefore is supplemented by the secondary market (prostitution) (Cameron, *The Economics of Sin. Rational Choice or No Choice At All?*, Edward Elgar, Cheltenham 2002, p. 184).

[17] But consider the very complex analysis in Laqueur, *Solitary Sex. A Cultural History of Masturbation*, Zone Books, New York, 2003.

[18] From a feminist perspective "Seen as a bargaining matter, the effect of forbidding prostitution is clear. Money has disproportionate value because it is fluid and fungible. Limiting the negotiability of currency in the sexual market renders the currency of money less powerful. If money cannot be offered outright, the male-female negotiation must be disguised. For example, a date uses both money and time, and thus the price goes up. Accordingly, the laws against prostitution are important not only for what they seek to prohibit directly, but also for their indirect effect on the availability of prostitutes as cheap, mostly female sexual labor, lowering the price for the rest of the sexual work force" (Hirshman, Larson, *Hard Bargains. The Politics of Sex*, Oxford U.P., New York, 1998, at p. 260).

These very simplistic remarks are meant to point out how many different aspects must be taken into account in a regulatory framework. Contract law by itself is insufficient to govern a market as anomalous as that for sex.

c. *Sex and sexual ability as a human right*

There is a further ambivalence in sex that renders the regulation of sex markets full of contradictions and open-ended. We have seen how sex is quite normally exchanged in a non-market, that of personal relations.

According to general mores sexual activity outside marriage or, at least outside of non-market relations, is considered immoral. On the other hand the law recognizes sexual potentiality and expression as a fundamental human right which merits protection.

The examples are quite obvious: if after an accident a person's sexual ability is seriously impaired the person will receive damages. In certain categories of tort a US court will award substantial general damages and astronomical punitive damages for loss of consortium. In the rating of physical impairment procured impotence is classified as one of the most serious bodily offences.

Sexual ability is an essential element in the right to form a family. It is widely debated if the denial of sexual activity to certain categories of persons, such as prisoners or the mentally retarded, is legitimate and has constitutional grounds.

The insurgence of new and deadly venereal diseases, such as AIDS, transmitted to unaware partners and, through genetic materials, to one's children, has raised questions of liability for careless sexual behaviour which one thought had been forgotten together with the substantial disappearance of syphilis in Western societies.[19]

For these reasons – both legal and social – sex, sexual health and sexual well-being are highly valued and have a price, at least on the tort market. It is, one might say, a wholesale price, in the sense that what is paid for, as compensation, is the whole (or a percentage) of a person's sexual ability. But it is difficult to set a price in one market and then set a rule that excludes fragmentation of the same good and renders single acts a *res extra commercium*.[20]

---

[19] Pollard Sacks, *Sex Torts*, 91 *Minn L. Rev*. 769 (2007) (with a proposal to apply a standard of strict liability to "sex tort liability"). The argument is further analysed by Ead., *Intentional Sex Torts*, 77 *Ford. L. Rev*. 1051 (2008). The issue is directly related to the vast debate on 'wrongful life' claims by children born with congenital defects caused by venereal diseases of one of their parents (typically syphilis contracted by the father). For a ground-breaking Italian decision see Trib. Piacenza 31.7.1950 (in *Foro Italiano* 1951, I, 987) and the ample discussion of the case by Rescigno, *Il danno da procreazione*, in *Riv. dir. civ*. 1956,I,614. For a comparative view of the 'wrongful life' debate see Markesinis, Unberath, *The German Law of Torts. A Comparative Treatise*, 4th ed., Hart, Oxford, 2002, p. 156ff.

[20] "Have commodified love, sexuality, marriages, family relationships, or personhood resulted from practices like awarding money damages for pain and suffering, loss of consortium,

One could object that initially sexual services were given a price and only much later, towards the 20th century, was sexual integrity considered an essential part of a human being and damages paid in the case of its violation. But this does not change the connection between the two aspects and the fact that markets are never isolated and one market generally develops others.

A typical example is that of sexology: doctors and therapists are paid for restoring sexual disabilities. Sex enhancing drugs are prescribed and bought and it is debated, as we have seen, as to whether the national health service should pay for them.

These professions are highly qualified and respected. The services they render are in no way considered immoral and nobody questions the use to which their patients will put their restored ability: whether with their spouse; with a lover or mistress; or in prostitute sex.

There are obvious and flagrant human rights violations in human trafficking. But one should also consider that at the other end of the debate about sex there is a basic need which is also, albeit with limitations and conditions, protected as a fundamental right.

d. *Sexual freedom*

The other side of the coin, as regards sex, is sexual freedom as a fundamental right of a human being.

And the first aspect of this freedom is that of choosing to have no sex. Sexual freedom is historically protected by criminal law statutes that punish rape, sexual assaults of various kinds, down to sexual harassment.

In the great 19th century treaties on penal law these were classified as crimes against sexual freedom, akin to those against individual freedom.

These offences have always been severely punished and have as obvious consequences a damage award. Sexual integrity, especially female, was highly prized, and the enactment of the crime of seduction with the (unfulfilled) promise of marriage was meant to preserve the virginity of the bride.

In this case, therefore, a market price is also given to (unlawful) sexual acts.

To this extremely important facet of sexuality, nowadays, one must add sexual freedom as expressed through the decriminalisation initially, and legal recognition subsequently of homosexual relations.

---

and wrongful death or compensating women upon divorce for unpaid household and family labor?" (Lucas, *The Currency of Sex. Prostitution, Law, and Commodification*, in Ertman, Williams (eds.), *Rethinking Commodification. Cases and Readings in Law and Culture*, NYU Press, New York 2005, p. 248 (at p. 264). See however Calabresi, *An Introduction to Legal Thought: Four Approaches to Law and to the Allocation of Body Parts*, in 55 *Stanford L. Rev*. 2113 (2003) who points out (at p. 2148) that for a long time the courts in the US had a very different approach towards male and female capacity.

Sexual discrimination is unlawful in public offices, work places, and in housing contracts. Again, those whose freedom to decide into which sexual relations to enter has been violated will receive damages.

One can easily imagine contracts in which aspects of sexual freedom are (to use an expression abhorred in certain milieus) commodified: from dress codes to the prohibition of having sexual relations with clients of the establishment; from the obligation not to marry for a certain number of years, to the sale of memoirs of sexual experiences.

Following a well-known pattern, the more freedom there is, the more will be offered on the market, and more side-markets will be created for collateral goods and services instrumental to the best use of that freedom.

e. *Sexual immorality: A notion that has made its time?*

The paradox this research started from was that if sexual immorality rendered contracts unenforceable, then millions of transactions every day fell under this rule. This prompted the search for a different rule, or at least, of a way to interpret differently that rule.

To look at things from an holistic perspective one conclusion is that the rule which made immoral contracts void or unenforceable was coherent with a society in which sex was hidden and not spoken of, and in which the courts were vested with the role of public guardians of individual and social morality.[21]

In a society in which sexuality is a fundamental right and sexual freedom the dominant condition it is extremely difficult, if not impossible, to maintain in life an immorality rule.[22]

However, what will substitute it appears to be a question which still requires a convincing answer.

---

[21] A role criticised over 50 years ago: "The courts cannot act as a moral agency and reach their decisions in accordance with the respective guilt of the parties" [Grodecki, *In pari delicto potior est conditio defendentis*, 71 *L. Quarterly R.* 254 (1955) (at p. 273)].

[22] "To disapprove mightily of illegality and turpitude, you have to have secure confidence in your righteousness and your own version of righteousness": Birks, *Recovering Value Transferred Under an Illegal Contract*, 1 *Theoretical Inq. L.* 155 (2000) (at p. 159).

BIBLIOGRAPHY

Abbott, Sharon A., *Motivations for Pursuing an Acting Career in Pornography*, in Weitzer, Ronald (ed.) *Sex for Sale: Prostitution, Pornography, and the Sex Industry*, Routledge, New York, 2000, p. 49.

Abrams, Kerry, *Immigration Law and the Regulation of Marriage*, 91 *Minn. L. Rev.* 1625 (2007)

Acton, William, *Prostitution considered in its moral, social, and sanitary aspects in London and other Large Cities and Garrison Towns with proposal for the control and prevention of its attendant evils*, Churchill, London (Ist ed. 1857, 2nd 1870)

Aggleton, Peter, *Men who sell sex*, UCL Press, London, 1998

Agustin, Laura Maria, *Sex at the margins: migration, labour markets and the rescue industry*, Zed Books, London, 2007

Albert, Rocio – Gomez, Fernando – Gutierrez Franco, Yanna, *Regulating Prostitution: A Comparative Law and Economics Approach*, [2007] published online at http://www.fedea.es/pub/Papers/2007/dt2007–30.pdf

Altman, Dennis, *Global Sex*, U. Chicago Press, Chicago, 2001

Ambruster, Christian, Comment to the *Prostitutiongesetz*, in the *Münchener Kommentar zum BGB*, 5th ed., Beck, Munich, 2006

Archard, David, *Sexual Consent*, Westview Press, Boulder, Co. 1998

Association Henri Capitant, *Travaux Journées Lilloises (1957)*, Dalloz, Paris, 1960

Avery, Dianne – Craine, Marion, *Branded: Corporate Image, Sexual Stereotyping, and the New Face of Capitalism*, 14 *Duke J. Gender L. & Pol'y* 13 (2007)

Baird, Stephen R., *Moral Intervention in the Trademark Arena: Banning the Registration of Scandalous and Immoral Trademarks*, 83 *Trademark Rep.* 661 (1993)

Balos, Beverly – Fellows, Mary Louise, *A Matter of Prostitution: Becoming Respectable*, 74 *N.Y.U. L. Rev. 1220* (1999)

Barlow, Anne, *Cohabitants and the Law*, 3rd ed., Butterworths, London, 2001.

Barlow, Anne – Duncan, Simon – James, Grace – Park, Alison, *Cohabitation, Marriage and the Law. Social Change and Legal Reform in the 21st Century*, Hart, Oxford, 2005

Barton, Chris, *Cohabitation Contracts*, Gower, Aldershot, 1985

Beale, Hugh – Hartkamp, Arthur – Kotz, Hein – Tallon, Denis, *Cases, Materials and Text on Contract Law*, Hart, Oxford, 2002

Becker, Mary – Bowman, Cynthia G. – Torrey, Morrison, *Cases and Materials on Feminist Jurisprudence. Taking Women Seriously*, West, St. Paul, 1994

Bellassai, Sandro, *La legge del desiderio. Il progetto Merlin e l'Italia degli anni Cinquanta*, Carocci, Rome 2006

Bellizzi, Antonio, *Contratto illecito, reato e irripetibilità ob turpem causam*, Giappichelli, Turin, 1999

Benjamin, Harry, – Masters, R. E. L., *Prostitution and Morality*, Julian Press, New York, 1964, at p. 275

Bergin, Kathleen A., *Sexualized Advocacy: The Ascendant Backlash against Female Lawyers*, 18 *Yale J.L. & Feminism* 191 (2006)

Bernstein, Elizabeth, *The Meaning of the Purchase. Desire, Demand and the Commerce of Sex*, 2 *Ethnography* 389 (2001)

Biesanz, Zach, *Dildos, Artificial Vaginas, and Phtalates: How Toxic Sex Toys Illustrate a Broader Problem for Consumer Protection*, 25 *Law & Ineq.* 203 (2007)

Bindel, Julie – Kelly, Liz, *A Critical Examination of Responses to Prostitution in Four Countries: Victoria, Australia, Ireland, the Netherlands, and Sweden*, London Metropolitan University 2003 available at www.endviolenceagainstwomen.org.uk

Bingham, Nicole, *Nevada Sex Trade: A Gamble for the Workers*, 10 *Yale J.L. & Feminism* 69, (1998)

Birks, Peter, *Recovering Value Transferred Under an Illegal Contract*, 1 *Theoretical Inq. L.* 155 (2000)

Boyle, Frances M. – Glennon, Shirley – Najman, Jake M. – Turrell, Gavin – Western, John S. – Wood, Carole, *The Sex Industry: A Survey of Sex Workers in Queensland, Australia*, Ashgate, Aldershot, 1997
Brewis, Joanna – Linstead, Stephen, *Sex, Work and Sex Work. Eroticizing Organization*, Routledge, London 2000
Brock, Deborah R., *Making Work, Making Trouble: Prostitution as a Social Problem*, U.Toronto Press, Toronto, 1998
Brooks-Gordon, Belinda, *The Price of Sex: Prostitution, Policy and Society*, Willan Pub., Cullompton, 2006
Brown, Dan, *Commercial Sex: Pornography*, in McAnulty, Richard D. – Burnette, M. Michele (eds.), *Sex and Sexuality*, Greenwood Press, Westport, Ct. 2006
Brown, T. Louise, *Sex slaves: the trafficking of women in Asia*, Virago, London, 2001
Bruch, Carol S., *Cohabitation in the Common Law Countries a Decade after Marvin: Settled in or Moving Ahead*, 22 *U.C. Davis L. Rev.* 717 (1989)
Buckley, R. A., *Illegality in Contract and Conceptual Reasoning*, 12 *Anglo-Am. L. Rev.* 280 (1983)
Buckley, R. A., *Illegality and Public Policy*, Sweet & Maxwell, London, 2002
Buckwalter, Ellen L. – Perinetti, Maria – Pollet, Susan L. – Salvaggio, Meredith S., *Modern Day Slavery in Our Own Backyard*, 12 *Wm. & Mary J. Women & L.* 403 (2006)
Bullough, Vern L. – McAnulty, Richard D., *The Sex Trade: Exotic Dancing and Prostitution*, in McAnulty, Richard D. – Burnette, M. Michele (eds.), *Sex and Sexuality*, vol. I, Praeger, Westport, Ct., 2006
Butler, Heather, *What Do You Call a Lesbian with Long Fingers? The Development of Lesbian and Dyke Pornography*, in L. Williams (ed.), *Porn Studies*, Duke U.P., Durham, 2004, pp. 167
Cabezas, Amalia Lucia, *Legal Challenges To and By Sex Workers/Prostitutes*, 48 *Clev. St. L. Rev.* 79 (2000)
Calabresi, Guido, *An Introduction to Legal Thought: Four Approaches to Law and to the Allocation of Body Parts*, in 55 *Stanford L. Rev.* 2113 (2003)
Calvert, Clay – Richards, Robert D., *Stripping Away First Amendment Rights: The Legislative Assault on Sexually Oriented Businesses*, 7 *N.Y.U. J. Legis. & Pub. Pol'y* 287 (2003)
Calverton, V. F., *Sex and Economics*, in *New Masses*, March 1927, p. 32
Cameron, Samuel, *The Economics of Sin. Rational Choice or No Choice At All?*, Edward Elgar, Cheltenham 2002
Cameron, Samuel, *Space, Risk and Opportunity: The Evolution of Paid Sex Markets*, in 41 *Urban Studies* 1643 (2004)
Cameron, Samuel – Collins, Alan, *Estimates of a Model of Male Participation in the Market for Female Heterosexual Prostitution Services*, 16 *EJL&E* 271 (2003)
Campbell, Rosie – O'Neill, Maggie, (eds.) *Sex Work Now*, Willan Pub., Cullompton 2006
Carchedi, Francesco – Stridbeck, Ulf – Tola, Vittoria, *Lo zoning possibile. Governance della prostituzione e della tratta delle donne. Il caso di Venezia, Sottocolma ed Amsterdam*, Franco Angeli, Milan 2008
Carpenter, Belinda J., *Re-Thinking Prostitution. Feminism, Sex, and the Self*, Peter Lang, New York, 2000
Carusi, Donato, *Contratto illecito e* soluti retentio, Jovene, Naples, 1995.
Case, Kevin, *Lewd and Immoral: Nude Dancing, Sexual Expression, and the First Amendment*, 81 *Chi.-Kent L. Rev.* 1185 (2006)
Chapkis, Wendy, *Power and Control in the Commercial Sex Trade* in Weitzer, Ronald (ed.) *Sex for Sale: Prostitution, Pornography, and the Sex Industry*, Routledge, New York, 2000, p. 181
Chavkin, David F., *Medicaid and Viagra: Restoring Potency to an Old Program*, in 11 *Health Matrix* 189 (2001)
Chawla, Romila, *Sex Tourism and Development*, Sonali Pub., New Delhi, 2004
Church Gibson – Roma Gibson, Pamela, (eds.), *Dirty Looks. Women, Pornography, Power*, British Film Institute, London, 1993
Clark, Anna, *Desire. A History of European Sexuality*, Routledge, New York, 2008
Collins, Alan – Judge, Guy, *Client Participation and the Regulatory Environment*, in Munro, Vanessa E. – Della Giusta, Marina (eds.), *Demanding Sex: Critical Reflections on the Regulation of Prostitution*, Ashgate, Burlington, Vt, 2008

Comment *Constitutional Protection of Obscene Material Against Censorship as Correlated with Copyright Protection of Obscene Material Against Infringement*, 31 *S. Cal. L. Rev.* 301 (1957)
Comment, *Justice beyond Borders: A Comparison of Australian and U.S. Child-Sex Tourism Laws*, 13 *Pac. Rim L. & Pol'y J.* 405 (2004)
Comment, *Life, Liberty, and the Pursuit of Viagra? Demand for "Lifestyle" Drugs Raises Legal and Public Policy Issues*, in 28 *Capital U.L. Rev.* 837 (2000)
Comment, *Mandated Medicaid Coverage of Viagra: Raising the Issues of Questionable Priorities, the Need for a Definition of Medical Necessity, and the Politics of Poverty*, in 44 *Loy. L. Rev.* 611 (1998)
Comment, *Prescription for Fairness: Health Insurance Reimbursement for Viagra and Contraceptives*, 35 *Tulsa L.J.* 399 (2000)
Comment, *Sex and the City: Zoning "Pornography Peddlers and Live Nude Shows"*, 49 *UCLA L. Rev.* 1139 (2002)
Comment, *Sex on the Internet: A Legal Click or an Illicit Click*, 38 *Cal. W.L.Rev.* 527 (2002)
Comment, *Substantive Due Process: Sex Toys after* Lawrence, 60 *Fla. L. Rev.* 507 (2008)
Comment, *U.S. Domestic Prosecution of the American International Sex Tourist: Efforts to Protect Children from Sexual Exploitation*, 94 *J. Crim. L. & Criminology* 415 (2003)
Comment, *The Hunkiest Little Whorehouse in Town is Looking for a Few Good Men, but Only to Work: The Constitutional Implications of Heidi Fleiss's Female Brothel*, 14 *Vill. Sports & Ent. L.J.* 77 (2007)
Comment, *We'd Better Treat Them Right: A Proposal for Occupational Cooperative Bargaining Associations of Sex Workers*, 9 *U. Pa. J. Lab. & Emp. L.* 679 (2007)
Comporti, Marco, *Negozio giuridico immorale e irripetibilità della prestazione "ob turpem causam" ex art. 2035 c.c.*, in *Giur. compl. cass. civ.* 1955, VI, 148
Cook, Jennifer, *Shaken from Her Pedestal: A Decade of New York City's Sex Industry under Siege*, 9 *N.Y. City L. Rev.* 121 (2005)
Corbin, Alain, *Les filles de noce. Misère sexuelle et prostitution*, Aubier Montaigne, Paris 1978
Corbin, Arthur L., *Corbin on Contracts. Illegal Bargains*, LexisNexis, Newark, NJ, 2002
Cornell, Drucilla, *At The Heart of Freedom. Feminism, Sex, & Equality*, Princeton U.P., Princeton, 1998
Courtney, Alice E. – Whipple, Thomas W., *Sex Stereotyping in Advertising*, Lexington Books, Lexington, Mass. 1983
Cowling, Mark – Reynolds, Paul, (eds.), *Making Sense of Sexual Consent*, Ashgate, Burlington. Vt., 2004
Crofts, Thomas – Summerfield, Tracy, *The Licensing of Sex Work: Regulating an Industry or Enforcing Public Morality*, 33 *UWAL Rev* 289
Dalla, Rochelle L., *Exposing the 'Pretty Woman' Myth. A Qualitative Investigation of Level Prostituted Women*, Lexington Books, Lanham, Md. 2006
Danna, Daniela, (ed.), *Prostitution and Public Life in Four European Capitals*, Carocci, Rome 2007 (and available on-line at http://www.danieladanna.it/)
Dank, Barry M., (ed.), *Sex Work & Sex Workers, Sexuality and Culture*, vol. 2, Transaction, New Brunswick, 1999
Dank, Barry M. – Refinetti, Roberto (eds.), *Sex Work & Sex Workers*, Transaction Pub., New Brunswick 1998
Davis, Kingsley, *The Sociology of Prostitution*, 2 *American Sociological Review* 744 (1937)
Davis, Nanette J., (ed.) *Prostitution. An International Handbook on Trends, Problems and Policies*, Greenwood Press, Westport, Ct, 1993
Davis, Theodore H., *Registration of Scandalous, Immoral, and Disparaging Matter under Section 2(a) of the Lanham Act: Can One Man's Vulgarity Be Another's Registered Trademark?* 54 *Ohio St. L.J.* 331 (1993)
De Albuquerque, Klaus, *Sex, Beach Boys, and Female Tourists in the Caribbean*, in Dank, Barry M., (ed.), *Sex Work & Sex Workers, Sexuality and Culture*, vol. 2, New Brunswick, Transaction, 1999, p. 87ff
Decker, John F., *Prostitution: Regulation and Control*, Littleton, Co., Rothman, 1979
DeLamater, John D., – Still, Margon, *Sexual Desire in Later Life*, in Stombler, Mindy – Baunach, Dawn M.- Burgess, Elisabeth O. – Donnelly, Denise – Simonds,Wendy (eds.), *Sex Matters. The Sexuality and Society Reader*, II ed., Pearson, Boston, 2007, p. 375

Della Giusta, Marina – Di Tommaso, Maria Laura – Strøm, Steinar, *Who is watching? The Market for Prostitution Services*, online *Journal of Population Economics* (2007)

Della Giusta, Marina – Di Tommaso, Maria Laura – Strøm, Steinar, *Sex Markets. A Denied Industry*, Routledge, Abingdon 2008

Devlin, Patrick, *The Enforcement of Morals*, OUP, London, 1959

Dickson, Sandra, *Sex in the City: Mapping Commercial Sex across London*, The Poppy Project, London 2004

Doais, Michel, *Travailleurs du sexe*, VLB, Montreal, 2003

Dorat Des Monts, Roger, *La cause immorale*, Rousseau, Paris, 1956

Dufour, Pierre, *Histoire de la prostitution chez tous les peuples du monde depuis l'antiquité la plus éculée jusqu'a nos jours*, (3 volumes), Seré Editeur, Paris, 1851–1852

Dworkin, Andrea, *Against the Male Flood: Censorship, Pornography and Equality*, in P. Smith (ed.), *Feminist Jurisprudence*, OUP, New York, 1993, p. 449

Edlund, Lena – Korn, Evelyn, *A Theory of Prostitution*, 110 *J. Pol. Econ.* 181 (2002)

Ekberg, Gunila, *The Swedish Law That Prohibits the Purchase of Sexual Services*, in 10 *Violence Against Women* 1187 (2004)

Enonchong, Nelson, *Illegal Transactions*, LLP, London, 1998

Ertman, Martha M. – Williams, Joan C., (eds.), *Rethinking Commodification. Cases and Readings in Law and Culture*, NYU Press, New York, 2005

Estes, Yolanda, *Prostitution: A Subjective Position*, in Soble, Alan – Power, Nicholas (eds.), *The Philosophy of Sex. Contemporary Readings*, V ed., Rowman &Littlefield, Lanham, Md. 2008

European Network for HIV/STD Prevention in Prostitution, *Hustling for Health. Developing services for sex workers in Europe*, (1998), online at www.europap.net

Ezer, Nicole L., *The Intersection of Immigration Law and Family Law*, 40 *Fam. L.Q.* 339 (2006)

Feaver, Peter D. – Kling, Robert – Plofchan, Thomas K. Jr., *Sex as Contract: Abortion and Expanded Choice*, 4 *Stan. L. & Pol'y Rev.* 212 (1992)

Fehlberg, Belinda – Smyth, Bruce, *Binding Prenuptial Agreements in Australia: The First Year*, in Mulcahy, Linda – Wheeler, Sally, (eds.), *Feminist Perspectives on Contract Law*, Glasshouse, London 2005, p. 125

Fineman, Martha Albertson, *A Legal (And Otherwise) Realist Response to Sex as Contract*, 4 *Colum. J. Gender & L.* 128 (1994)

Flexner, Abraham, *Prostitution in Europe*, Grant Richards, London, 1914

Flowers, Amy, *The Fantasy Factory. An Insider's View of the Phone Sex Industry*, U. Penn. Press, Philadelphia 1998

Forkosh, Morris D., *Obscenity, Copyright, and the Arts*, 10 *New Eng. L. Rev.* 11 (1974)

Frank, Rainer, *The Status of Cohabitation in the Legal Systems of West Germany and Other West European Countries*, 33 *Am. J. Comp. L.* 185 (1985)

Freeman, Michael D. A. – Lyon, Christiana M., *Cohabitation without Marriage. An Essay in Law and Social Policy*, Gower, Aldershot, 1983

Gall, Gregor, *Sex Worker Union Organising: An International Study*, Palgrave, Basingstoke, 2006

Gangoli, Geetanjali – Westmarland, Nicole, *International Approaches to Prostitution. Law and Policy in Europe and Asia*, Policy Press, Bristol 2006

Garb, Sarah H., *Sex for Money is Sex for Money: The Illegality of Pornographic Film as Prostitution*, 13 *Law & Ineq.* 281 (1994)

Geadah, Yolande, *La prostitution: un métier comme un autre?*, VLB, Montreal, 2003

Gibbons, Llewellyn L., *Semiotics of the Scandalous and the Immoral and the Disparaging: Section 2(a) Trademark Law after Lawrence v. Texas*, 9 *Marq. Intell. Prop. L. Rev.* 187 (2005)

Glendon, Mary Ann, *The Transformation of Family Law. State, Law, and Family in the United States and Western Europe*, U.Chicago Press, Chicago, 1989

Gooderson, Richard N., *Turpitude and Title in England and India*, 1958 *Cambridge LJ* 199

Gott, Merryn, *Sexuality, Sexual Health and Ageing*, Open University Press, Maidenhead, 2005

Gould, Arthur, *The Criminalisation of Buying Sex: the Politics of Prostitution in Sweden*, 30 *Journal of Social Policy* 437 (2001)

Greer, Chris, *Sex Crime and the Media: Sex Offending and the Press in a Divided Society*, Willan Pub., Cullompton, 2003

Grodecki, Jan K., *In pari delicto potior est conditio defendentis*, 71 *L. Quarterly R.* 254 (1955)

Grubb, Andrew, (ed.), *The Law of Restitutions*, Butterworths, London, 2002

Guaracino, Jeff, *Gay and Lesbian Tourism. The Essential Guide for Marketing*, Elsevier, Amsterdam, 2007
Guillaume, Florence – Arn, Raphael, (eds.) *Cohabitation non maritale: Evolution récente en droit suisse et étranger. Actes du colloque de Lausanne du 23 février 2000*, Droz, Geneva, 2000
Guinn, David E. – Steglich, Elissa, (eds.), *In Modern Bondage: Sex Trafficking in the Americas*, Transnational Pub., Ardsley, N.Y., (c2003)
Gunther, Barrie, *Media Sex. What Are the Issues*, Lawrence Erlbaum, Mahwah, N.J., 2002
Haff, Nicole, *Health Care Coverage: Contraception and Viagra*, 7 *Georgetown J. Gender & L.* 1185 (2006)
Halavais, Alexander C., (ed.), *Cyberporn and Society*, Kendall/Hunt, Dubuque, 2006
Halsbury's *Laws of England*, 4th edition, Butterworths, London 2006
Hausbeck, Kathryn – Brents, Barbara G., *Inside Nevada's Brothel Industry, in* Weitzer, Ronald, (ed.) *Sex for Sale: Prostitution, Pornography, and the Sex Industry*, Routledge, New York, 2000, p. 217
Hausmann, Rainer – Hochloch, Gerhard, *Das Recht der nichtehelichen Lebensgemeinschaft*, Schmidt, Berlin, 1999
Hawkes, Gail, *A Sociology of Sex and Sexuality*, Open University Press, Philadelphia,1996
Hawkes, Gail, *Sex & Pleasure in Western Culture*, Polity, Cambridge 2004
Hawkes, Gail – Scott, John, (eds), *Perspectives in Human Sexuality*, OUP, Oxford, 2005
Hennigan, Peter C., *Property War: Prostitution, Red-Light Districts, and the Transformation of Public Nuisance Law in the Progressive Era*, 16 *Yale J.L. & Human.* 123 (2004)
Henriques, Fernando, *Prostitution and Society. A Survey*, MacGibbon & Kee London 1963
Hernandez, Tany Katerì, *"Sex in the [Foreign] City". Commodification and the Female Sex Tourist*, in Ertman, Martha M. – Williams, Joan C. (eds.), *Rethinking Commodification. Cases and Readings in Law and Culture*, NYU Press, New York, 2005, p. 222
Hirshman, Linda R. Larson, Jane E., *Hard Bargains. The Politics of Sex*, Oxford U.P., New York, 1998
Holmes, Oliver W., *The Path of the Law*, reprinted in *The Collected Works of Justice Holmes*, U. Chicago Press, 1994, vol.3, p. 391ff.
Honoré, Tony, *Sex Law in England*, Archon Books, Hamden, Ct., 1978
Honoré, Tony, *The Quest for Security: Employees, Tenants, Wives* (Hamlyn Lecture 1982), Stevens, London, 1982
Hubbard, Philip, *Sex and the City. Geographies of Prostitution in the Urban West*, Ashgate, Aldershot, 1999
Hunyor, Jonathon, *Short Skirts and the Sex Discrimination Act: 'What's Wrong With Being Sexy?'*, 31 *Alternative L.J.* 15 (2005)
Jackson, Suzanne H., *Marriages of Convenience: International Marriage Brokers, Mail-Order Brides, and Domestic Servitude*, 38 *U. Tol. L. Rev.* 895 (2007)
Jeannel, Julien, *De la prostitution dans les grandes villes au dix-neuvième siècle*, Baillière, Paris 1874
Jeffrey, Lesley Ann, *Sex and Borders: Gender, National Identity, and Prostitution Policy in Thailand*, UBC Press, Vancouver, 2002
Jeffrey, Lesley Ann – MacDonald, Gayle, *Sex Workers in the Maritimes Talk Back*, UBC Press, Vancouver 2006
Jeness, Valerie, *Making It Work. The Prostitutes' Rights Movement in Perspective*, De Gruyter, New York, 1993
Kaminski, Stephen T., *Must Employers Pay for Viagra? An "Americans with Disabilities Act" Analysis Post-Bragdon and Sutton*, in 4 *DePaul J. Health Care L.* 73 (2000)
Kelly, Linda, *Marriage for Sale: The Mail-Order Bride Industry and the Changing Value of Marriage*, 5 *J. Gender Race & Just.* 175 (2001)
Kempadoo, Kamala, (ed) *Sun, Sex, and Gold. Tourism and Sex Work in the Caribbean*, Rowman & Littlefield, Lanham Md, 1999
Kempadoo, Kamala, *Sexing the Caribbean. Gender Race, and Sexual Labor*, Routledge, New York, 2004
Kempadoo, Kamala, – Doezema, Jo (eds.), *Global Sex Workers. Rights, Resistance, and Redefinition*, Routledge, New York, 1998
Kneeland, George J., *Commercialized Prostitution in New York City*, Grant Richards, London, 1913

Kotiswaran, Prabha, *Preparing for Civil Disobedience: Indian Sex Workers and the Law*, 21 *Boston Coll. Third World L. J.* 161 (2001)
Kuo, Lenore, *Prostitution Policy. Revolutionizing Practice through a Gendered Perspective*, NYU Press, New York, 2002
Kirkman, Allison, *Ageing and Sexuality. The Final frontier for Positive Ageing?*, in Hawkes Gail – Scott, John (eds.), *Perspectives in Human Sexuality*, OUP, Oxford, 2005, p. 104
Kneeland, George J., *Commercialized Prostitution in New York City*, Grant Richards, London, 1913
Koppelman, Andrew, *Eros, Civilization, and Harry Clor*, 31 *N.Y.U. Rev. L. & Soc. Change* 855 (2007)
Kulick, Don, *Four Hundred Thousand Swedish Perverts*, 11 *GLQ- J. Lesbian & Gay Studies*, 205 (2005)
Lane, Frederick S., *Obscene Profits. The Entrepreneurs of Pornography in the Cyber Age*, Routledge, New York, 2000
Laqueur, Thomas W., *Solitary Sex. A Cultural History of Masturbation*, Zone Books, New York, 2003
Laumann, Edward O. – Ellinson, Stephen – Mahay, Jenna – Paik, Anthony – Youm, Yoosik, *The Sexual Organization of the City*, U. Chicago Press, Chicago, 2004
Law, Sylvia A., *Commercial Sex: Beyond Decriminalization*, 73 *S. Cal. L. Rev.* 523 (2000)
Leander, Karen, *Reflections on Sweden's Measures against Men's Violence against Women*, 5 *Social Policy and Society* 115 (2006)
Lehmann, Jens-Torsten, *Prostitution und gaststättenrechtliche Unsittlichkeit im Wandel der Zeit*, in *NVwZ* 2009, 888
Lemoncheck, Linda, *Loose Women, Lecherous Men*, Oxford U.P., New York 1997
Le Tourneau, Philippe, *La regle "nemo auditur"*, (th. Paris), LGDJ, Paris 1970
Lever, Janet – Dolnick, Deanne, *Clients and Call Girls: Seeking Sex and Intimacy*, in Weitzer, Ronald (ed.), *Sex for Sale: Prostitution, Pornography, and the Sex Industry*, Routledge, New York, 2000, p. 85ff
Levins, Hoag, *American Sex Machines. The Hidden Story of Sex at the US Patent Office*, Cincinnati, Adams Media 1996
Lewis, Jacqueline, *Controlling Lap Dancing: Law, Morality, and Sex Work*, Weitzer, Ronald (ed.), *Sex for Sale: Prostitution, Pornography, and the Sex Industry*, Routledge, New York, 2000, p. 203
Lewis, Jacqueline – Maticka-Tyndale, Eleanor, *Licensing Sex Work: Public Policy and Women's Lives*, 26 *Canadian Public Policy / Analyse de Politiques*, 437 (2000)
Lim, Lin Lean, (ed.), *The Sex Sector: The Economic and Social Bases of Prostitution in Southeast Asia*, ILO, Geneva, 1998
Lindee, Kirsten M., *Love, Honor, or Control: Domestic Violence, Trafficking, and the Questions of How to Regulate the Mail-Order Bride Industry*, 16 *Colum. J. Gender & L.* 551 (2007)
Liu, Xuemei, *An Effective Punishment Scheme to Reduce Extramarital Affairs: An Economic Approach*, 25 *EJL&E* 167 (2008)
Loe, Meiha, *The Rise of Viagra. How the Little Blue Pill Changed Sex in America*, NYU Press, New York, 2004
Lucas, Ann, *The Currency of Sex. Prostitution, Law, and Commodification*, in M. Ertman, Martha, C. Williams, Joan (eds.), *Rethinking Commodification. Cases and Readings in Law and Culture*, NYU Press, New York 2005, p. 248
Luciani, Massimo, *Il lavoro autonomo della prostituta*, in *Quad. cost.* 2002, 398
MacKinnon, Catherine A., *Sexual Harassment of Working Women. A Case of Sex Discrimination*, Yale U.P., New Haven, Ct., 1979
MacKinnon, Catherine A., *Only Words*, Harvard U.P., 1993
MacKinnon, Catherine A., *Pornography as Trafficking*, 26 *Mich. J. Intern. Law* 993 (2005)
MacKinnon, Catherine A., *Women's Lives – Men's Laws*, Belknap Press, Cambridge, Ma., 2005
MacQueen, Hector – Cockrell, Alfred, *Illegal Contracts*, in Zimmermann, Reinhard – Visser, Daniel – Reid, Kenneth, *Mixed Legal Systems in Comparative Perspective. Property and Obligations in Scotland and South Africa*, OUP, Oxford, 2004, p. 143 ff.
Majer, Christian Friedrich, *Sittenwidrigkeit und das Prostitutionsgesetz bei Vermarktung und Vermittlung*, in NJW 2008, 1926
Manchester, Colin, *Sex Shops and the Law*, Gower, Aldershot, 1986

Manderson, Lenore – Jolly, Margaret (eds.), *Sites of Desire, Economies of Pleasure. Sexualities in Asia and the Pacific*, U. Chicago Press, Chicago, 1997
Marcks, Peter, Comment to the *Prostitutiongesetz*, in Landmann, Robert A. – Rohmer, Gustav (eds.), *Gewerbeordnung und Erganzende Vorschriften*, Beck, Munich, 2009, § 14
Marella, Maria Rosaria, *Bocca di Rosa, Roxanne e le altre: considerazioni in tema di sesso, mercato e autonomia privata*, in 2 *Polemos*, issue 2/2008, p. 35
Marguenaud, Jean-Pierre, *Les droits de la femme prostituée a l'épreuve du proxenetisme de l'Etat*, in *Revue Trimestrielle Droit Civil* 2007, 730
Markesinis, Basil M., *Good and Evil in Art and Law: An Extended Essay*, Spinger, Vienna, 2007
Markesinis, Basil M., *The Duality of Genius*, Jan Sramek Verlag, Vienna, 2008
Markesinis, Basil M. – Unberath, Hannes, *The German Law of Torts. A Comparative Treatise*, 4th ed., Hart, Oxford, 2002
Markesinis, Basil M. – Fedtke, Jörg, *Engaging with Foreign Law*, Hart, Oxford 2009
Mason-Grant, Jason, *Pornography Embodied. From Speech to Sexual Practice*, Rowman & Littlefield, Lanham, Md., 2004
Matter, Mohamed Y., *Trafficking in Persons: An Annotated Legal Bibliography*, 96 *Law Libr. J.* 669 (2004)
Matthews, Roger, *Prostitution, Politics and Policy*, Routledge, London, 2008
McAnulty, Richard D. – Burnette, Michele M. (eds.), *Sex and Sexuality*, vol. I, Praeger, Westport, Ct., 2006
McGee, Robert W., *If Dwarf Tossing Is Outlawed, Only Outlaws Will Toss Dwarfs: Is Dwarf Tossing a Victimless Crime?*, 38 *Am. J. Juris.* 335 (1993)
McGinley, Ann C., *Harassment of Sex(y) Workers: Applying Title VII to Sexualized Industries*, 18 *Yale J.L. & Feminism* 65 (2006)
McLaren, Angus, *Impotency: A Cultural History*, Chicago, Chicago U.P. 2007
McNair, Brian, *Striptease Culture. Sex, Media and the Democratization of Desire*, Routledge, London 2002
Monto, Martin A., *Why Men Seek out Prostitutes*, in Weitzer, Ronald (ed.) *Sex for Sale: Prostitution, Pornography, and the Sex Industry*, Routledge, New York, 2000, p. 67ff
Monzini, Paola, *Sex Traffic: Prostitution, Crime, and Exploitation*, Zed Books, London, 2005
Mulcahy, Linda – Wheeler, Sally (eds.), *Feminist Perspectives on Contract Law*, Glasshouse, London 2005
Mullings, Beverley, *Globalization, Tourism and the International Sex Trade,* in Kempadoo, Kamala, (ed) *Sun, Sex, and Gold. Tourism and Sex Work in the Caribbean*, Rowman & Littlefield, Lanham Md., 1999, p. 55ff
Munro, Vanessa E. – Della Giusta, Marina (eds.), *Demanding Sex: Critical Reflections on the Regulation of Prostitution*, Ashgate, Burlington, Vt, 2008
Murray, Kristen, *Labour Regulation in the Legal Sex Industry in Victoria*, 16 *Austr. J. Labour L.* 321 (2003)
Newsome, Holli B., *Mail Dominance: A Critical Look at the International Marriage Broker Regulation Act and Its Sufficiency in Curtailing Mail-order Bride Domestic Abuse*, 29 *Campbell L. Rev.* 291 (2007)
Note, *A Guide for Municipalities on the Validity of Licensing and Regulating Oriental-Style Hostess Bars as Escort*, 14 *Whittier L. Rev.* 249 (1993)
Note, *A New Sexual Revolution?: Viagra as Pandora's Box for the Elderly*, 7 *Elder L.J.* 409 (1999)
Note, *Anonymity and International Law Enforcement in Cyberspace*, 7 *Fordham Intell. Prop. Media & Ent. L.J.* 231 (1996)
Note, *Child Sex Tourism Legislation under the Protect Act: Does It Really Protect?* 79 *St. John's L. Rev.* 445 (2005)
Note, *E-Rated Industry: Fair Use of Sheep or Infringing Goat?*, 6 *Vand. J. Ent. L. & Prac.* 291 (2003)
Note, *Extraterritorial Accountability: An Assessment of the Effectiveness of Child Sex Tourism Laws*, 28 *Loy. L.A. Int'l & Comp. L. Rev.* 641 (2006)
Note, *Fornication, Cohabitation, and the Constitution*, 77 *Mich. L. Rev.* 255 (1978)
Note, *Immorality, Obscenity and the Law of Copyright*, 6 *S.D. L. Rev.* 109 (1961)
Note, *Jobs and Borders*, 118 *Harv. L. Rev.* 2171 (2005)
Note, *Patent Law for New Medical Uses of Known Compounds and Pfizer's Viagra Patent*, in 46 *IDEA* 283 (2006)

Note, *Self-Disparaging Trademarks and Social Change: Factoring the Reappropriation of Slurs into Section 2(a) of the Lanham Act*, 106 *Colum. L. Rev.* 388 (2006)

Note, *Sex, But Not the City: Adult-Entertainment Zoning, the First Amendment, and Residential and Rural Municipalities*, 46 *Boston College L. Rev.* 625 (2005)

Note, *The Best Little Whorehouse Is Not in Texas: How Nevada's Prostitution Laws Serve Public Policy, and How Those Laws May Be Improved*, 6 *Nev. L.J.* 217 (2005)

Note, *The International Marriage Broker Regulation Act: Protecting Foreign Women or Punishing American Men?*, 29 *Campbell L. Rev.* 317 (2007)

Note, *Trademark Law and Free Speech: Protection for Scandalous and Disparaging Marks*, 42 *Harv. C.R.-C.L. L. Rev.* 451 (2007).

Nussbaum, Martha C, *"Whether from Reason or Prejudice": Taking Money for Bodily Services*, 27 *J. Legal Stud.* 693 (1998) [partly republished in Ertman, Martha M. – Williams, Joan C. (eds.), *Rethinking Commodification. Cases and Readings in Law and Culture*, NYU Press, New York 2005, p. 243]

O'Connell Davidson, Julia, *Prostitution, Power and Freedom*, Polity, Cambridge, 1998

O'Connell Davidson, Julia – Sanchez Taylor, Jacqueline, *Fantasy Islands. Exploring the Demand for Sex Tourism*, in Kempadoo, Kamala (ed.), *Sun, Sex, and Gold. Tourism and Sex Work in the Caribbean*, Rowman & Littlefield, Lanham, Md, 1999, p. 47 ff

O'Malley, Thomas, *Sexual Offences. Law, Policy and Punishment*, Sweet & Maxwell, Dublin, 1996

Outshoorn, Joyce (ed.), *The Politics of Prostitution. Women Movements, Democratic States and the Globalisation of Sex Commerce*, Cambridge U.P., Cambridge 2004

Outshoorn, Joyce, *Comparative Prostitution Politics and the Case for State Feminism*, in Outshoorn, Joyce (ed.), *The Politics of Prostitution. Women Movements, Democratic States and the Globalisation of Sex Commerce*, Cambridge U.P., Cambridge 2004, p. 265

Pa, Monica, *Beyond the Pleasure Principle, The Criminalization of Consensual Sadomasochistic Sex*, 11 *Tex J. Women & L.* 51 (2001)

Padilla, Mark, *Caribbean Pleasure Industry. Tourism, Sexuality, and AIDS in the Dominican Republic*, U. Chicago Press, Chicago, 2007

Parry, Martin, *The Law Relating to Cohabitation*, 3rd ed., Sweet&Maxwell, London, 1993

Pateman, Carole, *The Sexual Contract*, Polity, Cambridge 1988

Phillips, Jeremy, *Copyright in Obscene Works: Some British and American Problems*, 6 *Anglo-Am. L. Rev.* 138 (1977)

Pitts, Marian K. – Smith, Anthony M. A. – Grierson, Jeffrey – O'Brien, Mary – Misson, Sebastian, *Who Pays for Sex and Why? An Analysis of Social and Motivational Factors Associated with Male Clients of Sex Workers*, 33 *Archives of Sexual Behavior* 353 (2004)

Pollard Sacks, Deana, *Sex Torts*, 91 *Minn L. Rev.* 769 (2007)

Pollard Sacks, Deana, *Intentional Sex Torts*, 77 *Ford. L. Rev.* 1051 (2008)

Posner, Eric A., *Law and Social Norms*, Harvard U.P., Cambridge, Ma., 2000

Posner, Richard A., *Sex and Reason*, Harvard U.P., Cambridge, Ma., 1992

Posner, Richard A. – Silbaugh, Katharine B., *A Guide to America's Sex Laws*, U. Chicago Press, Chicago, 1996

Poulin, Richard, *La mondialisation des industries du sexe. Prostitution, pornographie, traite des femmes et des enfants*, Interligne, Ottawa 2004

Py, Bruno *Prostitution, Proxénétisme, Racolage*, in *Rep. Pen. Dalloz*, Paris, 2006

Radin, Margaret Jane, *Market Inalienability*, in Smith, Patricia (ed.), *Feminist Jurisprudence*, OUP, New York, 1993, p. 389

Radin, Margaret Jane, *Contested Commodities*, in Ertman, Martha M. – Williams, Joan C. (eds.), *Rethinking Commodification. Cases and Readings in Law and Culture*, NYU Press, New York 2005, p. 81

Raymond, Georges, *Messageries roses et droit des contrats*, in *Contrats, conc., consom.* 1994, chron. 4

Reichert, Tom – Lambiase, Jacqueline (eds.), *Sex in Advertising: Perspectives on the Erotic Appeal*, Lawrence Erlbaum Ass., Mahwah, N.J., 2002

Reichert, Tom, *The Erotic History of Advertising*, Prometheus, Amherst, N.Y., 2003

Reinicke, Kenneth, *La prostituzione in Danimarca*, in Carchedi, Francesco – Stridbeck, Ulf – Tola, Vittoria, *Lo zoning possibile. Governance della prostituzione e della tratta delle donne. Il caso di Venezia, Sottocolma ed Amsterdam*, Franco Angeli, Milan 2008, p. 156

Rescigno, Pietro, *Il danno da procreazione*, in *Rivista diritto civile* 1956, I, 614

Rescigno, Pietro, "*In pari causa turpitudinis*", in *Rivista diritto civile* 1966, I, 1
Resta, Giorgio, *La disponibilità dei diritti fondamentali e i limiti della dignità*, in *Rivista diritto civile* 2002, II, 801
Reynolds, Helen, *The Economics of Prostitution*, C. C. Thomas, Springfield, Ill., 1986
Rich, Grant Jewell - Guidroz, Kathleen, *Smart Girls Who Like Sex: Telephone Sex Workers*, in Weitzer, Ronald (ed.) *Sex for Sale: Prostitution, Pornography, and the Sex Industry*, Routledge, New York, 2000, p. 35ff.
Ringdal, Nils, *Love for Sale. A Global History of Prostitution*, Atlantic Books, London, 2004
Ripert, Georges, *La règle morale dans les obligations civiles*, LGDJ, Paris, 1949
Roach, Catherine M., *Stripping, Sex, and Popular Culture*, Berg, Oxford, 2007
Rogers, Edward S., *Copyright and Morals*, 18 *Mich. L. Rev.* 390 (1920)
Rolph, Cecil H. (ed.), *Does Pornography Matter?* Routledge, London, 1961
Rook, Peter Ward, Robert, *Rook & Ward on Sexual Offences. Law and Practice*, Sweet & Maxwell, London, 2004
Ropelato, Jerry, *Pornography statistics 2007*, available at: www.internet-filter-review.toptenreviews.com
Rosewarne, Lauren, *Sex in Public. Women, Outdoor Advertising and Public Policy*, Cambridge Scholars Pub., Newcastle 2007
Rubellin-Devichi, Jacqueline, *Des concubinages. Droit interne - Droit international - Droit comparé*, Litec, Paris, 2002.
Ryan, Chris - Hall, Michael C., *Sex Tourism: Marginal People and Liminalities*, Routledge, London, 2001
Sanders, Teela, *Sex Work. A Risky Business*, Willan Pub., Cullompton 2005
Sanders, Teela, *Blinded by Morality? Prostitution Policy in the UK*, in *Capital & Class* n° 86, p. 9 (2005)
Sanders, Teela, *Paying for Pleasure. Men who Buy Sex*, Willan Pub., Cullompton, 2008
Sanger, William W., *The History of Prostitution: Its Extent, Causes and Effects Throughout the World*, The Medical Pub., New York 1910
Savatier, René, *Le droit, l'amour et la liberté*, 2nd ed., LGDJ, Paris, 1963
Scheffler, Uwe, *Von Telefonsex, Sittenwidrigkeit und Betrug*, in *JuS*, 1996, p. 1070
Schröer, Thomas, *Bordellbetriebe und Öffentliches Baurecht*, in *NZBau* 2009, 166
Scott, George Ryley, *A History of Prostitution*, Torchstream Books, London, 1954
Scoular, Jane - O'Neill, Maggie, *Legal Incursions into Supply/Demand: Criminalising and Responsabilising the Buyers and Sellers of Sex in the UK*, in Munro, Vanessa E. - Della Giusta, Marina (eds.), *Demanding Sex: Critical Reflections on the Regulation of Prostitution*, Ashgate, Burlington, Vt, 2008
Scottish Administration, *Being Outside - Constructing a Response to Street Prostitution* (December 2004)
Scrutton, Roger, *Sexual Desire. A Philosophical Investigation*, Weidenfeld & Nicholson, London, 1986
Shamoon, Deborah, *Office Sluts and Rebel Flowers: The Pleasure of Japanese Pornographic Comics for Women*, in Williams, Linda, (ed.), *Porn Studies*, Duke U.P., Durham, 2004, pp. 77
Sklar, Maggie, *Nude Dancing*, 5 *Geo. J. Gender & L.* 95 (2004)
Smith, Patricia, (ed.), *Feminist Jurisprudence*, OUP, New York, 1993
Soble, Alan, *Pornography and the Social Sciences*, in Soble, Alan - Power, Nicholas (eds.), *The Philosophy of Sex. Contemporary readings*, V ed., Rowman & Littlefield, Lanham, Md. 2008
Soble, Alan - Power, Nicholas, (eds.), *The Philosophy of Sex. Contemporary readings*, V ed., Rowman & Littlefield, Lanham, Md. 2008
Soper, Donald, in Rolph, Cecil H. (ed.), *Does Pornography Matter?* Routledge, London, 1961, p. 41
Spector, Jessica, (ed.), *Prostitution and Pornography. Philosophical Debate about the Sex Industry*, Stanford U. P., Stanford, 2006
Steinman, Kathy J., *Sex Tourism and the Child: Latin America's and the United States' Failure to Prosecute Sex Tourists*, 13 *Hastings Women's L.J.* 53 (2002)
Stombler, Mindy - Baunach, Dawn M. - Burgess, Elisabeth O. - Donnelly, Denise - Simonds, Wendy (eds), *Sex Matters. The Sexuality and Society Reader*, II ed., Pearson, Boston, 2007, p. 375

Stridbeck, Ulf, *La compravendita di prestazioni sessuali in Svezia e Olanda. Regolamentazione ed esperienze locali*, in Carchedi, Francesco – Stridbeck, Ulf – Tola, Vittoria, *Lo zoning possibile. Governance della prostituzione e della tratta delle donne. Il caso di Venezia, Sottocolma ed Amsterdam*, Franco Angeli, Milan, 2008, p. 84ff.

Strossen, Nadine, *Defending Pornography. Free Speech, Sex, and the Fight for Women's Rights*, Doubleday, New York, 1995

Stychin, Carl F., *Law's Desire. Sexuality and the Limits of Justice*, Routledge, London, 1995

Sullivan, Barbara, *The Politics of Sex. Prostitution and Pornography in Australia Since 1945*, Cambridge U.P., Cambridge, 1997

Sullivan, Barbara, *Prostitution and Consent: Beyond the Liberal Dichotomy of 'Free or Forced'*, in Cowling, Mark – Reynolds, Paul (eds.), *Making Sense of Sexual Consent*, Ashgate, Burlington. Vt., 2004, p. 127

Svanstrom, Yvonne, *Criminalising the John – a Swedish Gender Model?*, in Outshoorn, Joyce (ed.) *The Politics of Prostitution. Women Movements, Democratic States and the Globalisation of Sex Commerce*, Cambridge U.P., Cambridge, 2004, p. 225

Svanstrom, Yvonne, *Prostitution in Sweden: Debates and Policies 1980–2004*, in Gangoli, Geetanjali – Westmarland, Nicole, *International Approaches to Prostitution. Law and Policy in Europe and Asia*, Policy Press, Bristol 2006, p. 67ff

Teichman, Doron, *Sex, Shame, and the Law: An Economic Perspective on Megan's Laws*, 42 *Harv. J. on Legis.* 355 (2005)

Terry, Nicolas P., *Prescriptions sans Frontières (or How I Stopped Worrying About Viagra on the Web but Grew Concerned About the Future of Healthcare Delivery)*, 4 *Yale J. Health Pol'y L. & Ethics* 183 (2004)

Thomas, Joe A., *Gay Male Video Pornography: Past, Present, and Future*, in Weitzer, Ronald (ed.) *Sex for Sale: Prostitution, Pornography, and the Sex Industry*, Routledge, New York, 2000, p. 49

Thompson, Susan E., *Prostitution – A Choice Ignored*, 21 *Women's Rts. L. Rep.* 217 (2000)

Thorbek, Susanne – Pattanaik, Bandana (eds.), *Transnational Prostitution. Changing Global Patterns*, Zed Books, London 2002

Treitmatter, Rodger, *Sex Sells!: The Media's Journey from Repression to Obsession*, Westview Press, Boulder, Co, 2004

UK Law Commission *Illegal Transactions: The Effect of Illegality on Contracts and Trust. A Consultation Paper* (no. 154), HMSO, London 1999

UK Home Office, *Paying the Price: A Consultation Paper on Prostitution*, June 2004

Vaccaro, Concetta Maria, *I comportanenti sessuali degli italiani. Falsi miti e nuove normalità*, Franco Angeli, Milan, 2003

van Doorninck, Marieke, *A Business Like any Other? Managing the Sex Industry in the Netherlands*, in Thorbek, Susanne – Pattanaik, Bandana (eds.), *Transnational Prostitution. Changing Global Patterns*, Zed Books, London 2002, p. 193

Various Authors, Proceedings of the conference on "*Economic Justice for Sex Workers*", in 10 *Hastings Women's L.J.* 1–252 (1999)

Vassalli, Filippo, *Del* Ius in corpus *del* debitum coniugale *e della servitù d'amore, ovverosia la dogmatica ludicra*, Bardi, Rome, 1944

von Galen, Margarete, *Prostitution and the Law in Germany*, 3 *Cardozo Women's L.J.* 349 (1996)

Waitt, Gordon – Markwell, Kevin, *Gay Tourism. Culture and Context*, Haworth Hospitality Press, New York, 2006

Walker, Kristen, *Damned Whores and the Border Police: Sex Workers and Refugee Status in Australia*, 31 *Melb. U. L. Rev.* 938 (2007)

Waskul, Dennis D., *Self-Games and Body-Play. Personhood in Online Chat and Cybersex*, Peter Lang, New York, 2003

Waskul, Dennis D., (ed.), *Net.sexxx. Readings on Sex, Pornography and the Internet*, Peter Lang, New York, 2004

Waskul, Dennis D. – Douglass, Mark – Edgley, Charles, *Outercourse: Body and Self in Text Cybersex*, in Waskul, Dennis D. (ed.), *Net.sexxx. Readings on Sex, Pornography and the Internet*, Peter Lang, New York, 2004, p.13ff

Waskul, Dennis D. *The Naked Self: Body and Self in Televideo Cybersex*, in Waskul, Dennis D. (ed.), *Net.sexxx. Readings on Sex, Pornography and the Internet*, Peter Lang, New York, 2004. p. 35ff

Weitzer, Ronald, (ed.) *Sex for Sale: Prostitution, Pornography, and the Sex Industry*, Routledge, New York, 2000
Weitzer, Ronald, *The Politics of Prostitution in America*, in Weitzer, Ronald (ed.) *Sex for Sale: Prostitution, Pornography, and the Sex Industry*, Routledge, New York, 2000, p. 159
Wendtland, Holger, Comment to the *Prostitutiongesetz*, in Bamberger, Heinz Georg - Roth, Herbert (eds.), *Online-Kommentar zum BGB*, Beck, Munich (updated to 1.5.2009)
Wertheimer, Alan, *Consent to Sexual Relations*, Cambridge U.P., Cambridge, 2003
Williams, Christine L., *Sexual Harassment in Organizations: A Critique of Current Research and Policy*, in Dank, Barry M. - Refinetti, Roberto (eds.), *Sexual Harassment & Sexual Consent*, Transaction Pub., New Brunswick 1998, p. 19ff
Williams, Linda, (ed.), *Porn Studies*, Duke U.P., Durham, 2004
Williston, Samuel, *A Treatise on the Law of Contracts* (4th edition by Lord, Richard A.), Lawyers Coop., Rochester, N.Y., 1997
Wolgast, Elisabeth, *Pornography and the Tyranny of the Majority*, in Smith, Patricia (ed.), *Feminist Jurisprudence*, OUP, New York, 1993, p. 431
Wonders, Nancy A. - Michalowsky, Raymond, *Bodies, Borders, and Sex Tourism in a Globalized World: A Tale of Two Cities - Amsterdam and Havana*, 48 *Soc. Probs.* 545 (2001)
Zelizer, Viviana A., *Money, Power, and Sex*, 18 *Yale J.L. & Feminism* 303 (2006)
Zeno-Zencovich, Vincenzo, *"Sex and the contract": dal mercimonio al mercato*, in *Riv. trim. dir. proc. civ.* 2007, 1191
Zeno-Zencovich, Vincenzo, *Freedom of Expression. A Critical and Comparative Analysis*, London, Routledge-Cavendish, 2008
Zimmermann, Reinhard - Visser, Daniel - Reid, Kenneth, *Mixed Legal Systems in Comparative Perspective. Property and Obligations in Scotland and South Africa*, OUP, Oxford, 2004
Zoppini, Andrea, *Le successioni in diritto comparato*, UTET, Turin, 2002

INDEX

Abetting 19fn, 20fn, 21
abolitionism 106fn, 116fn
Adultery 57fn, 85fn, 86fn, 122fn
AIDS 60fn, 124
allocation rules 47
aphrodisiacs 36ff, 64, 109, 122, 123
appraisal 54fn
assault 34fn, 125
assignment 26, 110

Barriers to entry 3
bathhouses 6fn, 75fn
bikini 21
billing 26fn
bondage 33fn
books 31fn
bookstores 31, 56fn, 58
brothel 3, 6fn, 8fn, 13fn, 15fn, 17fn, 20fn, 21, 49fn, 53, 54fn, 56fn, 61fn, 64fn, 79fn, 93fn, 98, 101fn, 109
buggery 88, 105

Causation 22, 65fn, (nota 6)
censorship 42fn
child custody 83, 97fn
child pornography and prostitution 1, 11, 42, 49fn, 59, 66, 80fn, 105
Cialis 36, 37
collateral contracts 22
collective bargaining 82
commodification 74ff, 87, 91fn, 103, 104, 110fn, 124fn, 126
conditions 66, 110, 118
condoms 20
conflict of laws 60
conjugal fidelity 2, 6, 83
consent 33f, 36, 38, 53fn, 65, 66, 73, 86fn, 89fn, 91, 102, 104, 121fn
consumer law 18, 27, 63ff, 92, 94fn
contracts
- advertising 26fn, 55fn
- distribution 35fn, 54
- employment 20, 54 63, 71, 72, 76fn, 77, 78, 106
- insurance 20, 21fn, 22
- loan 21fn
- rent 19, 21fn, 50, 54, 78fn, 88fn
- sale 3, 29, 30, 32, 33, 35, 39fn, 41, 44, 46, 47, 55, 64ff, 78fn, 111, 126
- transport 20, 66
cooperation 11
copyright 40ff

Damages 16, 18, 19fn, 20fn, 24fn, 39, 41, 44fn, 54fn, 66, 72fn, 88fn, 98, 99, 110, 124, 125, 126
dance clubs 6fn, 23, 24, 55fn
de-criminalization 17, 18, 82fn, 115
deceit 29fn, 54fn
deceptive practices 66ff
dignity 36, 51, 52, 69ff, 76, 78, 84fn
dildos 35fn, 63, 120
dismissal 72fn
discrimination (among businesses) 51fn, 58fn
discrimination (among persons) 2, 14fn, 61fn, 71, 72, 88, 89, 103, 106, 110, 112, 126
discrimination (among products) 111
divorce 84fn, 125fn
donation 83, 84ff
dress codes 72, 75fn, 126
drugs 37, 38fn, 46, 64, 65, 75, 125

E-commerce 32fn, 64
econometrics 7
economic realities test 81fn
enforceability 17, 18, 19, 20fn, 21, 22, 26, 32, 38, 42, 49fn, 55, 56, 60, 64, 83, 89, 94fn, 95fn, 100, 110, 126
equality 22, 29, 58, 88, 104, 106fn
escorts 8, 49, 56fn, 91fn, 93
extra-territoriality 59, 60

Female sex tourism 31, 61fn, 106, 107
feminism 1fn, 5, 15fn, 29, 30fn, 60, 71, 73fn, 74, 75fn, 76fn, 80, 91, 103ff, 107, 109, 110fn, 116, 120, 121fn,123fn
firm 49ff, 54
free movement 111, 112
freedom of expression 24fn, 29, 30, 51fn, 52, 56fn, 58fn, 71
fornication 85, 105
fraud 54fn, 65, 66, 67fn, 92fn
fundamental rights 27fn, 30, 34, 36, 52, 57, 70, 71, 73, 88fn, 92fn, 124, 125, 126

Gambling 68fn, 101
gay tourism 61
gift 24, 83, 84, 89fn
globalisation 103, 120

Harassment 2, 72, 104, 125
health insurance 37, 79, 81
hedonism 119

homosexuals 14, 26fn, 29, 33, 34fn, 43fn, 53, 61fn, 88, 89, 104, 107, 125
house prostitution 8, 35, 85
human trafficking 1, 3, 11, 71, 77fn, 82fn, 91, 92, 103fn, 104, 106, 108, 113, 114fn, 125

Illegal contracts 16, 17, 20fn, 31, 36, 37, 38, 49fn, 53fn, 54, 56, 60, 78, 85fn, 89fn, 93, 98, 99, 100, 101
IMBRA 90ff
immoral contracts 11, 12, 18, 19, 21fn, 32, 39, 41, 98, 126 101fn
implied terms 11, 110
import/export 105, 110, 111, 113
impotence 37, 124
incentives 7fn, 109
inefficiency 50, 98, 99, 105, 107fn, 110
inflatable dolls 111
inheritance law 86
intent of parties 22, 71, 87, 88, 92, 94fn, 99fn
invalidity 21, 22, 30fn, 31, 36, 37, 39fn, 45, 54, 56, 71, 84, 89fn, 92, 98, 100fn

Labour law 69ff
lap-dancing 23ff, 53, 69, 117fn
legal feminism (see feminism)
lesbian 29fn, 43fn, 53, 61fn
licensing 30fn, 45, 54fn, 55ff, 79, 80fn, 93fn, 111fn, 116
litigation 99
loss of consortium 124

Marriage 5, 10fn, 19, 43fn, 73fn, 83, 84, 85, 86fn, 123fn, 124, 125
marriage brokerage 63fn, 88ff.
marriage of convenience 90, 91fn, 92
massage parlour 13fn, 49fn, 58fn, 59, 63, 67fn, 93fn
master/servant relationship 81
masturbation 14, 25, 53, 55fn, 123
misrepresentation 54fn
motive 32, 92, 93

National health service 37, 125
nexus of contracts 49
newsagents 32
newsstands 1, 31, 32fn
nightclubs 23fn, 24fn, 53ff
NIMBY 55, 102, 116fn
non-discrimination (see discrimination among persons)
nude entertainment 6, 9, 23fn, 24fn, 63, 70, 102
nullité de protection 18

Obligations 11, 19, 26, 76, 80, 83, 84, 85, 87, 117, 118, 121fn
offset 31fn
on-line dating 94ff
on-line sex 19, 65, 66, 117

Partnership 5fn, 49fn, 86, 97
passing off 41, 46, 47
patent 36fn, 44ff
payment 15fn, 18, 20fn, 23, 26, 27, 35fn, 53fn, 54fn, 65, 66ff, 89fn, 101fn, 109, 118
pay-per-view television 52
peep-show 15, 23ff, 67fn, 75fn
per capita spend 3
performance (of contract) 16, 24, 29, 53, 66, 83, 84fn, 87, 98, 110
personal data 65
pimp 5, 8fn, 18, 19, 76fn
porn videos 4, 7, 11, 30, 31, 51, 56fn, 61fn, 64
postal laws 40fn, 111
pre-paid cards 27, 66
premarital agreements 84ff
price 4, 8, 9, 10, 20fn, 35fn, 44, 47, 52, 124, 125
price dynamics 3
private autonomy 57, 71, 76fn, 98, 102, 108, 109
private international law
privé club 53ff
poems 41fn
promises 84, 85, 89, 90, 100, 118, 125
public policy 20, 21, 22, 32, 39, 40, 41fn, 42, 44, 45, 46, 49fn, 56, 84, 85, 87, 89fn, 90, 94fn, 101, 109, 112
publishing agreement 30fn, 31fn, 39fn, 41fn, 82fn

Rape 103, 125
real estate 57
red-light cinemas 53ff, 57
red light district 10fn, 57fn, 58, 107
rental of premises 19
reputation 9
restitution 16, 18, 19, 39, 98, 110fn

Sado-masochism 33ff, 53
sale by post 111
self-determination 6,70, 71, 86
sex-shops 10, 33, 53ff, 56fn, 57, 76fn, 102, 122
sex tourism 8, 9, 49fn, 59ff, 66, 79fn, 82, 91fn, 106, 107, 113, 114fn
sex toys 35fn
sexual freedom 33f, 37, 98, 125f
sexual potency 37
shareholders 51
slavery 71, 104
social clauses 114
social security 76fn, 77fn, 81fn, 116
sociology 2ff

sodomy 88
specific performance 83, 98, 110fn
spouses 5, 83, 84, 86, 89fn, 122
statistics 3ff, 8, 11, 17fn, 86fn, 92fn
stimulators 33, 38, 54fn, 55fn
street prostitution 8fn, 10fn, 17fn, 20, 49fn, 79, 107, 109
striptease 23ff, 49fn, 53, 54fn, 67fn, 69, 75fn, 93fn

Taxation 7fn, 27fn, 51, 78, 114, 116
telecommunications 4, 27, 63, 75, 115
telephone sex 6fn, 25ff, 49fn, 75fn, 93fn
television 51ff
trade unions 77
trademarks 44ff
transaction costs 121fn
transgender sex 30, 71, 106

Unfair terms 66f, 92fn

Venereal diseases 66, 85, 117, 124
Viagra 36ff
Vulgarity 45fn

Wages 76
warnings 30, 53fn, 65fn
warranties 110, 118
web chat 2fn, 14fn, 26fn, 27fn, 94
wife swapping 73

Zoning 31fn, 55ff, 106fn, 109, 116